American Pragmatism

American Pragmatism

An Introduction

Albert R. Spencer

polity

First published in 2020 by Polity Press

Polity Press
65 Bridge Street
Cambridge CB2 1UR, UK

Polity Press
101 Station Landing
Suite 300
Medford, MA 02155, USA

ISBN-13: 978-1-5095-2471-6
ISBN-13: 978-1-5095-2472-3(pb)

A catalogue record for this book is available from the British Library.

Library of Congress Cataloging-in-Publication Data

Names: Spencer, Albert R., author.
Title: American pragmatism : an introduction / Albert R. Spencer.
Description: Medford : Polity, 2019. | Includes bibliographical references
    and index. | Summary: "In this comprehensive introduction, Spencer
    presents a new story of the origins and development of American
    Pragmatism, from its emergence through the interaction of European and
    Indigenous American cultures to its contemporary status as a diverse,
    vibrant, and contested global philosophy. This is an indispensable guide
    for undergraduate students"-- Provided by publisher.
Identifiers: LCCN 2019023987 (print) | LCCN 2019023988 (ebook) | ISBN
    9781509524716 (hardback) | ISBN 9781509524723 (paperback) | ISBN
    9781509524754 (epub)
Subjects: LCSH: Pragmatism. | Philosophy, American.
Classification: LCC B944.P72 S64 2019 (print) | LCC B944.P72 (ebook) |
    DDC 144/.30973--dc23
LC record available at https://lccn.loc.gov/2019023987
LC ebook record available at https://lccn.loc.gov/2019023988

Typeset in 10.5 on 12.5 pt Sabon by
Servis Filmsetting Ltd, Stockport, Cheshire
Printed and bound in Great Britain by CPI Group (UK) Ltd, Croydon

For further information on Polity, visit our website: politybooks.com

Contents

Preface

This book surveys American pragmatism: its central themes, figures, and relevance to contemporary culture and philosophy. It will explore the following questions: What is American pragmatism? What is distinctly American about pragmatism, or any other philosophy? And what should be the proper boundaries of American pragmatism?

The book not only introduces the familiar figures (Peirce, James, Dewey), concepts (the pragmatic maxim, radical empiricism, the pattern of inquiry), and themes (fallibilism, meliorism, and pluralism) of American pragmatism but broadens the canon by including satellite figures (Royce, Addams, and DuBois) whose influence should be considered primary. It also intends to demonstrate pragmatism's contemporary relevance by showing its growing global influence and how its concepts and methods can be applied to current problems. Although it does not intend to pursue a critical thesis, this introduction explores how pragmatism emerges in response to America's transition from colony to superpower and how this transition, in turn, influences not only the development of pragmatism but its current relevance and future. In a nutshell, then, this study presents pragmatism as a philosophy of place that attempts to understand the meaning-making activities that shape the American experience. Thus it favors authors who engage with problems that emerge from the complex and tragic effects of settler colonialism and from the racial contract hidden behind the veil of American exceptionalism. It also presents contemporary pragmatism as a contested tradition. Some see it as a *theory of truth* established by the logician Charles S. Peirce, informed by experimental science, and designed to solve conceptual problems. Others see it as a *method of experience*, as it was defined by the psychologist William James and, later, by the educator John Dewey, who insisted upon honoring a plurality of human perspectives on ameliorating concrete problems.

Chapter 1 explains how the classical pragmatists (Peirce, James, and Royce), found pragmatism through their embrace of fallibilism – that is, through the recognition that even our most trusted knowledge is conditional and must continually be revised in light of new experience. They use this fallibilism to critique modern philosophy and to ameliorate the legacy of the Civil War. Chapter 2 describes how the Chicago pragmatists (Addams, Dewey, and Mead) deepen the social dimensions of pragmatism by using it to ameliorate the concrete problems of immigration and US expansion. Chapter 3 examines how the second generation of Harvard pragmatists (Santayana, DuBois, Kallen, and Locke) developed various forms of pluralism in order to challenge racism at home and totalitarianism abroad in the decades before World War II. Chapter 4 shows how the analytic pragmatists (Lewis, Quine, and Rorty) debunked the assumptions of logical positivism and transformed mainstream philosophy during the Cold War by drawing on the Peircean commitment to verification. Chapter 5 surveys the contemporary pragmatists who, during the eclipse of Jamesian pragmatism, engaged a variety of global traditions so as to find hope in an increasingly perilous world.

Before concluding this preface, a few logistical remarks are in place. First, owing to the effects of colonization, the etiquette of referring properly to the peoples of the western hemisphere remains a complicated issue and often varies according to the history of a particular nation, region, or people. Hence I follow the following conventions. When referring to the original inhabitants of the western hemisphere or their descendants, I use the term "indigenous peoples." Whenever I refer to the indigenous people who inhabit the United States in general, I use the term "American Indian." According to Thomas Norton-Smith, whose recommendation I'm following here, this term should be used in academic writing because it occurs in the numerous treaties between the United States and the indigenous peoples of the western hemisphere, as well as in state and national legislation. Norton-Smith also recommends this convention as a means of acknowledging and retaining the special legal status and rights guaranteed to American Indian peoples through treaties with the United States, in resistance to attempts to disenfranchise these peoples from such rights and protections simply by reclassifying them as another ethnic group. In all other cases I have sought to use the preferred name of the tribe or nation to which a person belongs, especially in the case of specific authors.

Second, this book approaches pragmatism through the critical lenses of settler colonialism, manifest destiny, and chattel slavery. Consequently it occasionally deals with tragic or graphic subject matter. Given the web of assumptions, institutions, and social practices that veil the ongoing impacts of these processes and keep them hidden from those whom they privilege, I deliberately include sources and information that accurately represent the dark realities of US history. I would like to apologize to any readers who may feel offended or who, having witnessed or endured these realities, prefer not to experience them again. Finally, the purpose of this book is not to be anti-American; on the contrary, I love this nation, its people, and its land. They are my home. But love, and even patriotism, often require critical analysis and an acknowledgment of the reality, scope, and magnitude of past problems, if healing is to occur.

Thus this book is only my representation of the rich variety of events, themes, locations, authors, works, and subjects that compose American pragmatism. My hope has been to write a narrative of pragmatism that is accessible to students and to curious readers – people who wish to know more about this tradition. However, I conceived and wrote this introduction to pragmatism during a period of difficult transition, both in the United States and globally. While I try to remain politically neutral in my commentary so as not to distract from the ideas and authors under discussion, this work was not composed in a vacuum. Indeed, paying due attention to context is a key commitment of the pragmatists; and Dewey calls us to reconstruct the past for the purpose of ameliorating the present and of imagining a better future. As a result, much of the content of this book has been selected to highlight moments in US history when this land and its people faced challenges similar to ones we face today.

Since the resources of American pragmatism are inexhaustible, there are many fascinating subjects that I could not discuss here, owing to limitations of time and space. If any of my readers notice any significant omissions, I hope the work as a whole will inspire them to devote their lives to the study of this thriving philosophical tradition – and maybe also to engage in the perpetual task of ameliorating the mistakes of the past.

Acknowledgments

Above all, I want to express unfathomable gratitude to those of my teachers who introduced me to pragmatism and, through their kindness, wisdom, and character, inspired me to study it: Roger Ward, Stuart Rosenbaum, and the late John J. McDermott, who created the collections, venues, and community necessary for the survival of pragmatism in the twentieth century and for its flourishing in the twenty-first.

Next I wish to thank the following people for their support during the development of this book: my wife, Tina, whose love, patience, and wisdom never end, for believing in me and my work even when I lacked self-belief; my brother-in-philosophy, Brady Romtvedt, for countless hours of conversation and for profound insights; Linda Eklund, for always supporting my career and scholarship; my mentors, Jeff Julum, Bill Karns, Bert Shaw, and Bob Williams, for reading multiple versions of the worst drafts of this work – and also for modeling lives of practical wisdom; my colleagues, Kyle Bromhall, Kevin Decker, Bennett Gilbert, Maurice Hamington, Aaron Massecar, Ian Patrick McHugh, and Noah Sharpsteen, for their constructive feedback on slightly more polished chapters; my cohort of SAAP-sters (members of the Society for the Advancement of American Philosophy) Justin Bell, John Giordano, David Henderson, Charlie Hobbs, Nate Jackson, V. Denise James, Zachary Piso, and Seth Vannatta, for expanding, refining, and challenging my understanding of pragmatism throughout the years; my students Ben Dunham, Ezra Goldberg, Ried Gustafson, Daniel Hettenbach, Tessa Livingstone, and Makenna Polan, for showing me how pragmatism continues to impact the lived experience of each generation; my friends Ted Van Alst, Paul Delahanty, and the late Miguel Reyes, for teaching me how to listen to this land and learn from the people who know it best, and for graciously helping me up when I stumbled along my journey to understand it; and the peoples of the Pacific Northwest whose traditional homelands sustain my life and work, specifically the Multnomah, the Kathlamet, the Clackamas, the Tumwater, the Watlala bands of the Chinook, the Tualatin Kalapuya and other Indigenous nations of the Columbia and Willamette Rivers. I honor the sacrifices of their ancestors, celebrate their legacy, and dedicate this book to ameliorating our tragic history.

I also thank my animal teachers: the crow, for surveying my subject; the spider, for weaving the connections; and the bison, for persevering until the end.

Last but certainly not least, I thank my daughter for being my hope.

An Introduction to
American Pragmatism

Most histories define pragmatism as a philosophical tradition begun in New England at the end of the nineteenth century, in the wake of the intellectual crisis of Darwinism and the social crisis of the American Civil War. The pragmatists insisted that the truth of a belief is best understood in terms of that belief's practical effects. Most of the founders of pragmatism were associated with Harvard University's Department of Philosophy; some were members of an informal group known as the Metaphysical Club who met regularly to discuss their criticisms of European philosophy. From this circle two polymaths emerged: the brilliant but troubled chemist–mathematician Charles Sanders Peirce (pronounced like "purse") and the gregarious but melancholic physician-psychologist William James. These men would maintain a lifelong personal and professional friendship, but one fraught with challenges and disagreement. Pragmatism arose from these tensions, which continue to fuel its vitality.

Philosophically, Peirce and James agreed that European thought (specifically, the idealism of Immanuel Kant and G. F. W. Hegel) had erred in its attempts to represent reality conceptually and advocated a return to our ordinary lived experience. As scientists, both trusted empirical evidence to be a superior ground for knowledge, yet they were fallibilists who acknowledged the limitations of the scientific method.

According to them, beliefs should function as hypotheses: they are provisional claims supported by the best available evidence and subject to revision in the light of future, possibly confounding evidence. On this view, a belief is true if it "works"—that is, if its application has the expected consequences.

Yet Peirce and James disagreed as to what type of empirical evidence should be privileged. Peirce's training as a scientist led him to prefer the incremental, but reliable, experimental evidence gathered methodically over time, whereas James's psychological research led him to prefer the more profound, but relative, insights gained through our subjective, lived experience. In fact Peirce would later rechristen his approach as "pragmaticism" in order to differentiate his work not only from James's, but also (and even more) from the work of those inspired by James's more radical approach. This tension between pragmatism's founders has not been resolved and has given birth to a variety of pragmatisms, both old and new; and thus the debate between Peirce and James continues. Is pragmatism a *theory of truth* inspired by experimental science and dedicated to the purpose of solving conceptual problems, or is it a *method of experience*, a pluralistic approach to knowledge that aspires to honor the diversity of human experience and has the purpose of ameliorating concrete social problems?

While it would be wrong to claim that subsequent pragmatists or affiliated philosophers deliberately or strictly adhered to this schismatic view of the origins of pragmatism, it is useful to consider where the heirs of Peirce and James fall along the spectrum it outlines. For example Josiah Royce, their contemporary, borrowed insights from both to craft his mature objective idealism; and John Dewey, the most prominent figure among twentieth-century pragmatists, sought to honor both through his emphasis on scientific inquiry dedicated to solving social problems. On the other hand, logicians such as C. I. Lewis used Peirce's pragmatic maxim to engage the logical positivists but had little use for James, whereas Richard Rorty dismissed Peirce's methodological rigor altogether in favor of a literary approach even more subjective than James's. Furthermore, most pragmatists—and certainly Peirce, James, and Dewey—are antidualists. While classical philosophical dualisms (mind–body, subject–object, free will–determinism, etc.) can function as useful frames for philosophical reflection, nearly all pragmatists contend that these distinctions are conceptual tools invented to organize and guide inquiry rather than necessary features of perennial problems. Insisting on the latter inevitably results in dualism's becoming an entrenched barrier to inquiry—what Alfred North Whitehead called "misplaced concreteness" (e.g. Whitehead 1967) and what Alfred Korzybski had in mind when he famously warned us that the map is not the territory "the thing mapped" (Korzybski 1933: 58, 247, etc.).

On the other hand, this approach risks oversimplifying pragmatism's significance in the intellectual history of the western hemisphere, marginalizing important voices that contributed to pragmatism's foundation and development and failing to fulfill pragmatism's commitment to addressing the concrete problems of lived experience. The brute reality is that America is a former colony that became a superpower. It still wrestles with the problems of sovereignty, race, and gender present at the inception of pragmatism, and pragmatism's progenitors witnessed the arrival of the responsibilities and temptations that accompanied the attainment of global hegemony. Their diagnosis and prognosis of this history explicitly influenced their work, alleviated contemporary ills, and inspired reform. We should learn from their example.

Now, at the beginning of the twenty-first century, pragmatists remain divided as to whether pragmatism should return to its philosophical origins as a theory of truth or expand its cultural boundaries while showing how it emerged from attempts to ameliorate settler colonialism. In consequence, this book will survey American pragmatism, its central themes, figures, and their relevance to contemporary culture and philosophy by exploring the following questions: What is American pragmatism? What is distinctly American about pragmatism or any other philosophy? And what should the proper boundaries of American pragmatism be? Although it will require the entire book to answer these questions adequately, it will be helpful to provide here a few preliminary and tentative answers, since these questions will frame and guide my inquiry.

Pragmatism as a Contested Tradition

What is American pragmatism? This Introduction already opened with an encyclopedic answer, but for convenience, pragmatism is a late nineteenth century American philosophical tradition conceived of by Peirce, enriched by James, systematized by Dewey, and developed by a variety of other authors throughout the twentieth century. At its core lies the assumption that *beliefs are inseparable from actions, therefore the truth of beliefs should be evaluated according to their consequences.* This assumption may seem minor, but it stems from pragmatism's perpetual criticism of dualism—the habit of philosophers throughout history to divide any subject into two opposing poles or positions: for example, mind–body, subject–object, science–religion, idealism–empiricism, theory–practice, nature–nurture, liberal–conservative, good–evil, and so on. The pragmatists argue that these dualisms are inventions, tools created by philosophers in order to aid their inquiry into a subject. Unfortunately, philosophers often forget that they created these tools and begin to see them as necessary to the inquiry or, worse, as essential features of the subject. As a result, they mistake the map for the territory. By contrast, pragmatists prefer to discover their answers for themselves, through direct *experience* and *experimentation.* Theory, maps, and the testimony can be useful, but sometimes we must disregard those tools when we encounter a roadblock, an abyss, a lacuna, an arroyo, or a cul-de-sac. We must adapt to changing circumstances.

As a result, pragmatists judge the value of ideas according to a variety of standards. First, they are *fallibilists,* which means that they believe all knowledge to be tentative and conditional. That's why even the most accurate maps or ideas must be revised. The territory constantly changes, experience constantly changes, therefore our knowledge must constantly adapt to changing circumstances. Usually circumstances change in predictable ways, but on occasion change is sudden and unexpected. In fact sometimes changes are so severe that we can never return to the stability we previously enjoyed. Therefore we must be content with responses that *ameliorate* the problem— that make our situation better than it was, but perhaps not as good as we want it to be. Experience shows that seeking perfection in a changing world usually causes more harm than good. True, we cannot guarantee that our deeds will be successful, but we are more likely to succeed if we share the *plurality* of our experiences, because we can learn more through cooperation than each one of us learns alone. We can also improve our likelihood of success if we *verify* the strengths and weakness of our ideas during the good times; and, when times get tough, as they surely will, the *hope* that our situation would eventually improve will sustain our struggles. Fortunately, surprises can be serendipitous as well as disastrous.

Each of the following chapters focuses on one of the themes contained in the next headings here and shows how various groups of pragmatists developed each idea. But this encyclopedic definition and practical narrative merely sketch the borders of pragmatism. If we want to explore the territory more fully, we must be aware of the pitfalls and challenges that may lie ahead. One minor confusion is the overlap between American philosophy and pragmatism: are they identical, or is pragmatism one philosophy among many developed in America? In practice, most scholars use the two terms as coextensive, but in theory their relationship is more complicated.

In *Genealogical Pragmatism*, John J. Stuhr (1997) distinguishes three uses of the label "American" when applied to philosophy or philosophers. First, "American" in the national sense refers to whether the philosopher so described is American. Second, "American" in the philosophical sense refers to whether the topics and methods so described are unique to the American philosophical tradition. Finally, philosophy can be said to be "American" in the cultural sense if it engages the content of "*American* culture or, more accurately, plural American cultures" (1997: 25).

6 American Pragmatism

American philosophy in the national sense

At first glance, American philosophy in the national sense appears to be a most straightforward notion; yet this notion hides from view some of the deepest challenges of understanding the origins, nature, and scope of pragmatism. Yes, there are clearly philosophers in the United States; and they are employed by institutions of higher education to teach and write philosophy. However, most professional philosophers who work in America do not consider themselves to be working in the tradition of American philosophy or of pragmatism in particular. This is so for at least three reasons.

First, why should any philosophy be relevant to a particular time, place, or culture? In the West, one usually assumes knowledge to be universal rather than particular. For example, we still study the Pythagorean theorem because the formula $a^2 + b^2 = c^2$ is ahistorical; it works today as well as it did in ancient Greece. By the same token it is acultural: it works regardless of the culture, beliefs, or identity of the person who applies the formula. Again, multiple ancient origins of the theorem corroborate this insight: its discovery predates the sixth century BC (Pythagoras's century) by more than one thousand years—in fact there is evidence of parallel discovery by geographically separated cultures such as Egyptian, Babylonian, and Indian. Now, it might be interesting to know *how* different cultures arrived at the theorem, but it is far more important to know *what* the theorem is. Similarly, when someone majors in mathematics or physics they rarely specialize in "American mathematics" or in "Bactrian physics." By analogy, if philosophy conceives of itself along similar lines, as a search for knowledge, should we not be more concerned with what their theories are and why they are relevant today than with understanding the biographical details of who developed an idea and how that idea emerged in response to where and when that person lived? The humanities focus on these details, but not the sciences. On the other hand, why do we refer to the formula by the name of a quasi-legendary Greek philosopher who most likely learned it from some other source and who could not have been the first to use it? This leads to the second reason why most professional philosophers in the United States do not see themselves as doing or specializing in American philosophy: mainstream philosophy conceives of itself as a science gradually expanding, clarifying, and revising a set of true or justified theories and concepts around certain topics in metaphysics, epistemology, and ethics. The historical reasons for the current professional paradigm in philosophy will be thoroughly discussed in chapter 4, but, in brief, the agenda was set in the mid-twentieth century by British and Austrian philosophers fleeing the rise and expansion of national socialism in Germany. As these luminaries and their students established themselves in philosophy departments, journals, and organizations across the United States, mainstream professional philosophy quickly began to favor the methods and subjects preferred by their tradition. Often referred to as *analytic philosophy*, this tradition focuses on the analysis of subjects such as science, mathematics, logic, and language, because those subjects promised to be more objective and empirical than metaphysics, ethics, and social–political philosophy. Analytic philosophy does not avoid these latter subjects, but when they receive attention their treatment is informed by the insights and methods offered by the former.

What is more, the analytic tradition does contend with a rival, but one that does not originate in America or identify with American philosophy either. This rival is known by the catchall "continential philosophy," because its theories, subjects, and methods descend from the various nineteenth- and twentieth-century European traditions that emerge from critical engagements with German idealism, such as Marxism, existentialism, phenomenology, hermeneutics, structuralism, psychoanalysis, and so on. Largely these traditions critique and abandon the assumption that knowledge can be universal or can progress. According to all of them, philosophy should be among the humanities because it functions best when it deconstructs the hidden assumptions of concepts, theories, or institutions so that all the latter may be reinterpreted in novel ways, usually ones that disrupt the authority of the status quo. Besides, there are still other contemporary traditions that do not fit easily into their own categories; such are feminism, critical race theory, or comparative philosophy. Just as chapter 4 will show pragmatism's engagement with the analytic tradition, chapter 5 will discuss the points of contact between pragmatism and various global traditions— for example pragmatism's parallels with existentialism, the relocation of the Frankfurt School to New York while Dewey and other pragmatists also resided there, and cross-border dialogue between pragmatism, American Indian authors, and Latin American writers. Once again, we will find pragmatism in the middle. It developed between these multiple traditions and in turn influenced them all. Also, its emphasis on practice at the expense of theory inspired the nascent social sciences as they emerged in the late nineteenth and twentieth centuries, at the boundary between the sciences and the humanities.

Nevertheless, while interest in pragmatism and American philosophy grew rapidly in the United States, a professional philosopher, if asked, would most likely describe herself as part of either the analytic or the continental tradition. In fact many might not even identify with a specific tradition at all, preferring to see themselves as specializing in a particular topic or issue rather than committed to any philosophical tradition. Consequently, most professional philosophers in the United States are not pragmatists and do not study American philosophers at all. Ironically, some of the most important figures in the history of American philosophy and pragmatism, for example George Santayana and Jürgen Habermas, were not Americans. This leads us to a third challenge about American philosophy in the national sense: who should qualify as an American philosopher? Just as the United States has difficulty clarifying, maintaining, and respecting its geopolitical boundaries, similar problems occur with regard to what figures should be included in the canons of both American philosophy and pragmatism.

James committed the first high-profile acts of retroactively enlisting historical thinkers to the tradition of pragmatism. He did so in the subtitle of his popular lectures, *Pragmatism:*

A New Name for Some Old Ways of Thinking (James 1907), and more substantially in his second lecture, "What Pragmatism Means," where he claims: "There is absolutely nothing new in the pragmatic method. Socrates was an adept at it. Aristotle used it methodically. Locke, Berkeley, and Hume made momentous contributions to truth by its means" (James 1968: 379). Dewey makes a similar point in his short 1930 intellectual autobiography, "From Absolutism to Experimentalism," when he insists: "Nothing could be more helpful to present philosophizing than a 'Back to Plato' movement provided we return to the dramatic, restless cooperatively inquiring Plato of the *Dialogues*, trying one mode of attack after another to see what it might yield; back to the Plato whose highest flight of metaphysics always terminated with a social and practical turn" (Dewey 1984: 154). If we take such views at face value, not only were the founders of American philosophy pragmatists, but ancient and modern philosophy were founded by pragmatists as well.

In a similar vein, contemporary scholars debate whether the American label should be dropped altogether. In "Essaying America," John Lysaker reconsiders the usefulness of applying a provincial label for any philosophy, American, pragmatist, or otherwise. He also returns to Ralph Waldo Emerson's "The American Scholar," a speech often cited as a founding document of American philosophy, and asks: "Where do we find ourselves?" (meaning, at this point in the story of the United States; Lysaker 2012: 534). Given the inescapable violence of American history, he demands that "we read history against the grain" by critiquing authoritarianism through an appeal to the authority of "countermemory," or else we risk further obfuscating or rationalizing the darker realities of American history (2012: 535). He admits that America is "not *reducible* to global empire" and that he still has more to learn from several American philosophers who challenged American imperialism; but, if we insist that this countertradition represents America better, we "threaten to render obscure if not illegible the American character that surrounded each and to which each movement is a decided protest." Concerning many of the authors whom this book will discuss, Lysaker concludes that they should be presented as "exceptions to a more pervasive national character," lest we belittle their courageous resistance to the dominant themes of their times (2012: 544). We should teach and read these authors in ways that highlight "points where they resist empire," but also in ways that expose "moments where they further empire, perhaps unwittingly" (2012: 545). Thus America should remain a subject of philosophical inquiry; yet he chooses to declare his independence from America until it can become a "more inclusive ideal, one covering the whole of the Americas, not just the United States" (2012: 547).

By contrast, Grant Silva argues that an anti-imperial identity of American philosophy is available now, if we can incorporate pragmatism into the wider narrative of the liberatory tradition of the Americas. In an article on the meaning of liberation for philosophy in America (Silva 2018), he envisages this inter-American philosophy as taking Emerson's "The American Scholar" to be one crucial declaration of independence among several others, such as Leopoldo Zea's "The Actual Function of Philosophy in Latin America" (1942) and Augusto Salazar Bondy's *Is There a Philosophy of Our America?* (1969). Just as Emerson hoped to declare the United States' cultural independence from Europe, Zea and Bondy sought to liberate Latin American philosophy and culture from the political, economic, and cultural hegemony of Europe's heir, the United States. Such an integration would establish a broader multicultural understanding not only of pragmatism, but of American identity and global philosophical thought. And it must use the work of critics such as Enrique Dussell, Aníbal Quijano, and Immanuel Wallerstein, who warn against the damage caused by narratives of world history that place Europe and the United States as the current centers of geopolitics and as the "main protagonists in world history" (Silva 2018: 4).

This introduction occupies the space between Lysaker and Silva, by looking back with a critical gaze on how American pragmatism emerges from its colonial past and in the hope of pointing toward new global and inter-American versions of pragmatism. While Lysaker's suspicion of the American label is warranted, pragmatism cannot be severed from its provincial origins, just as we cannot untangle ourselves from the complicated web of relations America represents. Pragmatism arises from the history of America as a collection of colonial states and of their independence; and the rise of the United States to superpower status is the history of our present global reality. Indeed, if we agree with Silva, the history of American pragmatism must be captured within the larger cultural history of the western hemisphere. Thus this introduction aspires to be an example of the *visionary pragmatism* described by V. Denise James (2013), which hopes to liberate the future of American pragmatism by acknowledging how the insights and biases of cultural context influence both the success and the failure of any philosophical project to ameliorate the urgent problems of lived experience. Its author also accepts that more work remains to be done to decolonize pragmatism, and humbly hopes that the present text will inspire and guide others without introducing new detours.

American philosophy in the philosophical sense

Returning to Stuhr, he argues that the essential character of pragmatism in the philosophical sense is a *method of experience* that uses philosophical inquiry to engage social problems. Stuhr bases this claim on introductory essays by the three mid-twentieth century scholars familiar with the tradition who articulated overlapping accounts of its content and approach. First, John Lachs insisted that pragmatism emphasizes human activity and daily life in order to avoid the perennial dualisms (e.g. subject–object, mind–body, individual–society) that mire most philosophical inquiry in esoteric discussions of abstract concepts. Likewise, John J. McDermott presented the project of pragmatism as consisting in "confronting and ameliorating concrete problems, such that the relevance of ideas in, and for, experience is preferred to their formalization in, and by, thought" (Stuhr 1997: 24). Finally, John E. Smith stressed pragmatism's "new emphasis on the roles of purpose and interest in determining

the direction and importance of reflection, the new understanding of the nature of experience, and the new focus on
community and the irreducibly social character of all human
undertakings, from science to religion" (ibid.). As we shall
see, Emerson anticipated this method of experience in "The
American Scholar"; the method will be present in the ethical
and social philosophy of James, but Dewey will explicitly
define it as *reconstruction*.

However, Stuhr (1997) does not mention that other contemporary scholars prefer to understand the philosophical
character of pragmatism in terms of its theoretical, not methodological, contributions to the history of philosophy. For
example, Robert Brandom (2011) admits the social dimension
of pragmatism, but presents the founders of pragmatism
(Peirce, James, and Dewey) as attempting to naturalize the
German idealism of Kant and Hegel through the integration
of the new scientific knowledge of the late nineteenth century,
specifically statistical mathematics, psychology, and evolutionary biology. Conversely, Cheryl Misak (2013) argues
that pragmatism attempts to naturalize the practical dimensions of Kant's philosophy, not his idealism. Specifically, in
Misak's view, Peirce agrees with Kant that philosophical
inquiry must begin with certain "regulative assumptions"
but insists these assumptions should be drawn from scientific
practice, not from theoretical analysis (Misak 2013: x–xi).
Therefore Misak asserts that pragmatism is best understood
as a *theory of truth* that acknowledges the limits of human
inquiry, for example how it is influenced by social factors,
but aspires to overcome them through the development of
more effective practices and conceptual tools. Furthermore,
she insists that we must rescue this "more objective kind of
pragmatism" from pragmatists like Richard Rorty and his
"classical predecessors (James and Dewey)" who hold "there
is no truth at which we might aim—only agreement within a
community or what works for an individual or what is found
to solve a problem" (2013: 3).

While Misak correctly identifies this tension as one element
present both at the inception of pragmatism and today, readers should form their own opinion as to the strengths and

weaknesses of the varieties of pragmatism discussed in this book. This tension will first be explored in chapter 1, where I examine the contrast between the theoretical pragmatism of Peirce and the methodological pragmatism of James. Then we shall see how the fissure revealed here led to parallel versions of pragmatism: the analytic pragmatism of the mid-twentieth century, examined in chapter 4, and the neo-pragmatism that emerged at the end of the century, examined in chapter 5. However, I urge my readers not to commit the fallacy of believing that an abstraction is a reality—that is, Whitehead's fallacy of misplaced concreteness, if I may recall his famous term for a second time in this Introduction. *These labels are heuristic constructs for recognizing important points of historical and theoretical divergence, rather than essential or irreconcilable divisions between members of the same philosophical family.*

Given that all pragmatists seek to overcome the dualisms and dogmatisms that block inquiry, it would be a sad irony if the tradition imploded in the twenty-first century as a result of its own inability to see past its own internal squabbles. Even Misak carefully admits that some pragmatists were simultaneously concerned about pragmatism as a theory of truth and as a method of experience, but prefers Peirce because James and Dewey "were not always clear about when they were engaged in one and when they were engaged in the other"; besides, the line between the two "tendencies can never be sharply delineated," since the "pragmatist account of truth links truth with practice" (Misak 2013, p. 4). To possess a comprehensive understanding of pragmatism, we must recognize these parallel definitions of its philosophical character, realize why they remain entangled, and develop a sufficient understanding of both branches—an understanding of the charitable kind, as good scholarship requires. However, we do not need to choose sides. Indeed, chapter 5 will conclude by considering how Huw Price's pragmatic naturalism recovers Peirce's demand for verification without reducing the varieties of Jamesian pluralism to a single theory or methodology.

American philosophy in the cultural sense

Given this distinction between pragmatism as a method of experience and pragmatism as a theory of truth with regard to the philosophical sense of "American," let us examine what it means to be an American philosopher in the cultural sense. Again, pragmatism in a cultural sense can be pursued in one of two ways: through contextual scholarship and through critical analysis. Contextual scholarship seeks to understand how various authors, movements, or the tradition as a whole has been informed by, and has responded to, the intellectual, social, and political realities of its context. This type of scholarship is vital if we wish to learn about any philosophical tradition, and even more so in the case of pragmatism, because many of its major figures consciously used the method of experience to engage their contemporary world. One of the first is *The American Angle of Vision*, a pamphlet first published in 1966, where, in Stuhr's words, McDermott suggests that American philosophy emerged as a response to the "reflective tradition" of Europe, specifically to the consequences of the sixteenth-century "triple revolution"—the discovery of the New World, the Protestant Reformation, and Copernicanism—on the "actual natural and social environment encountered in [seventeenth-century] America" (Stuhr 1997: 31).

Proceeding chronologically, Bruce Kuklick (1977) provides a thorough history of the professionalization of philosophy in general during the twentieth century and explains how this process shaped and was shaped by the work of the pragmatists as well as by other historical events. Cornel West (1989: 5) explains how American pragmatism avoided "perennial problems in the Western philosophical conversation" in favor of a "continuous cultural commentary or set of interpretations that attempt to explain America to itself at a particular historical moment." He does so not only by addressing established figures such as Emerson, James, and Dewey but also by canonizing several mid-century public intellectuals whose engagement with political issues deepened the social applications of pragmatism, namely

Sidney Hook, C. Wright Mills, W. E. B. DuBois, Reinhold Niebur, and Lionel Trilling. In a similar vein, Charlene Haddock Seigfried (1996) explores the historical contributions of women to the development of pragmatism in order to reveal resources relevant to contemporary philosophical and political discussions of feminism. Scott Pratt (2002) performs a similar analysis in order to track the historical and contemporary interactions between pragmatism and the thought of American Indians. Seigfried and Pratt also broaden the pragmatic canon just like West, by introducing several historical figures such as Charlotte Perkins Gilman and Sagoyewatha. Louis Menand presents one of the most popular and accessible contextualizations of pragmatism in *The Metaphysical Club* (Menand 2001), when he explains how this tradition emerges from its founder's attempts to ameliorate the intellectual, social, and political wounds of the American Civil War (1861–1865). Gail M. Hamner offers a similar contextual analysis in *American Pragmatism: A Religious Genealogy* (Hamner 2003), when she examines how the early pragmatists sought to resolve the tensions within the religious and secular cultures of late nineteenth-century New England such as Puritanism, Unitarianism, Jeffersonian republicanism, and the psychologies of Hermann von Helmholtz (1821–1894) and Wilhelm Wundt (1832–1920). Most recently, Carlin Romano (2012) argues that American cultural is inherently philosophical because Emerson's call for individual intellectual sovereignty has been heeded. Thus, almost two centuries later, the majority of Americans abide by Emerson's imperative "we will speak our own minds," not merely manifest in academia but distributed throughout all genres of literature, communications technology, and popular media.

Yet American philosophy in the cultural sense also includes critical analysis, which uses pragmatism's method of experience to engage current social problems. Most of the histories of pragmatism listed so far contextualize the past for the purpose of gaining new insights, relevant to current attempts to reconstruct present problems. Stuhr devotes the introduction to his *Genealogical Pragmatism* to clarifying these different senses of American philosophy in order to refine the method of experience in subsequent chapters and to apply it to concurrent topics in science, politics, business, and education. Colin Koopman (2009: 2) also refines the method of experience, first of all by recontextualizing historical figures so as to present pragmatism as a process of cultural transition, which redescribes the "philosophical practices of thought, critique, and inquiry such that these practices take place in time and through history." By understanding pragmatism in this way, Koopman presents it as a more fruitful alternative to established theories of ethics and politics, which obsess over hypothetical conceptual problems rather than over actual, concrete ones—or over the practical effects of theories when applied. Another valuable work of both contextual and critical scholarship is Erin McKenna and Scott Pratt's (2015) *American Philosophy: From Wounded Knee to the Present*. This tome not only provides a comprehensive survey of American philosophy in general but presents pragmatism as a philosophy of resistance that "challenges dogma and settled belief from a perspective that recognizes the pluralism of experience and the value of growth and change" (McKenna & Pratt 2015: 6).

If we wish to reduce pragmatism in the philosophical sense to a theory of truth, its cultural context can easily be excised; and then concerns about national boundaries become less relevant. We simply clarify the most essential components of Peirce's pragmatism, identify the historical and contemporary interlocutors who influenced their development, trace the impact of these ideas on the philosophical conversations that followed, then consider how they relate to current debates. This approach would be instructive and useful, but it risks a narrow view of pragmatism, a view that severs the tradition from the rich biographical and cultural experiences that founded its development and continue to inspire new generations of readers. Conversely, an approach that focuses only on the development of the method of experience risks a similar reduction, or being too inclusive and therefore superficial. Similarly, an introduction that focuses only on contextualizing pragmatism risks presenting it as a historical and consequently dead tradition, which does not speak to contemporary problems or debates, whereas overemphasizing critical analysis risks reducing pragmatism to one perspective, or else becoming entangled in contemporary political disputes that cloud the objective and alienate some readers—often the ones most in need of persuading. Therefore, as stated previously, this text aspires to *contextualize* its survey of American pragmatism as a philosophy of place, in the hope of establishing a critical perspective from which one can confront American exceptionalism as an epistemology of ignorance. The next section will define a set of analytic tools, so that they may be applied in the final section of the Introduction and throughout the book.

Pragmatism as a Philosophy of Place

When "American" is taken in the national sense, "America" clearly refers to a geographical entity of some sort; but which one? Although it functions as a synonym for the United States of America, this name can also refer to both continents of the western hemisphere. So then, are Canadians American? They are part of the continent but not part of the United States. Are Hawaiians American? Hawaii is a state, but it is not part of the North American continental plate. Are Puerto Ricans Americans? Their island is part of the continental plate and a US territory, but it is not one of the official United States. Its inhabitants are US citizens, but they cannot vote in national elections. Are Mexicans American? Are Hondurans American? Are Chileans American? These questions are not intended to be merely rhetorical or semantic; and they are not flippant either. Instead, they should unsettle our political and cultural assumptions about what is implied when the proper name "America" is used in any of the aforementioned senses. Geographers confront these issues every day and often refer to various philosophies of geography before they mark boundaries on a map. Furthermore, these boundaries are not trivial. They often determine the fate of people and destiny of nations: consider the Rio Grande, the

Mason–Dixon Line, the DMZ, the Balfour Agreement, or the Berlin Wall.

In *Place: A Short Introduction*, Tim Cresswell (2014) explains how place functions as a "key geographical concept," but also as "an interdisciplinary introduction to an issue that transcends geography, philosophy, or any other discipline." We enthusiastically study places such as America, or historical sites, or potential travel destinations, but we possess "very little considered understanding of what the word 'place'" means (2014: 1). Places are not merely locations or spaces, rather they are spaces endowed with meaning through the "place-making activities of people" (2014: 11). At the astronomical and quantum scales, the universe is, mostly, empty space. That is what makes this place, Earth, special: it the only location where we can live. Now, we may know where a party is located but be unable to find the place. Or you may be assigned a room—a space—on the second floor of a dormitory: that will be its location, but it won't feel like home—a place—until you hang your Dark Side of the Moon poster on the wall (a place-making gesture). Places exist in imagination or memory that never existed or no longer exist in space: Tatooine or Hogwarts, the Library of Alexandria or Cahokia. Furthermore, "places have space between them": we move through space to arrive at some place where we abide for a time before leaving to go somewhere else (2014: 11–15).

Everything we do, physically and mentally, occurs in some place. Places provide the settings for our experiences, contain the objects we experience, and determine the perspectives from which we experience the world. Thus, Cresswell argues, places are epistemologies because they are ways of understanding the world (2014: 18):

> When we look at the world as a world of places, we see different things. We see attachments and connections between people and places. We see worlds of meaning and experience. Sometimes this way of seeing can seem to be more an act of resistance against a rationalization of the world that focuses more on space than place. To think of an area of the

world as a rich and complicated interplay of people and the environment—as a place—is to free us from thinking of it as facts and figures.

As anyone with a broken heart knows, we may occupy the same location, but be in completely different places. The power of place determines our immediate experiences, the stimuli we notice, the thoughts we think, the emotions we feel, the depth of our understanding, the knowledge we gain, and the histories we remember. Critically, places provide the nourishment we need to survive and inform our identities.

Further, we continually transform spaces into places through our meaning-making activities, even if we are merely occupying a space; and, when contrasting senses of place overlap, misunderstanding and conflict can occur. Cresswell shares an example of contrasting senses of place that is very relevant to my discussion of American pragmatism (2014: 15):

> Consider the relationship between ... sea and land along the coast between Seattle and Vancouver. In his book *Passage to Juneau* the travel writer Jonathan Raban tells of his trip by boat along that shore ... Alongside his travel narrative he tells of the voyage of the explorer Captain Vancouver in his ship HMS *Discovery* in 1792. Vancouver's task was to map the coast and name it as he went—making it a place of empire. Naming is one of the ways space can be given meaning and become place. Vancouver's journal reports the seemingly nonsensical movements of natives in their canoes in the sea around them. Rather than taking a direct line from point A to point B the natives would take complicated routes that had no apparent logic. To the native canoeists their movements made perfect sense as they read the sea as a set of places associated with particular spirits and particular dangers. While the colonialists looked at the sea and saw blank space, the natives saw place.

This anecdote captures the pattern of misunderstandings and conflicts between natives and settlers that has shaped world history since humanity's tragic and painful reunion in 1492. Quoting directly from Raban (1999: 103), "[t]wo world-views were in collision; and the poverty of white accounts of these canoe journeys reflect the colonialists' blindness to the native sea. They didn't get it—couldn't grasp the fact that for Indians the water was a place, and the great bulk of the land was undifferentiated space."

If the western hemisphere is the *location* where these cosmologies meet through the people who embody them, then the *sense of place* that emerges from their interactions is America. The structure that largely determines these interactions is settler colonialism, in other words

> The specific formation of colonialism in which people come to a land inhabited by (Indigenous) people and declare that land to be their new home. Settler colonialism is about the pursuit of land, not just labor or resources. Settler colonialism is a persistent societal structure, not just an historical event or origin story for a nation-state. Settler colonialism has meant genocide of Indigenous peoples, the reconfiguring of Indigenous land into settler property. In the United States and other slave estates, it has also meant the theft of people from their homelands (in Africa) to become property of settlers to labor on stolen land. (Rowe & Tuck 2017: 4)

For generations, indigenous authors have stressed the primacy of place and the challenges of surviving the actions and consequences of settler colonialism. In his keynote address to a conference of the Native American and Indigenous Studies Association (NAISA) held at the University of Georgia in 2008, the Acoma Pueblo poet Simon J. Ortiz talks about the primacy of place: "Dai-stuudeh-eh wai. We are here today. Dzaadze-eeskha-haadih-steh-eh-nuh. We are nowhere else but here. We are here: in this place and in this moment. Right now, we are not anywhere else. It is important to be conscious of this. It is significant and so important that our very Existence is dependent upon this acknowledgement, realization, agreement, and acceptance" (Ortiz 2011: 285). Thus Ortiz invites his predominantly native audience to resist feeling "Americanized" by acknowledging how the identities of its members emerge from the meaning-making activities of language, land, and community. He stresses the sacred responsibility of each generation to preserve its cultural legacy while learning new ways to live in the two worlds created by colonization. Only courageous and "creative collaboration and syncretism" can overcome the "loss and disempowerment" of colonization (2011: 293).

Leslie Marmon Silko places America at the transition between the fourth world and the fifth. She describes how her ancestors, the Laguna Pueblos, escaped three other worlds before arriving in the fourth, the paradise of pre-Columbian America. To her and her people, 1492 marks the twilight of the fourth world; but the fifth world still gestates. This gestation involves the Americanization not only of the indigenous peoples of the western hemisphere, but also of the settlers. Her elders remind her to be patient, because the settlers have been in this place only for a short time: a mere five hundred years, in comparison to the twelve thousand years during which the "Pueblo and their paleo-Indian ancestors have lived continuously in the southwest of North America" (Silko 1996: 124). She elaborates on the elders' perspective (1996: 124–5):

> Still, they say, the longer Europeans or others live on these continents, the more they will become part of the Americas. The gravity of the continent under their feet begins this connection, which grows slowly in each generation. The process requires not hundreds, but thousands of years.

Thus settlers and natives do not simply default to roles of either active or passive participants in this process of Americanization. Both actively endure and participate in the process of making and protecting their separate and shared senses of place, but indigenous elders insist that the land itself is not a passive space of objects waiting to be endowed with meanings through human activity; rather the land is the *primary* agent in a larger spiritual process of meaning-making. They take comfort in "the prophecies foretelling the arrival of the Europeans to the Americas" and await the arrival of the fifth world, when the ways of the settlers, not their descendants, will disappear. This "spiritual process" has already begun and "no armies" can prevent it (1996: 125). Thus, if either Stuhr or Cresswell overlooked anything in their analyses of American identity or place, it was this: they did not make room for the possibility that *the land actively determines the meaning of American identity in the spiritual sense*. Fortunately, they did not preclude this possibility either; and neither does American pragmatism.

Indeed, most indigenous philosophers refer to these different attitudes to the authority and function of time and space in the abstract, or of history and place in the social world, as a fundamental cosmological difference between the natives' and the settlers' phenomenological experience of the land. Vine Deloria, Jr. (Lakota) makes this point abundantly clear in his book on traditional Native American religion titled *God Is Red* and originally published in 1972:

> American Indians hold their lands—places—as having the highest possible meaning, and all their statements are made with this reference point in mind. Immigrants review the movement of their ancestors across the continent as a steady progression of basically good events and experiences, thereby placing history—time—in the best possible light. When one group is concerned with the philosophical problem of space and the other with the philosophical problem of time, then the statements of either group do not make much sense when transferred from one context to the other without the proper consideration of what is taking place. (Quoted here from Deloria 1999: 61–2)

Despite this difference concerning the supremacy of time or space, Deloria asserts that the land remains the fundamental source of a people's identity and worldview. He reasons that, if "we look for the origin of peoples, we must discover religious experiences; as we look for the origins of religions, we must discover nations of people, and whichever way we look, it is to the lands on which the people reside and in which religions arise that is important" to look, rather than to temporal authorities such as a sacred text or religious tradition (1999: 142). By the same token, the symbols used to encode meaning—specifically, religious meaning—correspond to the geographic features of their place of origin. Therefore Deloria concludes (1999: 146):

Land must somehow have an unsuspected spiritual energy or identity that shapes and directs human activities. Religions must not be simple expressions of ethical and moral codes as we have been taught. They must be more complicated manifestations of the living earth itself and this aspect of religion is something that American Indians of all the peoples on earth represented.

Across the border, the American pragmatists also recognize the primacy and the activity of place. In a presidential address to the Society for the Advancement of American Philosophy titled "The Need for Reciprocity and Respect in Philosophy," Erin McKenna (2017: 11–12) discusses whether pragmatists should drop their association with the "American tag." She insists that they should not, and for the following reasons:

One reason is that it has come to stand in for a growing stable of thinkers working out of one kind of American experience of another. It is not just their location in "America," but the location of their thinking within the cultures and experiences of the pluralistic and changing place. While this includes a history of intolerance and imperialism, it also includes valuable responses to those tendencies.

Furthermore, she and Scott Pratt demonstrate, in a co-authored history, how American philosophy "took a variety of forms as it emerged in the encounter with the people and lands of North America." They argue thus:

One strand sought to tame the Americas and institute a particular vision of life drawn from the European enlightenment and bound to a conception of a single humanity governed by fixed and certain principles. The other strand grew in resistance to the invasion and sought pluralism with the recognition that fixed and final principles and certainty are not available options. (McKenna & Pratt 2015: 6)

The latter was manifest in practices of either "assimilation or exclusion," whereas the former resisted colonization through "transformative thinking that rejects settled truth, fixed goals, and endless progress." Assimilation, exclusion,

and resistance are all space-oriented terms and function as
meaning-making strategies for transforming space into place.
Thus resistance grounds itself by insisting that "thought is
situated, fallible and committed to the idea that liberation is
a placed and shared experience" (ibid.). Indeed, these theories and strategies of assimilation, exclusion, and resistance
stem from Pratt's earlier history, *Native Pragmatism* (Pratt
2002), which argues that pragmatism arose from the logic of
place originally practiced by the indigenous people of New
England, in resistance to the colonial attitude that justified
settler colonialism.

Thus, viewing pragmatism as a philosophy of place offers
several advantages. Not only does it link pragmatism to
indigenous thought, but it shows how place can influence the
content of philosophical ideas. As I have explained, the pragmatists consistently argued that philosophy occurs within a
context or location. This emphasis on place grounds their
theories in the material and social world, allowing them to
avoid or overcome many of the dualisms that plague philosophy, such as the oppositions between realism and idealism or
between the mind and the body, the subject–object distinction, and the separation of theory from practice. This also
means that the pragmatists appreciated how philosophical
inquiry should begin with and return to the concrete problems within our historical and geographical setting. Finally,
the pragmatists would also argue that our location is not
the only space that determines the direction and content of
inquiry. We reason not only from a geographic location but
also from a biological one: our bodies. We are not merely in
an environment, but part of our environment through the
space of our bodies. Furthermore, the spaces occupied by
our bodies are transformed by historical meaning-making
processes such as settler colonialism. In the next section I will
examine pragmatic theories of embodiment and show how, in
America, the body as a space has been transformed through
patriarchy and racism.

Pragmatism as an Embodied Philosophy

In *The Meaning of the Body: Aesthetics of Human Understanding*, Mark Johnson presents the most thorough account of pragmatism as an embodied philosophy. Drawing primarily on Dewey, James, and contemporary neuroscience, Johnson shows how both Dewey's theory of inquiry and his moral imagination correspond to contemporary neurophysiology. He argues that logical rules of inference do not exist independently of the human mind but are actually "just the patterns of thinking that we have discovered as having served us well in our prior inquiries, relative to certain values, purposes, and types of situations" (Johnson 2007: 109). Even our most abstract reasoning is conditioned by the patterns of our sensorimotor experiences, which are the product of biological structures in the brain (2007: 279). Consequently Johnson rejects the theories of language favored by analytic philosophers as unnecessarily dualistic insofar as they insist on semantics, syntax, or sets of other logical principles separate from the body and the brain. What is more, in earlier works co-authored with George Lakoff, Johnson also develops neuropragmatism (see Lakoff & Johnson 1980, 1999), a theory designed to show "that the body generates meaning even before one is self-conscious" and that "such meaning-making is aesthetic" (McKenna & Pratt 2015: 322). Thus the brain is the space where we both interpret the meanings of place and imagine the meanings that we use to transform space into place through language and the other activities of the body.

Likewise, in *Body Consciousness* Richard Shusterman (2008) presents somaesthetics as a pragmatic reconstruction of the body and art as means of philosophical inquiry. He rightfully claims that the body and art have been at best neglected and at worst denigrated throughout the history of western philosophy; and he develops a compelling critical framework by combining various eastern philosophies with twentieth-century philosophers who emphasized the importance of the body and art, specifically Dewey. Shusterman blames Plato for the bias that "the body distracts us from reality and the search for true knowledge by interrupting our attention with all sorts of sensational commotion and diverting our minds with all sorts of passions, fancies, and nonsense" (2008: 4) and that "[a]rt is dangerous politically ... because it purveys imitative falsehoods" and "appeals to the baser parts of the soul and overstimulates those unruly emotions that disturb the right order in the mind of the individual and the polis in general" (2008: 114). Thus Shusterman recovers the body and art, overcomes several false dualisms, resists aristocratic prejudices, and emphasizes the importance of instrumental value.

While these pragmatic accounts of embodied cognition focus on how the mind functions through the body to transform space into place, they do not place as much emphasis on how place transforms the body into a place of meaning. However, Shannon Sullivan (2001) accomplishes this task in her book *Living Across and Through Skins: Transactional Bodies, Pragmatism, and Feminism* by discussing how our skin functions as the space where, through meaning-making, activities occur. She extends Dewey's concept of the live organism transacting with its environment to show how the two—body and place—are caught in a loop of meaning-making activities:

> bodies do not stop at the edges of their skins and are not contained neatly and sharply within them. Rather, as Dewey eloquently puts it, organisms live "as much in processes across and 'through' skins as in processes 'within' skins." This does not mean that organisms transact in physical, chemical, or material senses only. While these are important examples of how transaction occurs, it is no less important that human transaction with the world takes place in social, political, and cultural senses as well. The suggestion that bodies and environments are transactionally co-constituted is not restricted to "natural" environments, as the word "environment" often is interpreted; "environment," in this case, includes the wide variety of cultural situations and surroundings that also make up the world. (Sullivan 2001: 1–2)

This reconceptualization of skin as a place of meaning-making not only shows how pragmatism can function as a philosophy of embodiment but allows us to see how historical structures such as settler colonialism endow places with meaning and how the meaning of our bodies changes, too, through our skin's transactions with those places and through the logics present in the environment.

Unlike Johnson and Shusterman, who emphasize embodiment in order to resist certain theoretical problems in epistemology and aesthetics, Sullivan has a philosophy of embodiment that allows her to explain and critique sociopolitical problems, specifically racism and patriarchy. The connection between skin as a place of meaning-making and racism should be obvious, since most cases of racism concern the racialization of skin differences: such differences are racialized in certain places, where they receive problematic meanings and responses. By explaining how skin functions as a space for and through which meanings are made, Sullivan provides a window through which we can see how a variety of cultural logics structure both place and our bodies. This applies not only to race and gender. Sullivan alludes to how it influences other forms of prejudice associated with bodies, such as ableism and speciesism. Likewise, in *Habits of Whiteness* (published in 2009), Terrence MacMullen applies the embodied philosophies of the pragmatist, specifically their emphasis on habit, to explicate the dissonance among white folk who do not explicitly possess racist beliefs yet are blind to how their patterns of behavior maintain segregation or discriminate against others. Thus the meanings associated with the body are the product of both a place's history of meanings and the meanings relevant to that body's specific time and place.

Two books that chart the history of how bodies in America have been gendered and raced through meaning-making activities are Carol Pateman's *The Sexual Contract* (published in 1988) and Charles Mills's *The Racial Contract* (Mills 1997), which modify the social contract theory developed by Hobbes, Locke, Rousseau, Kant, and others to address the concealed but omnipresent contracts that determine our social roles and privileges according to the types of bodies we inhabit. In theory, political sovereignty should flow not from the divine right of monarchs but from the consent of the governed. Philosophical discussions of the social contract focus on what the "ideal" social contract should be and on the circumstances under which contracts should be established, revised, or revoked. They do this by examining a cluster of topics, such as human behavior and its relation to various forms of government. Once these questions have been answered, social contract theorists consider what the specific principles of government, balance of powers, laws, rights, and privileges should be if we want to establish and maintain social order. Thus it follows that, if we can accurately describe human nature, then we can develop a form of government that is best suited to the needs of the populace and that can maintain social harmony. This principle rests on the assumption that, through open civil dialogue, the governed can rationally determine how they prefer to be governed.

In practice, history reveals that many people have been excluded from any dialogue of this kind; consequently the established social contracts deliberately or incidentally harm people who inhabit certain specific bodies. Thus Pateman questions the legitimacy of social contract theory because, historically, women have been excluded from participating in this dialogue owing to a prior *gender* or *sex contract*. The gender contract establishes patriarchal societies in which men control not only society but also female bodies.

In the same spirit, Charles Mills argues that the racial contract is more than a background element of the philosophies that inform social contract theory; it is explicitly stated in actual, historical social contracts. Using the US constitution as an example, one need only reference the Three-Fifths Compromise of 1787, which resolved how slaves would be counted when determining a state's total population for taxation and the number of seats each state would get in the House of Representatives. This compromise explicitly placed less value on slaves than on free people and allowed slaveholder interests in practice to determine the government agenda until the American Civil War in 1861.

Both the logic of settler colonialism and the gender and racial contracts hide behind the idea of American exceptionalism. While the United States and its citizens have accomplished several praiseworthy acts, this notion of a special destiny or, worse, the assumption of moral or spiritual superiority prevents its citizens from seeing the suffering they have caused and from recognizing the problems they must correct. Indeed, American exceptionalism often serves as an *epistemology of ignorance*: it constitutes a set of ideas, beliefs, and practices that stop individuals and communities from arriving at accurate conclusions. However, American exceptionalism also has the ability to inspire the best in Americans. Hence the task is not to dispel it but to reconstruct it with each generation, so that it may liberate minds rather than oppressing them. This transformative process happens only by thinking deeply about the American experience; and a long tradition exists of articulating what it means to be American.

Pragmatism as a Philosophy of Experience

While the previous sections traced indigenous and colonial contributions to the generative themes of pragmatism, these themes and others coalesce around the life and works of Ralph Waldo Emerson (1803–1882); and "The American Scholar," the address he delivered in 1837 to the Phi Beta Kappa Society, functions as pragmatism's founding document. Indeed it is a staple of most anthologies of American literature and philosophy. In that address, Emerson presents a rich and prophetic vision of what American thought should (and would) become, expounding not only the concepts that became American transcendentalism but also the themes central to American pragmatism. He delivers his address during a historical period often referred to as "the era of the common man," a time that many historians and scholars deem critical for the development of what would become America's national identity. This period begins with the Monroe Doctrine, issued in 1823, whereby the United States announces that it will no longer tolerate European colonialism in the western hemisphere; and it concludes with the Civil War of 1861–1865. This period would leave the United States free not only to expand its borders westward, into the territory it acquired through the Louisiana Purchase in 1803, but also to consolidate its power within the borders it had at the time.

That was also the era when writers articulated the ideologies of American exceptionalism, manifest destiny, and white supremacy that came to be woven into the country's cultural identity and shaped its political history. According to Deborah L. Madsen, American exceptionalism is the idea that "America and Americans are special, exceptional, because they are charged with saving the world from itself and, at the same time, America and Americans must sustain a high level of political and moral commitment to this exceptional destiny" (Madsen 1998: 2). Multiple historical sources testify to this idea, which continues to evolve; but the text most often referred to as marking its origin is John Winthrop's "A Model of Christian Charity," a speech from 1630 designed to inspire fellow members of the Massachusetts Bay Colony before embarking on the arduous journey to the New World, so that the city of Boston may be as a city upon a hill. During the era of the common man, the idea develops in two travelogues written by visitors to the United States: Lorenzo de Zavala's *Journey to the United States of North America* (originally published in 1834; see Zavala 2005) and Alexis de Tocqueville's *Democracy in America* (originally published in 1835). Both men were statesmen in Mexico and France (their respective countries) and were deeply inspired by the democratic way of life they witnessed in America while on tour. Of the two, Tocqueville's account remains the more popular and influential one; however, Zavala's stands out as the more insightful. I am following here José-Antonio Orosco's suggestion, made in an unpublished conference paper, that histories should place Emerson in comparison with Zavala in order to provide a critical view on American identity.

Tocqueville coins the term "American exceptionalism" to capture the United States' revolutionary origins, commitment to democracy, apparent freedom from class divisions, and ethos of personal industriousness that mark this country as unique. Zavala, too, sees the United States as a democratic utopia worth emulating and hopes to learn lessons that can be adopted by his fellow citizens in the newly independent and democratic Republic of Mexico. He begins his Prologue by exclaiming that "nothing can give more useful lessons in politics to my fellow citizens than the knowledge of the manners, customs, habits, and government of the United States, whose institutions they have so servilely copied" (Zavala 2005: 1). He believes that the United States' strong legal protections of private property allow "for a democracy in which citizens participate in all matters of state formation," whereas in the former colonies of the Spanish Empire there is an "absolute [material] separation between conquerors and conquered." According to Zavala, in Mexico this separation remains owing to "exceptional laws" that "perpetuate a privileged aristocracy that is antithetical to Republican ideas"; and he hopes to persuade his fellow Mexicans that they should be repealed, if Mexico wishes to enjoy a truly democratic culture (2005: 71).

However, Zavala's awareness of the complicated relationship between the United States and Mexico allows him to remain more critical than Tocqueville on the other two ideologies previously mentioned: manifest destiny and chattel slavery. First, Mexico already felt the "effects of the expansionist US policies of the Monroe Doctrine" under the guise of the "democratic protectionism" that would come to be known as manifest destiny, as Rivera (2005: viii) notes in his introductory study. In the decade since the Monroe Doctrine was issued, the United States had already expanded into two former territories of New Spain—Florida and Louisiana—at the expense of the Latin peoples who lived there, and thus the "American Republic was at the very doorstep of Mexico in its advance westward" (Rivera 2005: xviii). Coincidentally, Zavala would make friends with Stephen F. Austin, "the Father of Texas," and would soon further the American expansion, becoming involved in the formation of the Republic of Texas and its independence from Mexico. Nevertheless, Zavala recognized the emerging rivalry between these republics and wished to foster mutual respect, not submission to either the political or the moral authority of the elder one.

Nothing undercut the moral authority of the US more than its abhorrent, yet legal practice of chattel slavery, which Zavala condemns in no uncertain terms. As to "the states which permit slavery in our sister republic," he writes that "the philosopher cannot fail to feel the contrast that is noted between the two countries, nor fail to experience a pleasant memory for those who have abolished this degrading traffic and caused to disappear among us the vestiges of so humiliating a condition to the human race" (Zavala 2005: 20). Thus, if Mexico should use the United States as a model in establishing its national identity, slavery cannot be included, not only for moral reasons, but also because slavery prevents the "emergence of autonomous and liberal political peoplehood precisely because the representation of the people, the demos, was the normalized white colonial master" (Rivera 2005: ix). The aristocratic divisions between conqueror and conquered already hampered the emergence of a democratic culture in Mexico, and such a culture would become impossible if the country also attempted to incorporate the hypocrisy of slavery.

What Zavala recognizes better than Tocqueville is that American national identity is complicated by mutual contradictions and affinities between exceptionalism, manifest destiny, and chattel slavery. While there are certainly proud moments when the United States achieves the democratic and moral ideals that make it historically exceptional, far too often its brutal foreign and domestic policies undermine these achievements. It habitually insists on setting rules and norms, while reserving the right to break them when it serves national interests. Thus exceptionalism becomes a way to rationalize the nation's worst crimes, as the nation acts by taking exception to the rules rather than acting in an exceptionally just manner. The era of the common man epitomizes these contradictions. The era received its name from the populist expansion of democratic power that occurred at the time and from the celebration of the inherent dignity and contributions of the common man; yet this sharing of power did not extend to women, African slaves, or American Indians.

Indeed, the era of the common man is also known as the era of Jacksonian democracy and no figure in US history represents these contradictions better than Andrew Jackson himself, the seventh president of the United States. Son of recent Scotish–Irish immigrants to southern Appalachia, Jackson possessed a tough, aggressive, and rebellious personality from a young age. He became wealthy first as a lawyer, through the successful acquisition of lands originally reserved by treaty for the Tsalagi (Cherokee) and the Chickasaw, and would later acquire the Hermitage, a 640-acre cotton plantation worked by as many as 150 slaves. He obtained his first political office as member of the US House of Representatives for the state of Tennessee in 1796 and became famous for his successes as a general, in several engagements and wars against various groups of American Indians: the 1812 War, the Creek War (1813–1814), and the First Seminole War (1814–1818). Eventually these financial, political, and military achievements, combined with his populist commitment to the idea of fighting government corruption and excess, earned him two terms as president, from 1829 until 1837.

By far his most controversial act as president pertained to US–Indian relations; it was, specifically, his proposal to relocate the "five civilized tribes"—the Cherokee, the Choctaw, the Creek, the Chickasaw, and the Seminole—west of the Mississippi River. These tribes were referred to as civilized because they had organized themselves into modern nation states by drafting their own constitutions and incorporating other colonial practices such as literacy, private property, industry, and conversion to Christianity. Sadly, some of them even practiced slavery on cotton and tobacco plantations throughout their lands. Nevertheless, in 1830 Congress passed the Indian Removal Act, which authorized the president to negotiate terms for the relocation of these tribes to the newly created Indian Territory, located in present-day Oklahoma. Pleased with the success of his proposal, Jackson proudly made the following statement in his First Annual Message to Congress (December 8, 1829):

Humanity has often wept over the fate of the aborigines of this
country ... To follow to the tomb the last of his race and to
tread on the graves of extinct nations excite melancholy reflections. But true philanthropy reconciles the mind to these vicis-
situdes as it does to the extinction of one generation of people
to make room for another. In the monuments and fortresses
of an unknown people, spread over the extensive regions of
the West, we behold the memorials of a once powerful race,
which was exterminated or has disappeared to make room for
the existing savage tribes ... What good man would prefer a
country covered with forests and ranged by a few thousand
savages to our extensive Republic, studded with cities, towns,
and prosperous farms ... and filled with all the blessings of
liberty, civilization, and religion? (https://www.mtholyoke.
edu/acad/intrel/andrew.htm)

The contradiction between this early statement of manifest
destiny and American exceptionalism could not be starker.
Our first response should be to flip Jackson's question and
ask how any person of conscience could find it morally or
rationally acceptable to displace a sovereign people from its
ancestral lands in the name of expanding liberty and civilization. However, a more penetrating question would be to ask
what beliefs allow a person to rationalize such contradictions while maintaining both his image of himself as a decent
person and the notion of the United States as a just nation.
Emerson repudiated Jackson's colonialism and racism, but it
is more informative to see how, despite his opposition to the
president, Emerson also internalized settler colonialism and
the racial contract. Thus, while his work successfully reconstructs American exceptionalism according to the pluralistic
and democratic vision that inspires pragmatism, future pragmatists will need to reconstruct Emerson, lest they perpetuate
these biases.

Returning to Emerson, he delivered "The American
Scholar" against this political backdrop. Proud of the
popularity their young alumnus achieved the previous year
(1836) with the publication of his essay *Nature*, Harvard
College's Phi Beta Kappa Society invited him to inspire
their members at the beginning of the new academic year.

Undoubtedly the organizers expected him to deliver a stirring, but conventional, speech in celebration of "the achievements of American scholarship," as previous speakers had done (Goodman 2015: 170). They did not realize that Emerson was gripped by an identity crisis, prefigured by the death of his deeply beloved wife Ellen from tuberculosis in 1831, at the age of 19, and then by the tragic mental collapse and eventual death of his brother Edward in 1834. Emerson found that his training as a Unitarian minister provided little to no comfort for his grief; and he became increasingly frustrated by the rituals and practice of organized religion. In an 1832 sermon titled "The Lord's Supper" he criticizes Communion, the most important sacrament of Christianity, on the grounds that the ritual and the doctrines surrounding it had become false idols that inhibit rather than enabling the emotional and mystical states they should evoke: "Forms are as essential as bodies; but to exalt particular forms, to adhere to one form a moment after it is out-grown, is unreasonable, and it is alien to the spirit of Christ." He asserted that "[f]reedom is the essence of this faith," therefore the church and its rituals "should be as flexible as the wants of men. That form out of which the life and suitableness have departed, should be as worthless in its eyes as the dead leaves that are falling around us" (Emerson 2000: 107).

Emerson reconstructs himself by pulling together a plurality of new influences. In his book *American Philosophy before Pragmatism*, Russell Goodman (2015) explains how Emerson's early thought combined the political thought of American deists and democrats such as Benjamin Franklin and Thomas Jefferson with the progressive theology of Unitarianism. With regard to the latter, William Ellery Channing, his mentor at Harvard Divinity School, impressed upon him two ideas that would last throughout his entire work: the compatibility of "rational investigation and scientific discovery" with religious faith and experience; and the rejection of Calvinism's strict doctrine and threatening tone in favor of ecumenicalism and a spirit of congeniality (Goodman 2015: 148–150). However, this embrace of religious pluralism, free thought, and curiosity would lead Emerson to incorporate even more diverse influences into his philosophy, in the wake of his personal crises. His lifelong interest in the ancient Greeks deepened as he focused more on the mystical elements of Plato and the Neoplatonists. In 1832 he traveled to Europe, where he met not only John Stuart Mill, the great philosopher of utilitarianism and liberty, but also several major figures of British romanticism: the philosopher and satirist Thomas Carlyle and the poets Samuel Coleridge and William Wordsworth. These ancient and romantic influences allowed Emerson to surpass the detached Enlightenment of Franklin and Jefferson, and even Channing's open, but still conventional Unitarianism. The world was neither the marvelous creation of a divine yet distant watchmaker nor the legacy of a benevolent yet reasonable deity, best understood through the teaching of Jesus. Instead, Emerson beheld the world as a permanently unfolding miracle, intelligible to the mind and of a rational character, but best understood through an enthusiastic relationship with nature, punctuated by moments of personal rapture and revelation, rather than merely through scientific research or the authority of religious tradition and scripture (Goodman 2015: 148–153).

However, the factors that influenced Emerson were not just European, they were global; and one must appreciate the profound influence of Hinduism on his thought, particularly during the transitional period 1832–1837. Emerson lived during the "first great period of European Sanskrit scholarship" and encountered Hinduism through snippets published in *The Edinburgh Review* and through his own study of Charles Grant's 1897 poem *Restoration of Learning in the East*. During his crisis, Emerson read two lectures from Victor Cousin's *Course of the History of Philosophy* (published in 1829) that not only corrected and expanded his knowledge of Hinduism but helped him recognize Hinduism's explicit articulation of two ideas he implicitly held: the "basic vision of unity" behind "myriad forms"—specifically, God (Brahman) and the Soul (Atman); and an "attack on knowledge obtained from books, even the sacred Vedas," in favor of the authority of personal experience and insight (Goodman 2015: 627–628).

These themes are immediately manifest in Emerson's quin-
tessential works of this period—*Nature* from 1836, "The
American Scholar" from 1837, his "Divinity School Address"
from 1838, and "Circles"—a piece from 1841. In fact we find
an obvious expression of all these themes in his most famous
prose passage, the description of the "transparent eyeball" in
Nature:

> In the woods, we return to reason and faith. There I feel that
> nothing can befall me in life—no disgrace, no calamity (leav-
> ing me my eyes), which nature cannot repair. Standing on the
> bare ground—my head bathed by the blithe air and uplifted
> into infinite space—all mean egotism vanishes. I become a
> *transparent eyeball* [my emphasis]; I am nothing; I see all; the
> currents of the Universal Being circulate through me; I am
> part and parcel of God ... I am the lover of uncontained and
> immortal beauty. In the wilderness, I find something more
> dear and connate than in streets or villages. In the tranquil
> landscape, and especially in the distant line of the horizon,
> man beholds somewhat as beautiful as his own nature.
> (Emerson 2000: 6)

This passage contains all of Emerson's influences—poetic and
philosophical, secular and religious, western and eastern. It
also contains the theme that would unify his writing and
thought throughout his career: the resolution of philosophical
dualisms, not through reason or faith alone, but through their
union in moments of ecstatic communion between nature and
the individual.

Most important to my present inquiry is the fact that
nature is not merely a passive—or even a symbolic—setting
for philosophical or spiritual inquiry; it is a fellow interlocutor. It waits and longs to speak to us and with us; we
must only take the time to escape the idle chatter of society,
surrender to its rhythms, and attune ourselves to its voice.
The land speaks to Emerson and tells him that the time has
arrived for Americans to "enjoy an original relation to the
universe ... [to] have a poetry and philosophy of insight and
not of tradition, and a religion by revelation to us, and not
the history of theirs" (Emerson 2000: 3). Bruce Wilshire

interprets this call as setting Emerson's work "at a critical distance from Europe, the Old World, with its tired conflicts, castes, creeds—itemized worldviews" (Wilshire 2000: 3). By the time of Emerson, Europeans had been "settling on the North American continent and interacting with its indigenous peoples for 250 years," out of which a "distinctly Euro-American" critique arose, specifically a "dawning realization that proud European Enlightenment and surging 'progress' have outrun our life-support system as ancient children of Earth" (Wilshire 2000: 4). Consequently, Emerson's transcendentalism insists on the importance of place and passes this insight on to the pragmatists.

Thus, when Emerson delivers "The American Scholar," he stands at the center of global thought and marks the birth of America's cultural identity. He announces:

> Our day of dependence, our long apprenticeship to the learning of other lands, draws to a close. The millions, that around us are rushing into life, cannot always be fed on the sere remains of foreign harvests. Events, actions arise, that must be sung, that will sing themselves. Who can doubt, that poetry will revive and lead in a new age, as the star in the constellation Harp, which now flames in our zenith, astronomers announce, shall one day be the pole-star for a thousand years? (Emerson 2000: 43)

In this opening, Emerson appeals for liberation, but a liberation that occurs through transcendence to a higher state of unity. The past should not be abandoned, it should be used to feed the future. Scholarship, experience, and politics are not separate but interrelated domains, which enable the individual to articulate the events and wisdom of the age through new meaning-making activities. Earthbound poetry and science both illuminate the new knowledge of the universe and endow it with meaning. Only the power of outdated beliefs to separate the population and reduce the individual to specialized social functions hinders this transcendence. Fortunately, each one of us has the power to overcome this objectification by becoming self-reliant, by realizing that we must think for ourselves. Americans must create the new beliefs, science, and culture that will restore their sense of independence and renew their social cohesion.

In the remainder of the address Emerson prescribes three sources of education for regaining individual intellectual sovereignty and for achieving cultural independence: nature, books, and action. First, nature provides our physical as well as our mental sustenance; thus we must escape the constraints of society and return to nature in order to experience an original relationship with the universe, thereby restoring our confidence in the authority of our own perspective. Second, we must respect books as historical attempts made by others to articulate their original relationship with nature, so that they might share their experience with the world and with posterity. Paradoxically, their benefit decreases as their authority increases, because we become dependent on their vision instead of using their insights to enhance our own perspective. We have the right, if not the requirement, to question anyone and to assert our own genius. Consequently, the mandate of education is not only to supply professional credentials or vocational training, but to provide the knowledge and skills necessary to empower students to think for themselves, so they may achieve their full potential. This leads to Emerson's third prescription: action. Each of us must discover our own insights and hone our abilities so as to enrich the quality of our lives. Experience is our first and most important teacher.

Next Emerson outlines the responsibilities of the scholar. He states: "The office of the scholar is to cheer, to raise, and to guide men by showing them facts amidst appearances" (Emerson 2000: 52). The scholar must first of all trust himself, realizing that the masses will not adopt his vision uncritically. Therefore, rather than conforming to social expectations, he must be willing to make the personal sacrifices necessary for him to discover and articulate his vision. He will begin to recognize that "[t]he world of any moment is the merest appearance," where fleeting fads often present themselves as urgent necessities. In consequence he must remain confident, believe in the importance of his work, and not be distracted. Most importantly, he must be "free and brave," because new insights and revolutionary ideas inevitably threaten the status quo. If anything, resistance validates his vision's vitality. "The world is his, who can see through its pretension. What deafness, what stone-blind custom, what overgrown error you behold, is there only by sufferance—by your sufferance. See it to be a lie, and you have already dealt it its mortal blow." Finally, the scholar must resist the temptations that accompany success; and he must do so not only to maintain the integrity of his own character and vision, but because "[t]he main enterprise of the world for splendor, for extent, is the upbuilding of a man" (2000: 52–55).

Emerson concludes the address by linking the implications of these prescriptions to his present moment. While he carefully stresses that the universal is present in the experience of any particular person or context, he admits that each individual and era have unique messages to communicate. The present moment is always an "age of Revolution; when the old and new stand side by side, and admit of being compared when the energies of all men are searched by fear and by hope; when the historic glories of the old, can be compensated by the rich possibilities of the new"; thus "[t]his time, like all times, is a very good one, if we but know what to do with it." And at this moment Emerson announces the philosophical significance of America (2000: 57–58):

> I embrace the common, I explore and sit at the feet of the familiar, the low. Give me insight into to-day, and you may have the antique and future worlds. What would we really know the meaning of? The meal in the firkin; the milk in the pan; the ballad in the street; the news of the boat; the glance of the eye; the form and the gait of the body—show me the ultimate reason of these matters; show me the sublime presence of the highest spiritual cause lurking, as always it does lurk, in these suburbs and extremities of nature; let me see every trifle bristling with the polarity that ranges it instantly on an eternal law; and the shop, the plough, and the ledger, referred to the like cause by which light undulates and poets sing—and the world lies no longer a dull miscellany and lumber-room, but has form and order; there is no trifle; there is no puzzle; but one design unites and animates the farthest pinnacle and the lowest trench.

In a sense, Emerson's method is the message. As a philosophical idea, America represents the sovereignty of the individual to liberate herself from the shackles of society, so that she may experience her own vision and renew the present age by sharing her truth and acting upon it. Thus the American scholar is the one who will "take up into himself all the ability of the time, all the contributions of the past, all the hopes of the future," because "in yourself is the law of all nature, and you know not yet how a globule of sap ascends; in yourself slumbers the whole of Reason; it is for you to know all, it is for you to dare all" (2000: 59).

In conclusion, Emerson establishes four key themes upon which pragmatism will be founded: experience, naturalism, democracy, and activism. As seen in the last paragraph, Emerson reminds us that all inquiry begins with, occurs within, and returns to our experience. While we should learn from and honor tradition, we should never be beholden to it. Thus, while his emphasis on experience alone links Emerson to the radical empiricism of James and to Dewey's aesthetics, his insistence that each generation and every person must evaluate historical ideas according to their relevance to present experience prefigures Dewey's method of reconstruction. Next, the greatest teacher in our experience is nature itself, and Emerson sees no inherent conflict between the careful insights of science investigation and mystical revelations. The empirical and the ecstatic are, both, crucial aspects of experience and we gain more by embracing their constructive interplay than by reducing one to the other. This establishes the rich holistic naturalism found all throughout pragmatism, from Peircean concepts like *musement* and *agapism* to James's lecture series *The Varieties of Religious Experience* (first published in 1902). Even more secular pragmatists like Santayana and Dewey devote a considerable amount of their work to charitably understanding the mystical from a naturalistic perspective. This holistic naturalism also anticipates the pragmatic penchant for avoiding and critiquing the vestigial dualisms of philosophy rather than ameliorating them. Finally, Emerson captures the democratic spirit of America when he suggests that more riches are to be found through immersion in common, everyday experiences and concerns than through sophisticated escapes into purely intellectual realms. If philosophy cannot explain how it coheres with, or how it impacts, everyday experience, we should suspect obscurantism. Besides, everyone has unique experiences, and thus specific insights that only this person can share; no one should be discounted on principle.

These commitments made Emerson one of the most important public activists of his day and anticipated the social projects of the Chicago pragmatists. Emerson condemned the Indian Removal Act and other US policies of expansion, advocated the abolition of slavery, and supported women's suffrage. Granted, he still shared several of the problematic biases of his time. According to the historian Peter Field, "[e]ven as [Emerson's] views evolved, they often appear contradictory; they can be simultaneously insightful, incipiently radical, and baldly racist." He "remained convinced that the characteristics that made the United States, for all its flaws, the great nation of the world were largely product of its Saxon heritage and history" (Field 2001: 3). Thus Emerson's defense of "political and social democracy" continued to rest "on the inherent intelligence of one race rather than imagining a polity based upon the capacity for self-culture inhering in all people regardless of color" (2001: 25). Likewise, Robert D. Richardson (1995) observes that Emerson's lecture "The Peace Principle" (delivered in 1838) defended pacifism, but only in the abstract, as it made no mention of the ongoing Seminole War; and Bethany Schneider (2008) explains how Emerson's rebuke of the Indian Removal Act in his famous "Letter to President Martin Van Buren" of 1838 spoke more of damage to the nation's moral identity than of the abhorrent suffering the Act caused to the Cherokee.

Despite these problematic beliefs, Emerson proved to be one of the most important advocates for social justice in the nineteenth century. The popularity of his writings and lectures positioned him as the mainstream conscience of his generation; and he continues to inspire readers today. He certainly inspired his godson, William James, as well as Dewey. On Emerson's centennial on May 25, 1903, both philosophers delivered public eulogies in his honor. By that time, pragmatism had been established for decades and had left a clear impression of its founders. James described Emerson as "proclaim[ing] the sovereignty of the living individual" by revealing that "[t]he point of any pen can be an epitome of reality; the commonest person's act, if genuinely actuated, can lay hold on eternity" (James 1968: 583). He also claimed that Emerson was a "real seer" who "could perceive the full squalor of the individual fact" as well as its transfiguration (1968: 586). Likewise, Dewey emphasized Emerson's empowerment of the individual and his insights into the nature of democracy. He viewed Emerson as reminding us that "every individual is at once the focus and the channel of mankind's long and wide endeavor, that all nature exists for the education of the human soul," and that we must restore "to the common man that which in the name of religion, of philosophy, of art and of morality, has been embezzled from the common store and appropriated to sectarian and class use" (Dewey 1981: 29). Thus, in his view, Emerson should be remembered as the "prophet and herald of any system which democracy may henceforth construct and hold by, and that when democracy has articulated itself, it will have no difficulty in finding itself already proposed in Emerson" (1981: 30). Even Peirce admitted—in an autobiographical essay titled "The Law of the Mind" and first published in 1892—that being "born and reared in the neighborhood of Concord ... at the time when Emerson, Hedge, and their friends [the Transcendentalists] were disseminating" their ideas, "it is probabl[e] that some cultured bacilli, some benignant form of the disease was implanted in my soul, unawares, and that now, after long incubating, it comes to the surface, modified, by mathematical conceptions and by training in physical investigations" (Peirce 1992: 313).

– 1 –

Fallibilism and the
Classical Pragmatists

Pragmatism begins conventionally with the friendship between Charles Sanders Peirce and William James and with their overlapping critiques of modern philosophy. Both men benefited from unique and privileged upbringings, which placed them in a position to critique nineteenth-century philosophy and to assimilate the American experience into their responses. Peirce was the son of Benjamin Peirce, an eminent research mathematician who taught at Harvard University for nearly fifty years and, while he inherited his father's talent for mathematics, science, and logic, he did not inherit his father's steadfastness. From an early age, Peirce suffered from a variety of medical, personal, and social problems that routinely disrupted his life work. As a result, Peirce never published a single comprehensive summary of his mature thought, but it is possible to get glimpses of a profound and systematic philosophy from his published articles and unpublished manuscripts.

James was the son of Henry James Sr., a wealthy businessman and theologian who spared no expense to see that his son enjoyed the finest education and was exposed to the best cultural experiences. James's intellect, much like Peirce's, thrived under these conditions, but early physical ailments plagued him too and often resulted in bouts of depression. Unlike Peirce, James developed more constructive means of coping with his maladies and, if anything, his melancholy often produced his most valuable insights. In fact it can be argued that his youthful listlessness led to the formative experiences that inspired him to become a psychologist and philosopher rather than pursuing a more conventional career as a physician, as he originally intended. Furthermore, James possessed the necessary temperament not only to spend his entire career at Harvard but to write voluminously, including several philosophical masterpieces. Thus, in interpreting James, the challenge is to appreciate how his thought matured throughout his life.

Hence this chapter will examine Peirce's development of the *pragmatic maxim* as an alternative to the foundationalism of René Descartes, then William James's development of *radical empiricism* as an alternative to the skepticism of David Hume. It will then contrast Peirce's and James's rival forms of pragmatism and highlight how this rift cuts across pragmatism throughout the twentieth century and remains a point of contention. Finally, the chapter will discuss the contributions of the two philosophers' friend and colleague Josiah Royce and how his *philosophy of loyalty* functions as a foil and extension of their pragmatisms. These concepts represent the theme of *fallibilism*—the idea that even the best supported claim is conditional upon, and subject to revision in the light of, future evidence and experience. Fallibilism not only serves as a unifying theme among the classical pragmatists but grounds pragmatism's general theory of knowledge and its unique contribution as a critique and as an alternative to modern philosophy.

Fallibilism, Epistemology, and Scientific Inquiry

As discussed in the previous chapter, Emerson's request that each individual and each generation trust their own experience when constructing their original relation to nature anticipates fallibilism. Of all the themes discussed in this introduction, we shall see that fallibilism emerges as the most essential and unifying one. According to Emerson, we should be suspicious of tradition because all accounts of nature, scientific or religious, are fallible. No one sees reality in its entirety, no one can communicate one's insights without error, and, even if one could, we may fail to understand or to apply those past insights properly. More importantly, experience is in a constant state of flux; thus even the best concepts and methods must be adapted to present circumstances. However, the fact of fallibility does not legitimate the common caricature according to which the pragmatists are total relativists who believe that truth does not exist or is just personal advantage and that all claims are equally valid. Rather the pragmatists believe that "fallibility is an irreducible dimension of the human condition: empirical belief can never be certain, exact, absolute, final. The abandoned 'quest for certainty' is replaced by piecemeal, multi-directional efforts to verify and warrant beliefs. The possibility of belief revision is never erased" (Stuhr 2000: 3).

While the pragmatists certainly inherit an idea of fallibilism from Emerson, scholars also assert that it is further informed by other sources. In *The Metaphysical Club*, Louis Menand (2001) insists that it emerges as a consequence of the Civil War. Many Americans blamed the war on polarized and intractable beliefs about slavery and worried that "certitude leads to violence" (2001: 61). Meanwhile, Charles Darwin's *Origin of the Species*, published in 1859, revolutionized biology and intellectual thought by dispelling not only prior religious and scientific beliefs about the origins and diversification of species, but—as we shall see Dewey explaining (in the next chapter)—the deeper ontological assumption, which goes back to Aristotle, that natural beings have a static essence and that beings or processes have a fixed purpose or ultimate goal. Nicholas Rescher (1998) argues that Peirce's fallibilism is informed by his experience as a laboratory scientist; thus it does not insist "on the falsity of our scientific claims but rather on their tentativity as inevitable estimates: it does not hold that knowledge is unavailable here, but rather that it is always provisional." Still others, for example Douglas Anderson (2008), locate pragmatism's commitment to fallibilism in Peirce's assertion that chance is a fundamental part of the cosmos—an assertion in contrast with the absolutist ontologies articulated by Kant and Hegel that dominated contemporary philosophical discussions. While we need not reduce pragmatism's commitment to fallibilism to a single historical source, this commitment is essential to the philosophies of both Peirce and James and develops through their friendship, overlapping critiques of modern philosophy. Historically, epistemology—that is, the theory of knowledge—has been a central part of philosophy. From classical antiquity on, many philosophical master-pieces and careers have focused on such questions as: What is knowledge? How do we know whether a claim is true? Should we prefer arguments or evidence in support of our knowledge? Is knowledge universally true at all times and in all places for everyone, or is it relative to cultural and historical contexts? What is the difference between facts and opinions? Are there differences between scientific, moral, and aesthetic knowledge? Are there any limits to what can be known and, if so, what are they? While these issues and questions are addressed by philosophers in all ages and cul-tures, they become critically important in the era of modern philosophy, as European culture transitioned from depend-ence on religious authority and superstition to secular politics and scientific inquiry. Philosophers hoped to settle disputes and create better societies based on rationality, coopera-tion, and scientific knowledge, thus determining the criterion for knowledge; and the best method for discovering it was crucial.

Inspired by mathematics, René Descartes (1596–1650) insisted upon seeking a set of basic axioms that could be deduced through a method of doubt. If any belief could be doubted, it should be dismissed, until only indubitable beliefs remained. These were innate ideas and would function as a stable and objective foundation for all other knowledge, since they could be determined through rational investigation, inde-pendently of experience. Unfortunately, each of Descartes' innate ideas (God, infinity, and substance) has been chal-lenged; and his emphasis on rationality further entrenched the dualism between the mind and the body. Conversely,

John Locke (1632–1704) would return to Aristotle's preference for evidence over reason by reviving the concept of
tabula rasa. Rather than possessing innate ideas, we are born
as blank slates and acquire knowledge through our senses,
which are the source of our experience. Eventually, David
Hume (1711–1776) advanced Locke's empiricism to several
perplexing conclusions. If all knowledge is obtained through
the senses, then we do not have direct experience of several
concepts we take for granted—such as causality, the self, and
induction.

At the turn of the nineteenth century European philosophy
was caught between Descartes' foundationalism, which led
to dualism, and Hume's empiricism, which led to skepticism.
Should philosophy continue the search for indubitable foundational principles, or should it content itself with probing
the limits of human reason? Most philosophers of the time
would develop various forms of idealism in response. Idealism
proposes that our knowledge consists of mental representations of the world rather than being a direct experience of
it. While Vedanta and Plato serve as ancient examples of
idealism, modern idealisms avoided the temptation to ground
knowledge in supernatural postulates, such as Brahman or the
Forms, and attempted instead to find the structures common
to experience that make our claims intelligible. Immanuel
Kant (1724–1804) argued that the categories of time and
space function as necessary structures of our experience; and
Georg Wilhelm Friedrich Hegel (1770–1831) proposed the
thesis that knowledge emerges over time through dialectics—
the historical process of rational discourse. I shall return to
Descartes and Hume shortly, to show how Peirce and James
raised specific critiques of their ideas, and our examination of
Royce will be the first to highlight the influence of idealism on
the development of pragmatism. In the nineteenth century the
rate of scientific progress was increasing rapidly, deepening
human understanding and demonstrating the power of the
scientific method to investigate phenomena. While revolutionary theories were proposed in all major fields, none was
more radical than Charles Darwin's (1809–1882) suggestion
that the diversification of species resulted from changes in the

population of organisms that were due to pressure exercised by the laws of natural selection over vast spans of time. Even if philosophers had questions about the nature of knowledge that remained unsettled, scientists were beginning to find answers to perennial questions about the natural world.

Thus pragmatism emerged at the crossroad between two axes: the philosophical tension between foundationalism and skepticism; and the disciplinary tension between philosophy and science as types of epistemic inquiry. Several of pragmatism's founders were experimental scientists. Peirce earned a BSc in chemistry from Harvard in 1863, served as a geographer for the US Coast and Geodetic Survey for several decades (1859–1891), and was elected to the National Academy of Sciences in 1877. James accompanied Louis Agassiz's expedition to Brazil and along the Amazon (1861–1865), earned an MD from the Harvard Medical School in 1869, and was president of the American Psychological Association in 1894—as was Dewey five years later, in 1899, and then Josiah Royce in 1901. Thus a deep respect for the scientific method is at the heart of pragmatism and informs its fallibilism, which in turn serves as a response to the dilemma of choosing between foundationalism and skepticism. The pragmatists recognized that the power of the scientific method lies not in its ability to uncover indubitable truths about the world but in its ability to falsify hypotheses and replace them with new ones, which better explain, predict, and control the natural phenomena.

A recent example of fallibilism in science is the reclassification of Pluto as a dwarf planet. Since prehistory, humans have observed and recorded the behavior of the objects in the night sky and, while the procession of the majority of them remains "fixed," a handful—Mercury, Venus, Mars, Jupiter, and Saturn—appear to move in less regular patterns. The ancient Greeks named these objects "planets" (πλανῆται, a noun derived from the verb πλανάω, πλανᾶν, "wander") because they were the only visible celestial objects in the sky that behaved in this manner. With the invention of the telescope at the beginning of the seventeenth century, new evidence stretched the application of the descriptor "planet." Galileo discovered that the Earth was a fellow planet rather than the center of the universe and that some planets, such as Jupiter, had their own satellites. In time, the other outer planets were discovered (Uranus in 1781 and Neptune in 1846). When Pluto was discovered in 1930, the number of wanderers stabilized for several generations until further discoveries with regard to its mass and orbit troubled Pluto's status and eventually the definition of a planet.

Then in 1992, a second trans-Neptunian object was discovered in the Kuiper Belt—the region inhabited by Pluto; and this inspired astronomers to begin scanning the region for other large objects. More were quickly discovered. Several are nearly the mass of Pluto, such as Sedna and Haumea (discovered in 2003 and 2004 respectively); some also possess their own moons, such as Quaoar and Makemake (discovered in 2002 and 2005 respectively); and one—Eris, discovered in 2005— is more massive. These discoveries provoked a crisis: does the solar system contain fourteen planets (or probably more), or do we need to change our definition of a planet in light of the new evidence?

The International Astronomical Union (IAU) formally defined a planet for the first time as a result of these findings; and in 2006 it reclassified Pluto, the asteroid Ceres, and the other newly discovered objects as "dwarf planets." The public outcry was enormous and has continued for a decade, because many felt that the demotion of Pluto was an insult and some even considered it to indicate the unreliability of science as an institution. Few appreciated the exciting implications of this announcement. Before 2006 we believed we lived in a solar system with only a handful of neighboring worlds. Now we know we have dozens, possibly hundreds of neighbors waiting to be explored! In fact, during the revision of this book, the IAU announced the discovery of two new trans-Neptunian objects: FarOut (11/2018 @ 120AU) and FarFarOut (2/2019 @ 140AU). Both were discovered while searching for the postulated Planet Nine, an object estimated to be the mass of Neptune, which may still lurk in the farthest reaches of the solar system. Thus we did not lose a planet; we gained a deeper understanding of star systems, our own and others. This reclassification demonstrates how our scientific knowledge is conditional and always open to revision when confronted with enough evidence.

Scientific knowledge is never "certain," "indubitable," or "foundational" in the Cartesian sense; rather it is practical, tentative, and always subject to revision in the light of future experience, evidence, or experimentation. It is fallible but pragmatic. Skepticism retreats in the face of the technological benefits provided by this provisional knowledge. While it may be impossible to verify causality or the reliability of induction through our sense experience, it is difficult to deny the advantages of an internal combustion engine over a steam engine, of a telegraph over semaphore flags, or of penicillin over folk remedies. Most importantly, fallibilism enables progress without reducing it to a single goal or metric. Since we can never have certainty, fallibilism implies continual, possibly perpetual expansion, improvement, and refinement of knowledge. As we shall see, this openness to growth supports most of the themes I will explore in subsequent chapters, specifically amelioration, pluralism, and hope, as well as the pragmatists' general (although not exclusive) preference for progressive politics. Now that fallibilism has been defined and related to its historical context, let us see how Peirce and James developed it through their respective critique of Descartes and Hume.

Charles Sanders Peirce (1839–1914) and the Pragmatic Maxim

As mentioned from the outset, Peirce's personal problems and lack of professionalism prevented him from writing a single summative work. However, he was incredibly prolific and, even though most of his work remains unpublished, there are glimpses of an intricate systematic philosophy between the lines of his more popular articles. Of crucial importance are three early essays: "Some Consequences of the Four Incapacities" (1868), "The Fixation of Belief" (1877), and "How to Make Our Ideas Clear" (1878). In these articles Peirce presents his criticisms of Descartes and articulates the basic notions he develops throughout his work: inquiry, habit, vagueness, and the pragmatic maxim. With these basic notions in hand, I will turn to his deep epistemological and metaphysical ideas, specifically his understanding of final opinion and his objective idealism.

Peirce begins "Some Consequences of the Four Incapacities" with a discussion of how Descartes' epistemology replaced the epistemology of the previous epoch: the work of the scholastics, which was heavily influenced by medieval Christian theology. This point of departure primes us as to Peirce's own ambitions. He intends to make a replacement similar to Descartes': just as Descartes needed to replace the medieval worldview to support the science of the Renaissance, Peirce needs to replace modern epistemology to support contemporary science. Yet, rather than focusing on the philosophers of the previous generation (Kant and Hegel), he aims for a deeper revision, which questions the basic assumptions of modernity. He argues that Descartes made four key replacements that modified scholastic thought: (1) the replacement of dogma with "universal doubt"; (2) the replacement of religious authority with "individual consciousness" as the arbiter of certainty; (3) the replacement of "multiform argumentation" with the method of a "single thread of inference depending often upon inconspicuous premises"; and (4) the replacement of faith in search for understanding with the suggestion that some phenomena are ultimately inexplicable (Peirce 1992: 28). He then critiques each of these replacements, one by one.

First, universal doubt is impossible because we all begin inquiry with prejudices, most of which are unrecognized. Although there may be some methodological benefits to assuming doubt for the sake of argument, Peirce argues the degree of doubt advocated by Descartes is at best superficial and at worst counterproductive. This insight is fairly common among undergraduates when they first read the *Meditations*. While most readers enjoy contemplating the questions Descartes proposes, few sound-minded people seriously doubt the reliability of their senses, whether they are asleep or dreaming, or whether an evil genius interferes with their thoughts. More pragmatic students (in the vulgar sense of the term) even wonder why these questions are relevant beyond allowing one to meet general education requirements, to answer trivia questions, or to impress guests at cocktail parties. Peirce would partially agree; but his deeper point is that we can never escape our assumptions. We inquire with them or through them and cannot suspend them at will. But, to be reliable, our beliefs do not need to be indubitable. Despite their flaws, they have successfully guided us to the present moment and can continue to be useful tools for further inquiry until proven otherwise.

Second, our individual consciousness cannot be the arbiter of certainty because we never reason in true isolation. Thinking does not occur in a vacuum; and, just as we start from our prejudices (as mentioned above), we inherited those beliefs from other people and refine them through further interaction. Thus thinking always occurs in a community; for even hermits in a cave or students in a library basement reflect on the ideas of other people or converse with authors via their books. This does not mean that we must submit to the authority of a particular tradition, say, scholasticism, but we must recruit the assistance of others in order to gain knowledge. If we were truly isolated, we would most likely have little cause to question our beliefs and no way to verify whether they are true. Therefore we cannot reliably engage in the form of individual philosophical inquiry Descartes proposes. Instead we gain knowledge through the process of investigating our doubts until we reach some sense of satisfaction. We may then share our personal conclusions with others, which may provoke further doubts and inquiry. If our conclusions do not provoke further doubts in our self or others, we may tentatively assume that they are true, until they are contradicted or troubled by future experiences. This process will be discussed later on, when I turn to Peirce's "The Fixation of Belief."

Third, rather than investigating the traditional topics of the scholastics (How many angels can dance on the head of a pin? Can God, who is omnipotent, create an object he could not move?) or insisting on Descartes' systematic search for foundational principles and subsequently moving from basic to more complex ideas, Peirce again advocates a middle approach. Our knowledge is neither a menagerie of ideas nor a chain where one idea necessarily connects to another, rather it is like a cable where individual fields are threads composed of multiple strands of argument that support one another, and these interdisciplinary threads are woven together to form larger cables. While some threads, arguments, and theories may be more critical than others, none of them is necessary to support the whole cable. Therefore they can be revised, updated, and replaced without requiring similar changes in the cable. Yet they are not completely separate areas of knowledge, since they provide support for one another. Thus, some repairs may require adjustments to other threads, and not only to those that are most frayed. Most importantly, we determine the veracity of our claims by subjecting them to some kind of empirical test; the cable or thread either will hold a weight or will break. Likewise, beliefs, when put into practice, will prove either true or false, as demonstrated by the consequences of acting upon them. This anticipates Peirce's pragmatic maxim as well as his definition of beliefs as habits of action.

Finally, we must not have faith either that all concepts are intelligible or that some will remain inexplicable. Both alternatives commit the fault of circular reasoning, because they assume the conclusion—the demonstrandum—to be true and use it as an opening premise in the inquiry. Some questions may be unanswerable, or all may eventually yield to investigation, but the outcome of any inquiry cannot be known from the outset. We must hope instead that all problems can be solved through inquiry, and we must remain confident about our current progress. Furthermore, because we use signs to symbolize our concepts, including ones that may ultimately be inexplicable (for example, *pi* and other irrational numbers), we can still reason about them by proxy and test them indirectly. Thus neither dogmatism nor skepticism is desirable, since both approaches function as blocks to inquiry. Some people assume that some questions have specific answers, others assume that some questions are unanswerable, but Peirce's pragmatism adopts an attitude of humble optimism: some inquiries will not be successful, but even failure confirms that some beliefs or hypotheses are incorrect.

Peirce also critiques Descartes in the 1878 essay "How to Make Our Ideas Clear." Here he focuses on Descartes' demand that our concepts be clear and distinct. Peirce interprets a clear idea to be "one which is so apprehended that it will be recognized wherever it is met... [and] no other will be mistaken for it." Likewise, he interprets a distinct idea as "one which contains nothing which is not clear" because "we can give a precise definition of it" (Peirce 1992: 124–125). He admits that clearness and distinctness are important epistemic values, but critiques Descartes on three grounds. First, clearness and distinctness are not properties of the concept, but rather feelings experienced by the inquirer. Second, there are other feelings that are relevant to inquiry, specifically doubt, which Descartes erroneously sees as problematic. And, finally, vagueness is as important to our concepts as clearness and distinctness, because it enables our concepts to be more pragmatic.

A concept may feel clear and distinct to an individual inquirer, but not to others. In fact a concept may even feel clear and distinct to a community of experts, or to an entire society, and still be false. This distinction is subtle but has profound implications. Peirce is suggesting that all forms of inquiry, including the most conceptually abstract disciplines, such as mathematics and physics, are ultimately subjective, because we judge a concept to be clear, distinct, or even true on the grounds that it *feels* clear, distinct, or true *to us*—either as individuals or as a group of inquirers. As we shall see, Peirce does not believe that knowledge is entirely subjective, since concepts must be tested through experiment or application, but he suggests that reasoning and inquiry are not purely objective. This implies that, when we evaluate the clearness, distinctness, soundness, or validity of any concept or argument we are engaging in a process of aesthetic judgment similar to that of evaluating the beauty of a painting. The subject may be different (arguments rather than paintings), the elements may be different (premises rather than shading), and the applied values may be different (clearness rather than proportion), but the processes are the same and even use some of the same values (for example, symmetry, parsimony, and harmony are relevant to both science and art).

Furthermore, the feelings of clearness and distinctness mark the end of inquiry, but they do not initiate it. As mentioned earlier, Peirce is skeptical of the artificial doubt adopted by Descartes, but Descartes' greater error was that he saw doubt as a problem rather than an opportunity. Instead, Peirce views doubt as the first stage of inquiry: "the action of thought is excited by the irritation of doubt and ceases when belief is attained; so that the production of belief is the sole function of thought" (Peirce 1992: 127). According to him, all knowledge is gained through a three-part process of inquiry: (1) we are motivated by the irritation of doubt (2) to engage in either formal or informal thinking in order to settle our doubts; and (3) when those doubts are appeased, we rest in a new belief, which conditions our habits of action until new doubts arise. Earlier on, in "The Fixation of Belief," Peirce discusses more thoroughly the psychology of doubt and the four most common methods for settling our doubts:

> Doubt is an uneasy and dissatisfied state from which we struggle to free ourselves and pass into the state of belief; while the latter is a calm and satisfactory state which we do not wish to avoid, or to change to a belief in anything else. On the contrary, we cling tenaciously, not merely to believing, but to believing just what we do believe. (1992: 114)

This passage describes not only the experience of doubt but also our most common response to it: tenaciously clinging to our current belief rather than revising or rejecting it in the light of new evidence.

In fact both of these phenomena, doubt and tenacity, have been researched in depth by twentieth-century psychologists. In a study titled *When Prophecy Fails*, Festinger, Riecken, and Schachter (1956) rename them "cognitive dissonance" and "belief perseverance" and narrate how they infiltrated a doomsday cult that believed that the world would end in a deluge on the morning of December 21, 1954. Even though the prediction failed, the three researchers noticed that many of the cult's adherents still clung to their faith, preferring to rationalize the outcome rather than rejecting their deeply held belief. While belief perseverance in the face of cognitive dissonance is more obvious among the faithful, both Peirce and Festinger and colleagues recognize that it is a universal habit of mind. We all assume our beliefs to be true, otherwise we would not hold them. Furthermore, it would be time-consuming (at best) or traumatic (at worst) to revise our core beliefs every time we are presented with conflicting evidence. Belief perseverance relates to several other habits of mind, now called cognitive biases (see Kahneman & Tversky 1972), which can inhibit our thinking. Examples include the confirmation bias, in which we unconsciously ignore counter-evidence and remember supporting evidence for our beliefs, and the backfire effect, in which our beliefs become stronger in proportion to the quality of the counterevidence presented.

Tenacity may be the most common method for "fixing" belief, but Peirce recognized three others that we may consciously or unconsciously adopt: the method of authority, the a priori method, and the scientific method. Rather than tenaciously clinging to our beliefs, we may, willingly or unwillingly, submit to an authority figure and adapt our beliefs to whatever it decrees, in order to settle our doubts. The nature of the authority figure is irrelevant. It can be personal (a parent) or remote (an organization), religious (a priesthood) or secular (a union), in fact it does not even have to be human (a Magic 8 Ball). The individual need only surrender her intellectual autonomy to another agent.

An alternative is the a priori method, in which a person settles her doubts according to established principles or criteria. These could be as simple and undeveloped as the maxim "a human being only acts selfishly" or as sophisticated as the Platonic notion that, as Peirce (1992: 119) puts it, "the distances of the celestial spheres from one another should be proportional to the different lengths of strings which produce harmonious chords." Political and religious ideologies can also fall under the a priori method, since they, too, produce automatic responses in their adherents when the latter are faced with a dilemma. Peirce admits that this method seems more "intellectual and respectable" because a priori principles are usually supported by some sort of argument, but at bottom they are really matters of taste (ibid.). We select them because they conform to our preferences.

Ultimately these two methods reduce to tenacity, because they preserve our beliefs and are determined by feelings and social pressures. As such, they merely stifle our doubts rather than helping us to learn and gain new knowledge. They are barriers to inquiry. Only the scientific method provides a means, independent of our preferences, of determining whether our beliefs are correct, because it uses external evidence to judge these beliefs rather than using our beliefs to judge the evidence. He describes the "fundamental hypothesis" of the scientific method as follows (1992: 120):

> There are real things, whose characters are entirely independent of our opinions about them; those realities affect our senses according to regular laws, and, though our sensations are as different as our relations to the objects, yet, by taking advantage of the laws of perception, we can ascertain by reasoning how things really are, and any man, if he have sufficient experience and reason enough about it, will be led to the one true conclusion.

We may disagree about the reality of climate change or about whether raising the minimum wage will hurt job growth and, if we resort to tenacity, authority, or a priori beliefs, we will continue to argue past one another; but, if we agree upon a means of empirically testing our beliefs independently of our opinions, we are more likely to advance our discussion, or at least to learn something new. The passage quoted above also previews Peirce's metaphysics, specifically his notion of "brute reality," which will be discussed soon; but, for now, I must finish my examination of "The Fixation of Belief" and show how it relates to Peirce's critique of Descartes.

Peirce's advocacy of the scientific method should not be seen as an appeal for scientism. We should avoid the temptation to reduce all disagreements to the current scientific consensus. Even though the scientific consensus is more likely to be correct than the consensus of other institutions, doing that would be another way of resorting to authority. More importantly, Peirce admits none of these methods is infallible and that each one of them has its advantages. The a priori method provides "comfortable conclusions ... until we are awakened from our pleasing dream by rough facts." The method of authority will "always govern the mass of mankind" and it is the "path of peace," but those who follow it will "never be convinced that dangerous reasoning ought not to be suppressed in some way." Finally, people who pursue tenacity are often "distinguished for their character": they "do not waste time in trying to make up their minds what they want." Unfortunately, tenacity is also "one of the splendid qualities which generally accompany brilliant, unlasting success" (1992: 121–122). Even the method of science has its risk and costs. It isn't easy to admit that we are wrong, or to give up cherished beliefs, but "what is more wholesome than any particular belief is integrity of belief," and failing to scrutinize a belief from "fear that it may turn out rotten is quite as immoral as it is disadvantageous" (1992: 123).

Returning to Peirce's critique of Descartes, we should aspire to make our ideas clear and distinct but, because these values are subjective, if they are the only values pursued, our inquiry is likely to devolve into the a priori method. If we are to be scientific, we must adopt additional values that are based on how our ideas interact with reality. Here Peirce introduces his *pragmatic maxim* (1992: 132):

> Consider what effects, which might conceivably have practical bearings, we conceive the object of our conception to have. Then, our conception of these effects is the whole of our conception of the object.

Our ideas and beliefs can be perfectly clear and distinct, and perfectly wrong when put into practice. In fact Descartes mind–body dualism can be seen as a solipsistic symptom of this problem. Beliefs are not exclusively internal phenomena. They structure our habits of mind and inevitably manifest themselves via our habits of action. Therefore we should always evaluate the veracity of our beliefs in terms of their practical consequences.

In fact, vague beliefs may often be more pragmatic than beliefs that are clear and distinct. Two of Peirce's greatest scientific achievements are his contributions to statistics and the methods he devised as a member of the US Coast and Geodetic Survey, to map and measure variations in the coastline and local gravity. These mathematical tools help predict phenomena by incorporating vagueness into their calculations. Coastlines change with the tides, and local gravity can fluctuate owing to subtle changes in topography, specifically altitude, but also owing to the position of the sun and the moon. An exact calculation may be impossible, unnecessary, or even counterproductive; therefore, in most situations, it is better to have a pragmatic estimate than a precise measurement. Likewise, statistics is a branch of mathematics dedicated to interpreting sets of data, usually for the purpose of prediction.

It is from a frequentist angle that Peirce focused on the nature of probability and on how to randomize experiments properly (see his articles "Illustrations of the Logic of Science," produced in 1877, and "A Theory of Probably Inference," in 1883), and in a moment I will discuss how the reality of tychism, or absolute chance, played a critical role in his cosmology. At a more everyday level, we can appreciate the value of vagueness over clarity when dressing for the weather. During winters in the Pacific Northwest, one need not know the exact temperature and humidity when planning what to wear. It will usually be cold and it will rain at some point during the day, so most people dress in layers and wear a hood. A more accurate forecast might be needed when planning for a hiking trip, a gala, a business meeting, or a sporting event, but these examples further demonstrate Peirce's point that the degree of accuracy needed is relative to the practicalities of the situation. Neither clearness nor distinctness should be the ultimate aims of our scientific or personal inquiries. They are important values, but our primary goal is to understand reality better and to develop more pragmatic ways to interact with it.

Thus, in these two essays, Peirce offers a thorough critique of the Cartesian assumptions that support most of modern philosophy. Despite the success of his approach, Descartes presented an idealized image of how we reason, whereas Peirce recognizes inquiry as a process *in medias res*—in the thick of things, without a preamble. While it may be noble and advisable to engage in the systematic meditations Descartes recommends, his approach is artificial and unlike most of our reasoning. Our thinking arises from our concrete experiences and has the purpose of making us understand and control our lives better. Our beliefs function as habits that influence our reasoning and manifest themselves in our actions. If these beliefs bring about good consequences, we continue to act upon them; but, if they lead us into error, doubt arises and we initiate some kind of inquiry to fix them. Frequently we adopt a method that stifles our doubts rather than investigating them.

While this may be permissible and even advantageous in many situations, we should challenge ourselves to practice the method of science by tailoring our beliefs to the best available evidence. Comparing our beliefs to brute reality is the only means we have for evaluating them independently of our own personal and social preferences. If we fail to do so, sooner or later brute reality will not tolerate our sheltered beliefs. We will suffer some serious consequence—what is commonly known as a "reality check." We must also accept that both our methods of inquiry and the beliefs they yield are inherently fallible. Even the most thoroughly tested and supported belief may prove false and there are no guarantees that any method, even science, will necessarily lead to truth. Despite these limitations, skepticism is unwarranted because progress is possible even if attaining Cartesian certainty is impossible.

In the final pages of these essays, Peirce articulates his own logic and epistemology. First, he concludes "Some Consequences of the Four Incapacities" by proposing an alternative system of logic. Since Aristotle, classical logic has described and investigated two forms of inference: deduction and induction. Deduction is reasoning with concepts; it uses inference and implication and is best illustrated in mathematics. By definition, a triangle is a two-dimensional figure that possesses certain properties, such as three sides and three interior angles. These properties imply others, which are described by mathematical theorems or axioms, for example the Pythagorean theorem, or the Euclidean postulate that the interior angles of a triangle will always total 180°. Using these properties and their implications, we can solve a mathematical proof or make other inferences, for example find the measure of a missing side or angle, respectively. Therefore, if an argument is valid and its premises are all true, the conclusion is necessarily true because it is logically implied by the premises. Descartes initiated modern philosophy by attempting to use doubt and deductive reasoning to discover foundational principles that are necessarily true, and his heirs spent the next centuries attempting to bridge the gap between conceptual reasoning and our empirical experience. Deductive reasoning may yield indubitable conclusions, but those conclusions are about concepts and may not match reality.

By contrast, induction is a type of reasoning that uses evidence and the foundational logic of science. If I drop a raw egg from a height of one meter onto a concrete floor, it will probably break. Therefore I may infer that if I drop an egg it will break; but, unlike in the case of the triangle, where the interior angles will always total 180°, I cannot assume that every egg will break when dropped. If I boil an egg, it may not break from the height of one meter. If I drop a raw egg onto a rubber floor, it may remain intact. Alternatively, if I drop it from a lower height, it may not break. Furthermore, even if I drop a dozen raw eggs, one at a time, onto a concrete floor from the original one-meter height, it is possible, even if unlikely, that one or more remain intact as a result of unknown factors that prevent, say, the last egg from breaking (shell thickness, whether the narrow or the wide end hits first, etc.). Thus the likelihood of my inductive claim—also known as a hypothesis—increases in proportion to (1) the specificity of the conditions under which an egg will break and that I can identify; and (2) the number of times I test the hypothesis. However, unlike in deductive reasoning, where the premises necessarily imply the conclusion via definition and implication, here even the most specific and supported hypothesis could be wrong. David Hume labeled this limitation "the problem of induction"; and it functioned as a key component of his skepticism. Induction rests on the assumption that the future will be like the past, yet we have no guarantee that such an assumption is true.

In many ways, the versions of pragmatism proposed by Peirce and later pragmatists engage these limitations of deduction and induction. We will see in chapter 4 how the analytic pragmatists address the gap between deduction and induction by articulating the conditions under which our conceptual reasoning must be verified by empirical evidence. James argues that our concepts function as promissory notes and shortcuts that allow us to engage the natural world more efficiently, but do not have validity independently of our experience. Dewey incorporates the problem of induction into the heart of his ontology via his notion of the precarious. While our social and biological environments are usually stable, Dewey calls attention to the fact that our situation can become precarious at any moment, without warning. This uncertainty and the provisional nature of knowledge is *the* problem of experience. All of the above are also examples of fallibilism. Even under the best of circumstances, our knowledge is provisional; therefore we must be content to develop pragmatic strategies and methods that humbly accept these limitations and focus on concrete problems.

Peirce is the source of this insight, but he also introduces a third form of reasoning, which ameliorates the shortcomings of deduction and induction: abduction. Abduction is reasoning via imagination; and, although it has always existed, it is rarely associated with deduction and induction. Most people are in the habit of seeing art and literature as wholly separate from math and science, but pragmatists were suspicious of any kind of dualism and, while Peirce was not as interested in the humanities as Dewey, George Santayana, Alain Locke, or Richard Rorty, he nevertheless recognized the importance of aesthetics and imagination in all forms of reasoning. Even in my examples of deductive and inductive reasoning, imagination plays a vital role. While the conclusion of a mathematical proof is contained in the premises, there is usually no single, best, or correct way to get that proof. In the triangle example, one could use the properties of the sides or those of the angles to reach the same valid conclusion. In most cases there is no logically necessary reason to select one path over the other; the choice is a matter of preference. Furthermore, complicated proofs often require imagination in the form of experimentation. A student will sometimes attempt to get a proof, only to discover that the path she is pursuing does not work; and then she will have to imagine an alternative path. In fact, how students get a proof usually reflects their personality, and occasionally they surprise their teachers by developing a novel strategy for solving an old problem. On the whole, inductive reasoning depends upon the proposal of new hypotheses to test as well as upon new ways of testing hypotheses, and the history of science abounds in anecdotes about serendipitous breakthroughs that came from dreams, accidents, baths, and other, even weirder sources.

Thus reason functions in three ways according to Peirce: deduction analyses concepts, induction predicts on the basis of evidence and experimentation, and abduction imagines new implications and hypotheses. Most importantly, knowledge grows through abduction, because this is the only mode of reasoning that introduces new possibilities. Furthermore, this triadic division of human reason, to which he refers as the "irreducibility of thirdness," can be found throughout Peirce's systematic philosophy and each of the three parts will be discussed. Returning to "How to Make Our Ideas Clear," Peirce concludes that essay by showing how knowledge arises from the application of logic, in other words from inquiry, and an analogous triadic relationship between inquiry, brute reality, and final opinion.

When we inquire, we attempt to describe, understand, and predict reality, which Peirce (1992: 137) defines as "that whose characters are independent of what anybody may think them to be." As stated earlier, Peirce eschews Descartes' skepticism as to whether physical reality exists independently of our mental perceptions; he accepts the existence of reality as independent of the mind and as the cause of mental phenomena because "all the sensations which they [real things] excite emerge into consciousness in the form of beliefs" (ibid.). He will often pair the term "reality" with the adjective "brute," to emphasize reality's manner of impinging upon our beliefs, regardless of our desires. I may believe that I can summit Mt. Everest and may have good evidence for so believing (e.g. past climbs, study of past expeditions, excellent equipment, a talented and experienced team, etc.), but until I make the attempt and encounter the brute reality of the mountain my belief remains unverified. Thus inquiry and brute reality have a symbiotic relationship. Encounters with brute reality create the doubt that motivates inquiry; and we test the products of inquiry, our beliefs, by applying them to reality. The scientific method, specifically experimentation, is a formalized version of this process, in which hypotheses are developed on the basis of the best available evidence and then an experiment is created to check a hypothesis against brute reality by observing its consequences in a controlled environment.

Knowledge results from this process, but, as mentioned, it is always fallible because even the most well-supported hypothesis may prove false under unknown circumstances. Suppose that, after a year of fattening, a wild turkey would be most convinced of the benefits of farm life on the morning of a feast day. Again, this example represents Hume's problem of induction and the impossibility of certainty, but by recognizing fallibilism we can maximize the likelihood of success (pragmatism) by constantly checking our hypothesis in a variety of controlled circumstances. However, I cannot do this alone but must recruit others, both to share the work and because they may notice anomalies, errors, and correlations that I miss or evidence that I interpret differently. Consider how the turkey might benefit by asking the old mule for his opinion on the seemingly endless supply of feed. In fact the opinions of others function as another brute fact that must be incorporated into our inquiry. Hence communal cooperation and disagreement strengthen the inquiry at all levels—deductive, inductive, and abductive. Consequently, the most reliable knowledge is produced by communities of inquirers who are experts in their field. Again, these communities are not infallible. Individuals may fall victim to the fallacies mentioned by Peirce in "The Fixation of Belief," or other social pressures may influence their work (for example, a new political regime might cut the funding for climate science), but the *method* of scientific inquiry remains the most reliable means for coping with fallibilism, because it seeks to tailor beliefs to reality through an ongoing process of objective and independent verification.

Therefore the goal of inquiry is not truth, but a final opinion. If we are committed to fallibilism we must admit that we can never know for certain that our beliefs are true. At best, we can know only that they are logically consistent and supported by evidence, cohere with expert opinion, and have not yet been falsified. This does not mean that truth is relative, because there may be a single best explanation for a specific phenomenon. Rather it is an admission that we cannot know when we have arrived at the correct belief. We do not know the truth before inquiry begins; and, when our doubts are settled, we *feel* we have found the truth, but we could be wrong. However, we can be confident that "the process of investigation, if only pushed far enough, will give one certain solution to every question to which they can be applied" because "[d]ifferent minds may set out with the most antagonistic views, but the progress of investigation carries them by a force outside of themselves [brute reality] to one and the same conclusion" (Peirce 1992: 138). Peirce believes that the truth emerges over time through this interplay between inquiry, reality, and community in the form of a final opinion: "The opinion which is fated to be ultimately agreed to by all who investigate, is what we mean by the truth, and the object represented in this opinion is the real" (1992: 139). This conclusion may seem pessimistic, since we surrender the hope of certainty, but Peirce describes it as an acceptance of the limitless potential of inquiry (1992: 140):

> Who would have said, a few years ago, that we could ever know of what substances stars are made whose light may have

been longer in reaching us than the human race has existed? ... Who can guess what would be the result of continuing the pursuit of science for ten thousand years, with the activity of the last hundred? ... how is it possible to say that there is any question which might not ultimately be solved?

The triadism manifest in Peirce's epistemological thought (induction, deduction, abduction; inquiry, brute reality, final opinion) can also be found in his metaphysical categories. The relationship between brute reality and truth in his epistemology provides a glimpse into his metaphysics. When pressed, Peirce would refer to his metaphysics as a form of objective idealism. He adopts the idealist position that our only access to reality is through our mental experiences; however, he believes that we can have objective knowledge about reality through the process of inquiry. Furthermore, the recurring triads found in inquiry (doubt, inquiry, belief), logic (deduction, induction, abduction) and epistemology (inquiry, brute reality, final opinion) function as a bridge between our mental experiences and the independent reality that corresponds to those experiences. In fact Peirce sees the irreducibility of thirdness as the fundamental architectonic of the universe. In "A Guess at the Riddle" (1887–1888) he eloquently describes the categories of firstness, secondness, and thirdness:

> The First is that whose being is simply in itself, not referring nor lying behind anything. The Second is that which is what it is by force of something to which it is second. The Third is that which is what it is owing to things between which it mediates and which it brings into relation to each other. (Peirce 1992: 248)

In brief, a first is the immediate object of experience, the second contrasts the first, and the third is the relationship between the first and the second. An example would be to think of a melody as a third made up of the interplay between notes (firsts) and intervals of rest (seconds). Furthermore, any first can simultaneously function as a second to another object, and the same holds for seconds and thirds. Thus a note can function as a second to another note or as a second to the interval of rest that precedes it, and a particular melody can function as a first (an introduction) or as a second (a chorus), when it is part of a larger third (a song). From these basic triadic relationships all greater complexity can be derived, and Peirce does not limit triadic relationships to the areas discussed but sees them as intrinsic to the nature of the cosmos.

In "Evolutionary Love" (1893), Peirce turns from rumination on Gilded Age politics to a discussion of how triadism functions through the evolution of the universe. He presents three possible explanations for the development of the universe: random chance, systematic laws, or deliberate choice. First, the universe could be the product of random chance, or what Peirce calls tychism. It is a fluke that the universe exists at all, and the phenomena we experience are ultimately chaotic and meaningless. Second, the universe could be the result of systematic laws, a process that Peirce calls here anancism and elsewhere synechism. On this hypothesis, the universe has existed perpetually and unfolds according to inevitable laws that have no exceptions. Finally, the universe could be created intentionally, by deliberate choice, in a scenario he refers to as agapism. In this scenario, the universe is created either through the choice of a divine intelligence or through the free choices of human action. Peirce provides a brief history of the philosophies and theologies that have emphasized one or another of these three as the most primitive element, yet he insists that all three are fundamental and that the world as we know it results from the interplay of three corresponding evolutionary forces: randomness, law (or necessity), and choice.

Building upon an idea expressed in an earlier essay, "The Architecture of Theories" (originally published in the first volume of *Monist* in 1891), Peirce advances a metaphysics of objective idealism where the matter that comprises the universe is "effete mind, inveterate habits becoming physical laws" (Peirce 1992: 293). The primitive elements of the universe are not dead matter but semi-conscious particles of mind that gradually acquire habits as they chaotically interact with one another (tychism). Over time, these habits repeat themselves so many times as to be identified as natural laws (synechism), and eventually they produce conscious beings capable of understanding and influencing those laws according to their own ends (agapism). Thus the universe evolves from randomness to order, first through the interaction of semi-conscious particles and then through a process of inquiry whereby we not only uncover the existing laws of nature but impose more structure on nature as we develop our own explanations of its behavior. More than revealing reality, inquiry shapes it; therefore final opinion is the last and most accurate description not just of reality, but of a reality fashioned by the minds that have investigated and manipulated it.

In sum, Peirce initiates pragmatism by developing an understanding of inquiry rooted in fallibilism. While we can strive for objectivity, inquiry is inherently subjective. We cannot be certain in the Cartesian sense that our beliefs are correct or that we have reached the end of our inquiry. Hence we must remain humble and acknowledge that even our most well-supported beliefs and theories could be disproved by new evidence. Our best correctives are empirical verification and communal inquiry. Ever the scientist and the socially inept, Peirce respects the latter, but his work favors the former. Furthermore, this split between the empirical and the social reveals not only a tension in Peirce's own thought, but the emergence of divisions in early pragmatism that continue to this day and are mirrored in the current split between analytic and continental philosophy. All pragmatists remain true to fallibilism, but they will emphasize one aspect over the other. James remains one of the first empirical psychologists, yet his philosophy relishes the subjective nature of experience. Royce articulates a system of logic that rivals Peirce's, but he excels at illuminating the individual's relationship with the community and the resolution of social conflict. As a result, some Peirce scholars find Peirce's main legacy in a system of verification that early twentieth-century philosophers raided in order to critique logical positivism; and they argue that this branch of pragmatism remains the most valuable and relevant one. Nevertheless, the social dimension of Peirce, especially his invention of semiotics, has arguably had a greater impact on pragmatism and continental philosophy. His notion of agapism resembles contemporary forms of constructivism by suggesting that human inquiry and human action shape knowledge and reality to some degree. In many ways, agapism foreshadows William James's (1968: 456) declaration that "[t]he world stands really malleable, waiting to receive its final touches at our hand ... Man engenders truth upon it" and warrants a shift of our attention to James's work.

William James (1842–1910) and Radical Empiricism

While Peirce and James were, both, exponents of the Cambridge, Massachusetts intellectual scene, their upbringing and careers could not be more divergent. As the son of a wealthy merchant and amateur theologian, James enjoyed every conceivable academic privilege. His godfather was Ralph Waldo Emerson, and his father would regularly host dinners with Emerson and other members of the transcendentalist circle, as well as other Harvard intellectuals. During his youth he traveled to Europe on two occasions and became fluent in French and German. He enrolled in the Harvard Medical School in 1864 but postponed his studies so he could accompany the naturalist Louis Agassiz on his expedition along the Amazon River in 1865. He finally finished his MD in 1869, but decided never to practice medicine. In hindsight, James clearly suffered from some form of chronic depression, but this early melancholy and listlessness is closely tied to his insights and pushed him towards psychology and philosophy, which he embraced for self-therapy as much as out of intellectual interest. His scientific training, like Peirce's, grounded his work in that it made him look for empirical evidence rather than intricate theories. But James's neurosis, unlike Peirce's, served as a resource and James became a founder of American psychology as well as of American philosophy thanks to his desire to study and articulate his subjective experience.

This leads to a different interpretive challenge when engaging with James's work. James wrote prolifically and, unlike

Peirce, successfully completed several masterworks during his career, specifically *The Principles of Psychology* of 1890, *The Varieties of Religious Experience*, published in 1902 (James 1958), and the 1909 *A Pluralistic Universe*. He often wrote for popular audiences, too, and his most inspiring and memorable passages are found in collections such as *The Will to Believe and Other Essays*, published in 1897, his public lectures on *Pragmatism* (James 1907), and the *Essays in Radical Empiricism* published posthumously, in 1912. As a result, scholars disagree as to which masterwork is authoritative and how one might best balance the rhetorical flourishes of James's popular work against the more deliberate and developed claims in his academic work. My approach here will be to examine how James's radical empiricism creates an alternative to the empiricism of David Hume by emphasizing fallibilism over skepticism. This approach will allow me to examine his most influential concept, that of the stream of consciousness, and to analyse its impact on James's epistemological, metaphysical, and ethical philosophy.

Just as Peirce's pragmatic maxim functions as a critique of Descartes' foundationalism, James's radical empiricism functions as a modification of Hume's skepticism. As empiricists, both James and Hume prefer experience to conceptual reasoning when it comes to the source of knowledge and both root their epistemology in psychology. In the 1793 *A Treatise of Human Nature*, Hume (2017: 1) argues that experience can be reduced to two components: impressions, "which enter with most force and violence" and include "all our sensations, passions and emotions"; and ideas, which are the "faint images of these in thinking and reasoning." Like Descartes' insistence upon clear and distinct perceptions, Hume's division of our experience into impressions and ideas is a useful heuristic, but yet another example of misplaced concreteness.

From this distinction between impressions and ideas Hume draws two other problematic conclusions. Since all our knowledge flows from impressions, Hume remains skeptical about claims of which we do not have direct experience. We cannot be certain about inductive claims, because we do not have experience of events that have not occurred; but this also applies to causality. When we play billiards we routinely claim that the cue ball causes other balls to move when it hits them. Hume points out that these loose statements about causality rest on two philosophical assumptions. First, they ignore the problem of induction, since they assume a necessary future outcome. While it is most likely the eight ball will move when struck by the cue ball, we are making an assumption about the future for which we do not have direct experience. It is possible, even if unlikely, that the eight ball will remain still, or explode, or vanish, or suddenly switch places with the nine ball, or any of infinite possibilities. Nor do we have any direct impression of the precise moment when the cue ball causes the eight ball to move. We never experience the exact moment in which causality occurs, because we could divide that moment infinitesimally, into always smaller units of time and space. In the circumstances, Hume prefers the name *constant conjunction* over *causality*. Certain events occur in a repeated sequence, often enough to create the expectation that a specific effect will occur after a specific cause, but this is an *idea* about the world, not an *impression* from the world. We form the habit of expecting constant conjunctions between particular events, rather than knowing causality as an objective feature of the world.

Not only does Hume doubt induction and causality, he also questions the self. Just as we have no direct impression of causality, we have no impression of the self. In this moment you are aware of several impressions and ideas. For example, you feel this book in your hands and you are thinking about Hume's theory of the self, but where, among those impressions and ideas, is an impression of yourself? According to Hume, we never have an impression of our self, because there is no specific feature of our experience that is constant or unique. The self is another idea we use to describe the collection or bundle of impressions and ideas we experience, but it is not itself among the impressions we experience. Besides, the self is always changing. Hence there is no single impression or idea that is essential to our identity.

Needless to say, Hume's conclusions are hard to accept.

Induction, causality, and the self seem to be fundamental aspects of our experience. Yet his arguments are difficult to refute if we are committed to empiricism. As a result, most historical responses to Hume, for example Immanuel Kant's, embrace idealism in order to overcome his skepticism. James challenges Hume by offering a richer empiricism:

> We now begin our study of the mind from within. Most books start with sensations, as the simplest mental facts, and proceed synthetically, constructing each higher stage from those below it. But this is abandoning the empirical method of investigation. No one ever had a simple sensation by itself. Consciousness, from our natal day, is of a teeming multiplicity of objects and relations, and what we call simple sensations are results of discriminative attention, pushed often to a very high degree. (James 1968: 21)

James doubts that experience can be reduced to Hume's two categories of impressions and ideas. In fact, here we see James introducing a theme that not only distinguishes him from Peirce and Royce but will influence Dewey and others: resistance to reductive dualisms in favor of more holistic and pluralistic accounts. Rather than studying experience by dividing it into two categories, James prefers to study it as we experience it: as a continuous, undifferentiated flow of intermingled thoughts, sensations, perceptions, emotions, and memories.

James referred to this flow as the stream of thought, but it is more popularly known as the stream of consciousness; and he outlines five key characteristics that differentiate his radical empiricism. First, consciousness is personal. To our knowledge, all thoughts and experiences belong to someone or something. You, my reader, are currently in your own stream of consciousness, to which I have no access, but while reading this book you allow your consciousness to mingle with an externalized version of my own; then I am no longer having these thoughts, nor do you have unrestricted access to my current experience or memories. All thoughts and experiences are owned by some particular conscious being.

Second, consciousness is constantly changing. As I write

this paragraph, my consciousness flows from the keys of my laptop to the rhythm of Black Sabbath's "Beyond the Wall of Sleep" in my headphones, until my wife messages me to ask if we can meet for lunch. I message her back, take a sip of stale coffee, pause to watch the pink blossoms of the mimosa tree outside my window bounce in the breeze, and return to the rhythm of writing until the next inevitable interruption arises. I imagine you are experiencing a similar cavalcade of thoughts and sensations as you grip this book in your hands and move your eyes left to right, line by line, top to bottom, page by page. Perhaps we can focus on a single thought or sensation without distraction, but not without the assistance of years of meditation or several cups of caffeine; and, even then, other objects will eventually bounce into our consciousness.

This thought leads to James's third characteristic of the stream of consciousness: it is continuous. While we organize and communicate our experiences using increments of time, these measures are abstractions created by the mind and imposed onto experience. They are not parts of experience itself. Consider how no moment or event has a precise ending or beginning. For example, class may be scheduled to start at 2:00 p.m., but when does our experience of a class begin? When you arrive, ten minutes early to get your favorite seat, or when I arrive, ten minutes late because I couldn't find a parking space? Does it end when you leave early, to be on time for your 4:00 p.m. shift, or when students for the next class start taking their seats, because my lecture rambled for too long? Even when there are periods of unconsciousness, like sleep, it can be difficult to remember the moment we slipped into oblivion, and when we awake we still have the impression that the interruption occurred as part of a sequence of experiences. Furthermore, while it is useful to classify our experiences according to type (thoughts, emotions, memories, sensations, etc.) if we wish to better understand and study them, these types of experiences are interwoven in our consciousness and often indistinguishable from one another. Returning to the previous example of writing, we constantly phase back and forth from sensation to thinking, to typing, to remembering—so much so that the phases of the activity cannot easily be reduced to simple categories. Thus there are no quantitative or qualitative breaks in experience. There are no edges, only fringe; and, while experience will take the shape of our interpretive vessels, it also drips, spills, and overflows as we pour it into those containers.

Fourth, we appear to be conscious of objects that are external to and independent of our mind. In this section, James bridges the gap between empiricism and idealism through an appeal to psychology. Because objects and events occur in my consciousness over which I have no control, I can be relatively assured that the empirical objective world exists independently of my mind. Furthermore, I can coordinate my experience of these objects with that of other conscious beings that act independently and have their own conscious experiences. Finally, those objects become the content of our own thoughts. This psychological argument strongly resembles Peirce's assertion that we gain knowledge through our communal inquiries into brute reality and that the content of thought arises independently of the mind (i.e. we have no power of introspection), except that James provides a more subjective description of this transaction. He uses a pack of cards as an example of the rich impression that a particular object makes upon our consciousness. A pack of cards does not simply represent itself but implies its location on a table, its content of fifty-two cards, its brand, the games it could be used to play, the card tricks we know, and so on. By the same token, any particular object is stuck within a *web of relations* to other objects, thoughts, and memories. As it enters our consciousness, it brings with it a flood of associations that extend over a period of time. Thus experience cannot be divided into Hume's self-contained, marble-like impressions and ideas. Even the simplest object of consciousness behaves like a wave that rises, crests, breaks, and crashes. It unfolds as an event in our mind.

Finally, consciousness constantly chooses among the objects of experience. The number of stimuli we receive in any given moment is overwhelming. We cannot be simultaneously conscious of them all; what is more, we need to focus on those stimuli in our environment that are the most interesting, the most relevant, or the most important for the purposes of survival and success. Thus the mind sifts the stream of consciousness to notice the most interesting and important objects of experience, while still passively receiving, but ignoring, the majority of the stimuli we encounter. As a result, consciousness fluctuates between three modes: attending to a specific stimulus, selecting a stimulus from a range of stimuli, and rejecting the majority of stimuli that fall outside our attention. In fact subsequent neurological research—such as Michael Gazzaniga and Roger Sperry's investigation into split-brain or callosal patients (i.e. patients who had the corpus callosum severed as part of the treatment for epileptic seizures)—has bolstered James's schema of consciousness. They discovered that, although the right and the left hemisphere of patients' brain could no longer communicate through a neural connection, those patients were able to have separate perceptions of particular objects and communicated them externally to the researchers. These studies led to the development of the theory of *brain lateralization*, according to which the hemispheres of the brain function independently and some cognitive functions are more dominant in one hemisphere than the other. As a result of lateralization, separate regions of the brain simultaneously engage in a diverse array of processes, most of which unconsciously or subconsciously sort out the constant cascade of sense data and organize it into the flow of experiences that are present to our conscious attention. Thus, for James, the self is this nexus that constantly selects, attends, and rejects stimuli from the flow of experiences.

In conclusion, James refutes Hume's skepticism by exchanging his dyadic empiricism, which is based on discrete impressions and ideas, with this richer notion of the stream of consciousness, where experience is continuous. We are not merely bundles of experiences, like boxes full of marbles, but an orchestra of continuous and redundant processes that deal with the continuous flow of sense experiences. Admittedly this orchestral view remains non-essentialist but captures well enough the novelty and richness of each individual self. The self cannot be reduced to a single monad, yet it is more than a mere collection of experiences. It is a habit of mental and embodied processes. Consequently, concepts and knowledge are patterns of habitual thought and behavior performed by individuals and groups. Concepts function as mental short-cuts that save time and effort, whereas knowledge results from those concepts found to be most reliable for achieving concrete ends. This epistemology differs little from Peirce's, except for starting in our subjective experience rather than in Peirce's more logical abstractions; but it departs radically from Descartes' need for indubitable foundational ideas and from Hume's resignation to limit knowledge to what we can experience directly. We are always in the flow of experience and our minds are always engaged in inquiry—that is, the process of making experience intelligible. We do not need foundational concepts because we are always cashing our beliefs by applying them to our situation and, while there are limits to our knowledge, these limits function more as fringes waiting to be explored and developed than as skepti-cal chasms that can never be crossed.

Furthermore, it is difficult to overstate the importance of the stream of consciousness on pragmatism as well as on twentieth-century thought and culture. While James describes the features common to all human experience, he also acknowledges its infinite variety and the uniqueness of individual experiences. This emphasis on the subject and on the element of novelty contrasts with Peirce's preference for method and probability; and, although the two approaches are not incompatible, this tension between Peircean conver-gence and Jamesian divergence defines the dynamic range of the varieties of pragmatism to come. Peirce sees inquiry as a communal project, whereas James sees it as a journey of personal discovery. Its psychological dimension allows James to emphasize the importance of the bodies that host these processes and experiences as well as their social extensions. A rich pluralism emerges that contextualizes the esoteric con-cerns of epistemology, metaphysics, and ethics in an embodied way, consistent with our experience and its peculiarities. This pluralism leads James to describe the universe as similar to "one of those dried human heads with which the Dyaks of

Borneo deck their lodges," where "the skull forms a solid nucleus; but innumerable feathers, leaves, strings, beads, and loose appendices of every description float and dangle from it, and save, that they terminate in it, seem to have nothing to do with one another" (James 1968: 197). The universe is intelligible at its core, but stranger than we expect it to be and resistant to our attempts to tame it. In many respects, the art and the literature of James's era endeavor to express this paradoxical unity between the familiar and the bizarre, the personal and the universal, as demonstrated by the poetry of T. S. Eliot, the paintings of Vincent Van Gogh, and the novels of Virginia Woolf.

This pluralism remains James's most significant contribution to pragmatism and culture, because it pays a tribute to our subjective experience without abandoning the scientific method. The advantages of this approach appear at their best in *The Varieties of Religious Experience*. As part of the Gifford Lectures on natural theology, James explores the subject of religion not by focusing on traditions, beliefs, or scriptures but by examining the roots of religion in our personal experience. By paying heed to the psychological aspect of religion, he avoids theological dogma and is able to study religion scientifically. He takes a pluralistic approach by performing an exhaustive survey of stories from across the globe. This massive catalog alone warrants the attention of anyone curious about the topic, but James astutely categorizes the stories according to certain criteria, for example sainthood, rather than according to their religion of origin, in order to analyse the commonalities and differences between them.

The most popular and anthologized chapter, entitled "Mysticism," exemplifies James's approach. In this chapter he identifies four marks of the religious experience that appear to be universal. The first two, ineffability and the noetic, he considers to be necessary conditions. For an experience to be mystical it must go beyond expression, transcend, be ineffable; and it must contain some transformative insight or knowledge, be noetic. The other two marks, transience and passivity, are optional, yet often present. Mystical experiences are usually rare and fleeting and happen unexpectedly, but there are people who claim to be in a constant mystical state (e.g. those in the state of samadhi), and various practices of religion—fasting, meditation, singing, flagellation, entheogens—intend to induce mystical experiences or at least increase their likelihood rather than allowing people to wait passively for one to occur. These four marks give legitimacy to a wide range of religious experiences, but they also imply that such experiences emerge from basic human nature; in other words they have natural rather than supernatural causes and can be explained through psychological and biological mechanisms. This suggestion might trouble many people of faith, but James sees here no threat to the legitimacy of these experiences or to the validity of their noetic insights. Always a pragmatist, James evaluates them on the basis of their consequences to the individual and her community. For example, if an alcoholic attends a Promise Keepers rally, experiences an intense moment of what he interprets to be God's grace, gives up alcohol, and dedicates himself to his family, career, and community, then we should not be too critical of the origins of that experience. Either way, we should be grateful that this person discovered a way to turn his life around; and we should do our best to support such efforts.

James also validated the use of entheogens, mind-altering hallucinogenic substances taken for spiritual exploration. In fact he and the other members of the Metaphysical Club, including Peirce, experimented with nitrous oxide and valued its limited ability to invoke oceanic states of consciousness. In 1898 James even submitted to the *Psychological Review* an article titled "Consciousness under Nitrous Oxide" in which he feigned anonymity in order to describe his own experiences and the insights he derived from the drug. After the gas settled the chatter of his conscious mind, he experienced a feeling of omniscience in which "[a] vast inrush of obvious and absolutely satisfying solutions to all possible problems overwhelmed my entire being, and an all-embracing unification of hitherto contending and apparently diverse aspects of truth took possession of my soul by force," allowing him to reconcile "Hegelianism itself with all other schools of philosophy in some higher synthesis" and filling him with "philanthropic

ecstasy." Needless to say, this state of reconciliation and ela-
tion vanished when the effects of the gas wore off, but it left
him with the impression that "[n]ormal human consciousness is only a narrow extract from a great sea of possible
human consciousness, of whose limits we know nothing"
(James 1968: 194). This openness to experimentation has
inspired curiosity in many generations of psychologists as
well as in lay people and made them willing to reconsider
the validity of a chemically induced religious experience. In
How to Change Your Mind, Michael Pollan (2018) provides
a thorough history of how James inspired the work of future
Harvard psychologists Timothy Leary and Richard Alpert
(among others), by establishing a precedent for scientific self-
experimentation with psychedelic substances such as LSD or
mescaline. Indeed, this attitude could well represent an even
larger part of James's legacy than the stream of consciousness, as it contributed to the countercultural revolution of the
late twentieth century; and, given the popular, critical, and
commercial success of Pollan's book, it may trigger another
cultural revolution in this century.

James would recount this episode in *The Varieties of
Religious Experience*; and it clearly influenced his projects
and later works. James not only helped to found American
philosophy, psychology, and comparative religion, he also
founded the American Society for Psychical Research in
1885. While this affiliation with parapsychology embarrasses
some scholars, it is an important indicator of his pluralism.
For James, the range of human experience is stupendously
rich, diverse, and novel. Mystical and psychic phenomena
may be rare and ultimately reducible to natural mechanisms,
but as recurring kinds of human experience they warrant
philosophical and scientific inquiry. Perhaps they should not
be prioritized, but they should not be dismissed out of hand
either. Recalling the shrunken heads of Borneo, there are
fringes to our experience and universe that may always remain
bizarre and inexplicable but should be investigated, even if
they perpetually resist or elude our inquiries. This pluralistic
openness can also be found in James's moral philosophy. For
James, ethics is not about adhering to unassailable principles

or about expedient problem-solving; it is about engaging in an effective process of moral inquiry that acknowledges the plurality of values and perspectives.

In "The Moral Philosopher and the Moral Life" (1891), he rejects the possibility of developing a normative ethical theory before acquiring experience that could be applied to any and all moral dilemmas. Because we live in a pluralistic universe, each situation is unique and we each bring our unique contributions to their resolution: "We all help to determine the content of the ethical philosophy," and thus "there can be no final truth in ethics any more than in physics, until the last man has had his experience and said his say" (James 1968: 610–611). Here again, we come across the relationship between pluralism and fallibilism; the goal of moral inquiry is to satisfy as many concrete demands as possible while recognizing the "tragically practical" fact that not all demands can be satisfied (1968: 621). Thus moral inquiry requires experimentation. We should implement the best available solution rather than relying on ideology or dogmatism. We should then study its effects or consequences and revise it in their light. It is here, in the development of pragmatism, that *amelioration*— the attempt to minimize the impact of moral crises rather than adopting an all-or-nothing solution—emerges as the preferred approach to social problems; and we shall see it more fully developed in the next chapter.

With James's help, Peirce's pragmatism spread far and wide, gaining many converts as well as critics. Examples include the theologian and Boston personalist Borden Parker Bowne, the German British humanist philosopher F. C. S. Schiller, and the French Jewish philosopher Henri-Louis Bergson; however, Josiah Royce emerges as the most important interlocutor of both Peirce and James. Although his philosophy is more idealist and religious than theirs, these differences shaped classical pragmatism, and his interaction with the two of them guided the development of his thought along pragmatist lines. Unlike Peirce and James, Royce emerged from a working-class background. His parents were pious settlers from Grass Valley, a California mining town in the western foothills of the Sierra Nevada mountain range, and these early experiences are at the base of much of his religious and communitarian philosophy. These folk sensibilities root Royce's version of pragmatism more deeply in the concrete, lived experience admired by James but often ignored by Peirce. Royce's adult life was filled with tragedy, specifically the depression, psychosis, and eventual suicide of his son Christopher. Thus Royce's fallibilism springs not from scientific research, like Peirce's, or from dilettante curiosity, like James's, but from his personal life and suffering.

This convergence of fallibilism, community, and religious identity is best demonstrated in his most popular work, *The Philosophy of Loyalty* (Royce 1908a). Although the book intends to establish a new foundation for ethics in the virtue of loyalty, it highlights all areas of Royce's thought and provides a fairly accessible account of his epistemology and metaphysics—certainly more accessible than the versions articulated in his earlier masterwork, *The World and the Individual* (Royce 1900). Royce argues we give meaning to our lives through our loyalties to the communities we join; and this is because we define ourselves through our interactions with others. But Royce recognizes that not all communities are worthy of our loyalty and warns against predatory causes that could exploit it. The best way to recognize a predatory cause is through its characteristic of disrespecting or undermining the loyalties that bind other communities together. To counteract such causes, we must be *loyal to loyalty* itself and express this commitment by supporting neighboring communities and causes. Conflicts will occur, but in the context of practicing loyalty to loyalty they should arise from contradictory hopes rather than from mere vice or prejudice. More importantly, through mutual respect and cultural exchange we may be inspired by the loyalties of others, take up their causes, or discover common loyalties we all can pursue.

Eventually, a *community of interpretation* emerges where knowledge is constantly reworked within and among diverse communities and, together, we increase the likelihood of successfully discovering the truth or realizing what Royce, coining a term that Martin Luther King will make famous, calls "the beloved community": an ideal social arrangement in which individuals and their particular communities still maintain their unique identities yet are united in a shared social identity, dedicated to understanding and attaining our highest ideals. While this hope may seem grandiose to some, Kipton Jensen explains how Royce's vision inspired significant social change through its influence on two important civil rights activists: Martin Luther King, Jr. and Howard Thurman. While he admits that critics correctly scrutinize the degree of this influence, Jensen provides detailed textual evidence of King's and Thurman's admiration for Royce and defends the view that all three regarded the beloved community as the ideal expression of a community of communities, so to speak, diverse but committed to "unconditional love, social justice, and an acknowledgement of the inviolable dignity of persons" (Jensen 2016: 254). Conversely, Tommy Curry (2018) fiercely criticizes Royce, revealing how various white supremacist influences led him to advocate policies of imperialism and scientific racism and also contributed to his absolutist metaphysics.

Consequently Royce remains a polarizing figure and, like Emerson, an example of how pragmatists developed strategies for coping with American racism and imperialism while still falling victim to the prejudices of their times. Unlike Peirce and James, Royce devoted more of his career to social and political concerns; but scholars still offer revealing treatments of both their cultural vision and blindness. In *Damn Great Empires!*, Alexander Livingston (2016) argues that James recognized how the philosophical desire for certainty and the political desire for empire were two sides of the same coin and that his pluralism sought to resist these totalizing impulses. Conversely, V. Denise James (2013: 43) suggests that, if we read William James side by side with the contemporary black liberation activist Anna J. Cooper, a comparison between the two of them reveals how James often formulated his ideas in a way that "precludes the acceptance of other individuals' worldviews and meaningful interpretations of their experience." Crucially, V. D. James does not dismiss William James on these grounds, as she recognizes his genuine desire to be pluralistic and inclusive of diverse backgrounds. Instead she argues that attending to the limitations that are due to the biases of his context is "compelling because it acknowledges the feelings many of us have that move us to want to do social justice work despite professional strictures that may support writing in a certain way about social justice but seem to prohibit other ways of knowing, working, and acting toward social justice" (2013: 44).

Meanwhile, both Robert Talisse (2005) and Lara Trout (2010) have reconstructed Peirce's views so as to develop their own political philosophies. In *Democracy after Liberalism*, Talisse (2005) employs Peirce's fallibilism and epistemic perfectionism to critique the visions of liberal democracy proposed by John Dewey, John Rawls, and Richard Rorty; in *The Politics of Survival*, Trout (2010) applies Peirce's theories to social justice issues by focusing on the critical importance of embodiment and community to inquiry. Furthermore, these two last examples remind us that, while the origins of pragmatism are closely tied to the emergence of American progressivism, pragmatism has no necessary political valence. Its emphasis on pluralism extends to conservative as well as to liberal voices. Seth Vannatta (2014) provides the best survey of this topic; he also traces the early influence of Edmund Burke on pragmatism and explains how the latter contributed in turn to the legal philosophies of conservative jurists and legal scholars such as Oliver Wendell Holmes, Jr. and Richard Posner. More importantly, Curry (2018) reminds us that, while pragmatism may have encouraged social justice and policies of decolonization, we must not ignore the ways in which racist assumptions shaped it too, especially as we transition to the more socially engaged pragmatists in Chicago.

Scholars also note how racist or imperialist assumptions are manifest in the work of Jane Addams and John Dewey. Maurice Hamington (2005) addresses the fruitful but often complicated theme of the alliance between Addams and the activist Ida B. Wells. The key expression of this complexity is Addams's endorsement, during their public correspondence on the issue of lynching, of the racist myth held by "many whites that black men had a predilection for licentiously accosting and violating white women" (Hamington 2005: 172). Likewise, Kelly Vaughan (2018: 39) argues that, "despite an expressed commitment to full and equal rights for African American students," Dewey's pedagogy "normalized the experience of White students and implicitly endorsed accommodationist education reforms for African American children." This indicates that we should extend to the other pragmatists Hamington's (2005: 167) warning about Addams: "like many important theorists [she was] simultaneously ahead of her time and very much of her time." Thus, while the fallibilism of the classical pragmatists lays the groundwork for the melioristic activism and pluralistic theories of future generations of pragmatists, the work of these pioneers should not be accepted uncritically; rather we should admit their ignorance and prejudices and use the benefits of hindsight to reconstruct their ideas more inclusively, so as to make them meet the needs of our present age. Indeed, if we are loyal to fallibilism, we must remain sensitive not only to how contextual biases inhibit the ideas and actions of the pragmatists, but also to how the biases of our own culture and experience blind us as well. Fortunately the classical pragmatists prescribed the best cure for this ailment: an ever expanding and more diverse community of inquirers and activists.

– 2 –

Meliorism and the Chicago Pragmatists

If the first wave of pragmatism originates from Peirce's and James's responses to the theoretical problems of nineteenth-century epistemology, the second wave of pragmatism originates from the responses of Jane Addams and John Dewey to the practical problems of turn-of-the-century Chicago. While the site of Chicago has always been a contested space due to its ideal strategic and economic location between the Mississippi River and Lake Michigan, the city's significance as a transportation hub was firmly established with the building of the Galena & Chicago Union Railroad and of the Illinois and Michigan Canal in 1848. When these railways and waterways opened, the city became connected to the world and waves of immigration soon followed, beginning with the Irish immigrants who labored to complete both projects. By 1880 the city's population reached 500,000 and would double twice within twenty years, reaching approximately 1.2 million in 1890 and 2 million in 1900. The city erected cheap tenement homes to accommodate this influx of humanity, which was soon followed by ghettoization, squalor, and exploitation, as exemplified in Upton Sinclair's novel *The Jungle* (1906).

Thus Chicago pragmatism begins in 1889, with the establishment of Hull House on the west side of Chicago, Illinois by Jane Addams and her partner Ellen Gates Starr.

Like Peirce and James, Addams benefited from a privileged upbringing. Her father, John Addams, owned a profitable mill in Cedarville and was an eighth-term Illinois state senator who regularly corresponded with Abraham Lincoln. He maintained a reputation of personal integrity and social conscience, both of which Jane inherited, and he encouraged his daughter to pursue her education. Unlike Peirce and James, Addams needed to work tirelessly to create the opportunities and projects that allowed her to develop and apply her talents in the face of gender oppression. Just as James's melancholy led him to investigate the intersections between psychology and philosophy, Addams would develop the habit of finding problems in need of solutions rather than developing solutions in need of problems. During a trip to Europe she visited Toynbee Hall, one of the first successful settlement houses dedicated to ameliorating the plight of London's impoverished working class, and she recognized the need for a similar settlement house in Chicago. Hull House eventually became a model of progressive outreach and through her twenty-five years of daily life with the women of Hull House she developed her concept of *sympathetic knowledge*—the recognition that social problems appear differently according to the observer's experiences. Consequently people of privilege have a responsibility to submit to the epistemic authority of those who are less empowered.

Despite the success of Hull House, no single person or project could hope to solve all of Chicago's problems and the turmoil continued to build. In 1894 railroad workers organized by the American Railway Union and led by Eugene V. Debs went on strike against the Pullman Company due to layoffs, decreased wages, and increased cost of living in the company town of Pullman, located on Chicago's South Side. At this moment John Dewey, a promising young scholar originally from Vermont, arrived to join the recently founded University of Chicago. Dewey, who was born into a modest family and had spent most of his time as a schoolteacher before pursuing philosophy, sympathized with the workers and saw their struggle as consistent with the social aims of his emerging philosophy. He had earned his PhD ten years

before, at Johns Hopkins University, and seemed destined
to become a typical neo-Hegelian scholar; but the pragmatic
sympathies of George Sylvester Morris, his mentor, a logic
class with Peirce, and his reading of James's *Principles of
Psychology* (1890) motivated him to consider how the methods of experimental science could be applied to philosophical
and social concerns, specifically to pedagogy.

When the university offered him the chair of the
Departments of Philosophy and Pedagogy, he recognized
Chicago as the perfect setting for putting his ideas into practice and for examining their results. Furthermore, Dewey had
met Addams two years before his new appointment, was
impressed with her work, and the two would remain colleagues for the remainder of their lives. In 1895 he founded his
own social project, the Laboratory School, which, like Hull
House, would not serve only as a venue for experimentation:
the experience he acquired there would inform and shape his
own philosophy. Rather than conceptualizing knowledge as
an affair of logical justification, his observation of children
supported his hypothesis that knowledge is generated through
a *pattern of inquiry*, namely through transactions with one's
social and material environment for the purpose of solving
the concrete problems of lived experience. His observation of
children also highlighted the influence of the Chicago pragmatists on the emerging social sciences, in that his pedagogy
demanded that theory be informed by social practice for the
purpose of ameliorating social problems.

Jane Addams (1860–1935) and Sympathetic Knowledge

Since its inception, the practical value of philosophy has
been questioned perpetually. When Aristophanes introduces
Socrates as a character in his comedy *Clouds*, he presents him
hanging upside down. The protagonist, Strepsiades, asks him
why he reposes in such a precarious state, to which Socrates
replies: "I'd never come up with a single thing about celestial
phenomena, if I did not suspend my mind up high, to mix
my subtle thoughts with what's like them—the air" (lines

275–279, in Ian Johnston's translation). Essentially Socrates confesses here to be the first "airhead"; and thus the venerable tradition of "philosopher jokes" was born. Pragmatists share Strepsiades's suspicion of philosophy; indeed, the tradition is named after it. Consider this quotation from Dewey's "The Need for a Recovery of Philosophy" (1917) which remains an astute indictment of professional philosophy:

> I believe that philosophy in America will be lost between chewing a historic cud long since reduced to woody fiber, or an apologetics for lost causes (lost to natural sciences), or a scholastic, schematic formalism, unless it can somehow bring to consciousness America's own needs and its own implicit principle of successful action. (Dewey 1981: 96)

Dewey recognized that philosophy earned its reputation for navel gazing by favoring these retreats into debates over historical minutiae or esoteric theories rather than facing everyday human problems. Meliorism, by contrast, is the idea that philosophy should engage and describe concrete social problems, favoring tangible improvement rather than escaping into history, theory, or utopian solutions. Undoubtedly the classical pragmatists' emphasis on making philosophy practical turned American thought in this direction, especially the ethical thought of James and the social thought of Royce. Yet these problems remained distant from the Harvard Yard, whereas on the streets of Chicago they were inescapable. How can one lecture on the mind–body problem when children are dying of malnutrition and disease in the ghettos? How can one lecture on the social contract when the city is paralysed by labor strikes? As we shall see, the Chicago pragmatists enriched pragmatism by starting from immediate social problems, by reasoning from the bottom up, and by allowing their practice to determine their theories. They lived with and served their communities. They were not afraid to get their hands dirty, and this deep populism represents the most "American" character of pragmatism.

The life and thought of Jane Addams beckons us as an excellent example of a concerned person dedicated to using

her talents and privileges to ameliorate the rapid transfor-
mations of her age. She was born into the upper echelons
of Illinois society, her father being a wealthy businessman
who made his fortune on an economic transition from early
investments in agrarian businesses like cattle and timber to
ownership of mills and textiles factories. He was also a founding member of the Illinois Republican Party, a state senator,
and a friend of Abraham Lincoln. These advantages and connections provided the precocious Jane Addams not only with
deep social insight and responsibility, but with the power
to create her own opportunities in a culture dismissive of
and hostile to an enterprising woman. In her youth, Addams
struggled to forge a sustaining career path and encountered
success as well as setbacks. The transformational moment in
her life occurred while on a trip to Europe in 1888 with her
life partner Ellen Gates Starr. Together they toured Toynbee
Hall in London, a settlement house dedicated to providing
young men with a place to live as well as with the training and
social support necessary for securing a successful trade in a
rapidly industrializing Britain.

Convinced that a similar experiment could help the city of
Chicago, she and Star established Hull House the following
year in order to provide lodging and support for immigrant
women. The two of them lived and worked with the women
of Hull House and its surrounding ghettos. While their program was nominally Christian, Addams and Starr had no
ideological commitments or political agenda. They intended
to meet the needs of their community, and allowed their
efforts to be informed by the experiences and insights of
the women they served. As a result, Hull House succeeded
far beyond anyone's expectations, becoming an exemplary
charitable institution that would inspire other social experiments and serve the city of Chicago into the twenty-first
century. While this grounding in service provides Addams's
thought with its vitality, it has unfairly been used to excuse
overlooking or even dismissing the value of her theoretical
work and its importance to the development of pragmatism.
Yet in her later works—*Democracy and Social Ethics* of 1902
and *Newer Ideas of Peace* of 1907—we see the development

of a theory of sympathetic knowledge that forms the basis of the meliorism and represents both pragmatism's engagement with social problems and a feminist approach.

While some of the language seems dated, informal, and needlessly theological, *Democracy and Social Ethics* provides a surprisingly contemporary framework for analysing social problems—a framework now known as sympathetic knowledge. Addams's introduction clarifies three themes.

First, it stresses the authority of social experience over science. This does not entail any denial of science. All the pragmatists, including Addams, recognize the value of empirical insight. Rather Addams assumes that "genuine experience" is not more likely to "lead us astray any more than scientific data"; that, more importantly, "social experience" provides "perspective ... sanity of judgment"; and that direct interaction with people and their communities "is the surest corrective of opinions concerning the social order, and concerning efforts, however humble, for its improvement" (Addams 1905: 7). Addams's attitude in this introduction represents, in short, a democratic humility that is willing to submit to the wisdom of the population one serves.

Second, this humility opens us to a more inclusive democratic community. As our social consciousness expands through the press, through literature, and through service, we develop a "new affinity for all men" and a realization that "much of the insensibility and hardness of the world is due to the lack of imagination which prevents a realization of the experiences of other people" (1905: 9). This affinity results in "identification with the common lot which is the essential idea of Democracy... the source and expression of social ethics" (1905: 11).

Finally, Addams blurs the dualism between theory and practice by emphasizing the efficacy of reform through common effort, as opposed to detached management or blind charity. Addams's work excels at highlighting the complementary aspects of knowledge and practice; and it does so by pointing out how the "educated and self-conscious members of the community" may more keenly feel the "perplexity" of social problems without forgetting that "the tentative and actual attempts at adjustment are largely coming through those who are simpler and less analytical" (1905: 12).

Her best demonstration of the application of sympathetic knowledge comes in the chapter "Charitable Efforts," where she applies it to the work of female charity visitors. She begins the chapter with a general claim, which informs her entire work: moral ideas develop and democracy requires "adjusting our conduct, which has become hardened into customs and habits, to these changing moral conceptions" (1905: 13). She then identifies not a particular social problem, but our understanding of charity itself, as the area most in need of moral amelioration. Charity lies at the intersection of two crucial democratic values: the common good and equality. If we are to pursue the common good, the privileged should help those less fortunate, but this "point of contact" between members of the population is inherently unequal. Thus the charitable relation itself must be reformed, lest it reinforce this inequality. Addams then contrasts two forms of charity by describing individuals who share different understandings and practices of it.

First she describes "the old-fashioned charitable man," who believes in merit-based charity, assuming that poverty results from "vice and laziness" whereas prosperity results from virtue and ambition (1905: 14). Thus he provides charity only for the worthy poor. This attitude reinforces his sense of superiority as well as the shame of those he claims to serve. David Huddleston's millionaire, who shares the same name with the film's eponymous hero in *The Big Lebowski* (dir. Joel and Ethan Coen 1998), is a good cinematic example of this type of charity. Prior to his first entrance, his butler, Brandt, introduces him as a successful philanthropic businessman commended for his support of the Little Lebowski Urban Achievers, "inner city kids of promise without the necessary means for a higher education." When he arrives, he impatiently chastizes the film's protagonist, "Dude" Lebowski, for being an unemployed bum "looking for a handout," claims that "every bum's life is his own responsibility regardless of who he chooses to blame," and brags about how he "went out and achieved" despite losing the use of his legs during the Korean War. By the end of the film we learn that the Big Lebowski's image and charity are façades: he married into wealth, mismanaged the family business, and was reassigned to charity work as a means of protecting his fragile ego. Ironically, the Big Lebowski is more of a bum than the Dude, which makes him the biggest bum in Los Angeles County; and this would place him high in the running for biggest bum worldwide.

Conversely, Addams imagines a charitable relation grounded in mutual respect and humility and instructs her female charity visitors to become and act as neighbors to the poor. Thus the first move toward sympathetic knowledge is to recognize that no meritocracy works behind most class distinctions and to put this recognition in the service of dispelling value judgments related to class:

> The daintily clad charity visitor who steps into the little house made untidy by the vigorous efforts of her hostess, the washerwoman, is no longer sure of her superiority to the latter; she recognizes that her hostess after all represents social value and industrial use, as over against her own parasitic cleanliness and a social standing attained only through status. (Addams 1905: 16)

In some respects, Addams anticipates what Peggy McIntosh (forthcoming) would label *privilege*; but this is privilege seen through the lens of socioeconomic class rather than race or gender. Acknowledging the virtue of the washerwoman allows the charity visitor to see past her own class assumptions and enables an equitable rather than a hierarchical relationship. The charity visitor must recognize how the economic fates of both women result from historical and systemic factors more than from moral successes or failures. Without this sympathetic knowledge, the charity visitor's service will be temporal, counterproductive, and occasionally harmful.

The remainder of the chapter "Charitable Efforts" catalogs specific examples of how these assumptions impede the charity visitor's ability to see the ethics and the logic of the washerwoman's daily life. With regard to money, marriage, and parenting, the realities of poverty require of an

individual to make different domestic and financial decisions
from those expected by an affluent person. Whereas the latter
would expect a poor person to save extra income in order to
improve his living conditions, "that saving, which seems quite
commendable in a comfortable part of town, appears almost
criminal in a poorer quarter where the next-door neighbor
needs food" (Addams 1905: 31). Likewise, the tendency of
young working women to spend most of their income on
expensive clothing perplexes the charity visitor, who can
"afford to be very simple, or even shabby as to her clothes,"
until she realizes that these clothes allow working women to
appear equal to affluent women in settings where they wish
to be judged favorably, for example at work, at school, or
at church (1905: 34–38). Finally, the seemingly inconsistent
wavering of impoverished parents between strict discipline
and indulgence toward their children is often informed by
the trauma of mourning and by the paradoxical guilt of a
bereaved parent—guilt for both failing to protect a lost child
and to enjoy a living one (1905: 32–34). While these behav-
iors may seem archaic, they are historical examples of class
prejudices that still persist.

Ultimately, Addams uses the recognition of privilege and
class assumptions for the purpose of teaching charity visitors
how to adopt a "neighborhood mind" rather than a charitable mind; she is attempting to make them understand "the
difference between the emotional kindness with which relief
is given by one poor neighbor, and the guarded care with
which relief is given by a charity visitor to a charity recipient"
(1905: 19). When neighbors help each other, "[t]here is the
greatest willingness to lend or borrow anything," because
the "economic condition of all alike is on a most precarious
level," so that "the ready outflow of sympathy and material
assistance [is] the most natural thing in the world" (1905:
19–20). Charity visitors must not only overcome their pity
for the washerwoman, nor merely admire her industriousness from a distance. They must become neighbors; and the
only means of accomplishing this transformation is through
shared experience. This transformation requires the creation
of *liminal spaces* such as Hull House, where people from

different communities can spend time together and become
familiar. It is not an abstract theoretical transformation, but a
concrete and physical one. Reading and learning about others
can increase sympathetic knowledge, but Addams came to see
that we must support it through embodied practices. Thus
she encouraged her volunteers to reside at Hull House along
with women from the community, because actually becoming
neighbors was the most effective and obvious way of building
this neighborly connection.

While this transformation of the charitable relation is
crucial for establishing sympathetic knowledge, Addams
applies the same kind of reform to other social concerns in
the subsequent pages of *Democracy and Social Ethics*. The
chapter "Filial Relations" discusses for women the need to
adapt to the changes in gender roles that resulted from mass
immigration and industrialization, so that young women may
be able to "secure a more active share in the community life"
instead of focusing, as expected, on familial and domestic
concerns (1905: 73). Addams describes the guilt felt by a
young woman, but this sentiment affected many college students of both genders (1905: 85–86):

> The daughter finds a constant and totally unnecessary conflict
> between the social and the family claims. In most cases the
> former is repressed and gives way to the family claim, because
> the latter is concrete and definitely asserted, while the social
> demand is vague and unformulated. In such instances the girl
> quietly submits, but she feels wronged whenever she allows
> her mind to dwell upon the situation. She either hides her
> hurt, and splendid reserves of enthusiasm and capacity go to
> waste, or her zeal and emotions turn inward, and the result is
> an unhappy woman, whose heart is consumed by vain regrets
> and desires.

In this case, the upwardly mobile youth recognizes that she
herself has become a place of social transformation. Social
change lies within her and manifests itself through her choices
and daily life. Sympathetic to her plight, Addams considers
how the education system can serve as a liminal space for
this transformation by teaching the young woman the social

values and habits necessary for a successful transition rather than placing on her the burden of social change (1905: 92).

Addams also applies sympathetic knowledge to a specific historical conflict: the devastating and violent Pullman Railroad Strike of 1894. "A Modern Lear," published in 1912, was first delivered as a speech during the strikes. There she draws an analogy between Shakespeare's King Lear and the industrialist George Pullman, whose authoritarian management caused the violent strike mentioned at the beginning of this chapter. Whereas Lear's failure was a private "domestic tragedy," Addams sees Pullman's analogous failure as a public "industrial tragedy" due to his inability to see how his early largesse to his workers, whom he provided with work, housing, and leisure, had become a means of control and oppression (Addams 1912: 132). Interestingly, Addams does not lay all the blame on Lear and on Pullman, but sees Cordelia and the rail workers as also failing to be sympathetic, albeit to a lesser degree, because they did benefit from their patriarch's indulgence; thus their rash reactions to a legitimate injustice unfortunately reinforce the authority's narrative of ingratitude.

Although there certainly are individual cases and social problems where the victims are totally blameless, Addams challenges us to recognize that sympathy should flow in both directions, because conflicts rarely reduce to simple dualisms between good and evil. Even when they do, the powerless find themselves caught in the delirium of the powerful; thus mutual sympathy increases the likelihood of success for both parties. Like Big Lebowski, Pullman, and Lear, the powerful frequently enjoy the luxury of self-pity, even in response to small slights. Addams writes (1912: 135):

> The shock of disaster upon egoism is apt to produce self-pity. It is possible that his self-pity and loneliness may have been so great and absorbing as to completely shut out from his mind a compunction of derelict duty. He may have been unconscious that men were charging him with a shirking of the issue.

Whether we are powerful or powerless, Addams reminds us that we all feel our grievances to be legitimate and must actively work to overcome self-pity by sympathizing with the others, no matter how different they are, if we hope to ameliorate conflict. Thus, for democracy to function, we must develop an educational system that teaches the old and the young, parents and children, men and women, owners and workers, the powerful and the powerless the skills and knowledge they need if they wish to sympathize across differences, reduce conflict, and become neighbors in the hope of "constantly [raising] the value and function of each member of the community however humble he may be" (Addams 1905: 178).

Once again, Addams recommends the school, specifically public education, as the crucial *liminal space* for this transformation to occur: "The democratic ideal demands of school that it shall give the child's own experience a social value; that it shall teach him to direct his own activities and adjust them to those of other people" (1905: 179–180). This passage, in fact the whole chapter that contains it, anticipates and echoes the ideas of Addams's friend, ally, and colleague, John Dewey, to whom I will turn soon.

With regard to education, Addams laments that the curriculum more often aligns with the desires of those in power than with the needs of vulnerable students and their communities. Thus standardized education reinforces social hierarchies, sets up sensitive students for failure, alienates working people from the value of education, specializes individuals, preparing them for tenuous jobs, and demeans crucial labor-intensive work.

David Simon's critically acclaimed television series *The Wire* (2002–2008) dramatized how separate social logics of this sort interact across parallel communities, for example in the complex relationship between law enforcement and the illegal drug trade in Baltimore, Maryland, which affected satellite communities such as unions, city politics, the press, and the educational system. In particular, Season 4 received high critical praise for masterfully dramatizing how pressure from hierarchical institutions undermined the attempts of public educators to meet the needs of inner-city students. We discover the dysfunction of the school system through the eyes of an outsider: Roland "Prez" Pryzblewski, a former police detective starting on a new career as a math teacher. On his first day, he fails to teach class owing to his students' rowdy behavior. Later on, at the faculty meeting, his administrators demand that he only teach content relevant to the standardized exam. This provision covers for spending time in math class teaching language arts, because the school needs more urgently to improve on that score, to prevent being taken over by the state. Expressing his dismay to fellow faculty, Prez asks two questions. First, how is he expected to teach his students the mathematics assessed by the exam, when they lack the socialization to learn effectively and the remedial skills needed for the exam content, and when he must devote a portion of his class time to teaching language arts? Second, how does preparing students for a specific exam teach them anything they can apply in their lives? The answers: you can't, and it doesn't. His colleagues advise him to put on his chalk board a question from the exam and keep it there, to fool observers into thinking that he is teaching for the exam while covertly teaching the students the math they need and making them accept the reality that standardized test scores do not exist for the students' benefit, but are there to provide authorities with a measurement for allocating funding and results for reelection campaigns. The standardized tests are political, not educational tools.

Ultimately the show portrays Prez as heroic despite his marginal successes, as he is an excellent representative of sympathetic knowledge and meliorism. He learns to see the students' rebellion not as malicious, but as an expression of their legitimate frustration, as they feel caught between the parallel logics of the street and the classroom. He finally reaches his students when he uses the game of craps to show them how learning to compute probability can increase their winnings.

Granted, this victory may be minor and fleeting, but all success is ultimately local, temporary, and we can never know its full impact. Toynbee Hall did not solve poverty in London but helped hundreds of families and inspired Hull House. In turn, Hull House helped Chicagoans for almost a hundred years; but it, too, ended. Meanwhile, Addams's experience and research continue to inspire and help others. This kind of uncertainty is the source of both the frustration and the joy of being an academic, a teacher, or a social worker: we have no idea how and to what degree our efforts will impact others.

John Dewey (1859–1952) and the Pattern of Inquiry

Scholars regard John Dewey as one of the key founders of pragmatism, alongside Peirce and James. And, indeed, special challenges surface when interpreting Dewey's work but, unlike in Peirce's and James's case, these barriers are not caused by his inability to organize his thoughts coherently or by significant conceptual shifts throughout his career. Ironically, his work is so vast and systematic that providing a comprehensive introduction to it proves impossible. He lived nearly ninety-three years, was prolific throughout his entire working life, and wrote several philosophical classics. Fortunately, although Dewey focused on different topics during his early, middle, and late career—a conventional division that corresponds roughly to three successive periods of tenure at the University of Michigan (1884–1894), at the University of Chicago (1894–1904), and at Columbia University in New York (1904–1930)—there are no major shifts in his thought. The pattern of inquiry that Dewey developed under the influence of Peirce, James, Addams, and, as we shall see, Charles Darwin runs throughout the entire corpus of his writings. It emerges from his early readings of the classical pragmatists, becomes funded by his collaboration in Chicago, then gets refined, systematized, and applied throughout his later work and projects.

Thus the main challenge of introducing Dewey is deciding which works, subjects, or themes to explore. There is, however, another problem that must be addressed, and it is one of approach: the problem of placing too much emphasis on the "founding fathers" of pragmatism. Doing so obscures or even discounts Addams's critical influence on Dewey and her role as a cofounder of pragmatism equal to her male colleagues.

To make this right, I will start with Addams's influence on Dewey's philosophy via the development of his pedagogy. Once this bottom-up influence is established and its relation to the origins and impact of the Chicago Laboratory School revealed, my introduction will move on to how Dewey presents a critique of idealism parallel to the critiques of realism provided by Peirce and James. Once projects and concepts have been sketched, I will survey the pattern of inquiry that can be found in Dewey's major works. Finally, I will examine how this synthesis of theory and practice contributes to the mutual influence between pragmatism and the emerging social sciences.

As described in the discussion of Addams, the decade that John Dewey spent at the University of Chicago from 1894 on was a time of radical social, professional, and personal change, both for the nation and for Dewey. America's rapid industrialization after the Civil War dramatically increased the general prosperity of the country, but also economic inequality. Dewey's personal life during this period was equally tumultuous; perhaps the Chicago decade was the most active period of his career. Within one year he moved his young family from Ann Arbor, Michigan to Chicago, became the chair of the Departments of Philosophy, Pedagogy, and Psychology, founded the Laboratory School, attended and delivered lectures at Hull House, and grieved the loss of his son Morris. Dewey's philosophy changed radically during these years and laid the groundwork for the ideas he would develop throughout his life.

Dewey began his career as a young Hegelian at Johns Hopkins University, but thanks to several factors (such as the influence of Peirce's logic class and William James's writings) he soon embraced pragmatism. Dewey changes course in 1896, with a piece entitled "The Reflex Arc in Psychology," where he uses ideas gleaned from James's *Principles of Psychology* to address the phenomenon of the reflex arc, specifically how and why our reflexes work in response to stimuli. Why does a curious child instantly recoil when she touches a candle flame? Dewey claims that the dualism between stimuli and reflex is a physiological version of much older philosophical dualisms, for example the metaphysical dualism between mind and body and the epistemological dualism between sensation and idea. And, in an argument reminiscent of James's notion of the continuity of experience, Dewey reaches the conclusion that contemporary psychology's problem is dualism itself. The study of the reflex arc had reached a similar impasse, because researchers demanded that the phenomena correspond to their theory rather than tailoring their theory to the phenomena. Dewey describes the impasse and the means of its removal as follows:

> Instead of interpreting the character of sensation, idea, and action from their place and function in sensorimotor circuit, we still incline to interpret the latter from our preconceived and preformulated ideas of rigid distinctions between sensations, thoughts and acts. The sensory stimulus is one thing, the central activity, standing for the idea, is another thing, and the motor discharge, standing for the act proper is a third. As a result, the reflex arc is not a comprehensive, or organic, unity, but a patchwork of disjointed parts, a mechanical conjunction of unallied processes. What is needed is that the principle underlying the idea of the reflex arc as the fundamental psychical unity shall react into and determine the values of its constitutive factors. More specifically, what is wanted is that sensory stimulus, central connections and motor responses shall be viewed, not as separate and complete entities in themselves, but as divisions of labor, functioning factors, within the single concrete whole, now designated the reflex arc. (Dewey 1981: 137)

Just as James argued that our consciousness does not divide itself up into discrete thoughts but streams from one thought to the next, Dewey argues here that the reflex arc is a continuous circuit between stimuli, perception, thought, and action. Organisms cycle so quickly through each phase that insisting that the phenomena can be reduced to discrete moments creates an artificial caricature of the reflex arc, and this is more likely to hamper further research than to increase our understanding. By reconstructing the reflex arc as a continuous process, Dewey revolutionized contemporary psychology. Even more, this insight into a reciprocal transaction between an organism and its environment whereby the two adapt to each other was to form the axis of Dewey's philosophy and determined his treatment of all other subjects.

Dewey first applies this insight to the subject of education in such a way that, of all his numerous, diverse, and outstanding achievements, the development of the concept of a *progressive education* brought him the greatest fame. Like the reflex arc in psychology, traditional education focuses on a dualistic, hierarchical, and didactic relationship between teacher and student. The teacher plays the active role of an authority who transmits knowledge to a passive student who must memorize it. Consequently, traditional education measures success either by the quality of the teacher's material and delivery of it or by the accuracy, breadth, and detail with which the student is able to recall this material. Therefore the standard methods are lecture, drill, exams, and essays. Thus the classroom becomes a scene familiar to many: the teacher is at the front of the room, speaking and moving freely, while students sit quietly in rows, focused on the lecture and jotting down notes.

Although many of the elite preparatory and higher education programs in the United States and other countries continue to use it, this structure excludes learners who are not neurotypical and reduces success to high grades, exam scores, and other quantitative metrics. Furthermore, these results often reinforce the various social distinctions that exist outside the classroom, despite the usually sincere intentions of administrators, who aspire to high standards of objectivity and excellence. While the teacher need not be as authoritarian as depicted in Pink Floyd's "Another Brick in the Wall, Part 2," the video and song masterfully express the typical angst, or at least boredom, that most students feel when enduring this type of pedagogy. Floyd's piece also captures the social implications of traditional education: children are isolated, imagination is ridiculed, difference is suppressed, the content becomes banal, and students, rather than being educated, are sorted for unclear, arbitrary, and possibility predatory social goals.

Returning to Dewey: when he arrived in Chicago, Dewey

possessed not only a clear vision of an alternative to traditional education but also the seed of his entire philosophy.
In "My Pedagogical Creed," which he published in 1897,
Dewey combines his insights from experience as an elementary school teacher with insights into pragmatism to assert
that education is the process through which the society
transmits its knowledge and culture to members of the next
generation. Therefore no process is more critical from a
social perspective; and Dewey would reform education so
as to make it a more active and engaged process, in which
all participants—the student, the teacher, the school—must
continually adapt in response to the needs of society and the
interests of learners. First, we must recognize that education
is not a merely formal activity that begins and ends when
the school bell rings but a native, continuous, and embodied
biological process, which begins at the moment of birth and
goes on until the moment of death. Consequently the school
should not be a regimented space separate from society, but a
place continuous with daily life where the learner participates
both in her own intellectual and moral development and in
the perpetuation of her culture. The teacher's function is not
to discipline students' behavior, transmit content, or prepare
them for a remote future but to enrich and enhance their
present learning experience so that they may develop, in addi-
tion to knowledge, abilities and skills that will allow them
to adapt or resolve problems as they arise. Thus education
functions as the "fundamental method of social progress and
reform," not through top-down coercive indoctrination but
by empowering the student to "share in the social consciousness" and in the process of "social reconstruction" (Dewey
1981: 452–453).

Under the influence of Addams, Dewey designs a curriculum
for the Laboratory School that will use progressive education
to ameliorate class divisions. Students start with domestic
occupations or hands-on everyday activities rather than with
abstract academic subjects such as arithmetic, grammar,
or the memorization of scientific and historical facts. This
approach ameliorates the class distinction between domestic
and professional work and captures the children's interest, as

it allows them to explore a subject freely, according to their preferred method. Then the instructor directs this interest toward the relevant academic content and skills by disclosing how these are relevant to the task at hand (which is something related to the subject that children wish to explore). This process mirrors the phases of the scientific method: students become habituated to using all their senses to observe the subject, then they progress to analysis, hypothesis, experimentation, and reflection. Most importantly, this pedagogical project mirrors not only science, but also democracy. Thus, students learn how to work cooperatively with each other and the instructor as they learn the necessary academic (1981: 456–461). This synthesis of education, scientific inquiry, and democratic participation forms the core of Dewey's pattern of inquiry and applies to philosophical subjects as well as to education, research, and politics.

Dewey explains this process with the help of the examples of sewing and weaving. First the instructor should distribute samples of the necessary raw materials—say flax, cotton, and wool—so that students may start with an immediate, tactile experience of the subject from which they can draw their own inferences by interacting with the material. Then the instructor should teach them how these materials and the basic tools associated with them can be used for basic domestic purposes. As the students put this lesson into practice, the teacher introduces the more specific academic content relevant to the task. Dewey famously remarks: "You can concentrate the history of all mankind into the evolution of the flax, cotton, and wool fibers into clothing" (1981: 463). Indeed, sensitive readers will recognize the subversive implication of Dewey's subject: the history of the United States had largely been determined by the problematic social arrangements necessary to grow, harvest, and process the cash crop of cotton. Starting with a concrete task rather than with abstract information, the learner discovers the "human significance" of the activity both in her daily work and in her academic studies. By integrating the two rather than reinforcing the artificial split between the hand and brain—a split with profound socioeconomic implications—students learn an important life skill, which fewer people possess in each generation. And in the process they also acquire problem-solving skills and experience with the task and the materials, all of which can be put to use in mathematics, history, science, and the like. Together, these examples contain the key components of what is commonly referred to as progressive education: experiential learning; an integrated curriculum; problem solving and critical thinking (in preference to memorization and testing); project-based, personalized and cooperative learning; lifelong learning; social skills. Most importantly, they allude to the social implications of the curriculum and suggest how the structure of education frames and informs our social and political opinions. Dewey warns:

> Until the instincts of construction and production are systematically laid hold of in the years of childhood and youth, until they are trained in social directions, enriched by historical interpretation, controlled and illuminated by scientific methods, we certainly are in no position even to locate the source of our economic evils, much less to deal with them effectively. (1981: 464)

Robert Westbrook contends that Dewey intended to use the Laboratory School to develop a curriculum that could have reformed the social divisions of industrial democracy; and he speculates that this institution would have become more "thoroughgoing and radical," if Dewey had the opportunity to continue (Westbrook 2005: 414–415). Dewey transfered to Columbia University when his wife was removed from her position as school principal, but fortunately he devoted the remainder of his life to articulating and expanding the lessons learned in Chicago under Addams's tutelage and at the Laboratory School.

Charlene Haddock Seigfried (1996) emphasizes that the cooperation between Addams and Dewey models how practical experience and theoretical insights can function to develop creative strategies for the most intractable social problems and that, for this reason, this relationship was of great importance to the development of pragmatism in the twentieth century. She observes: "Hull House was not so much an example of

Dewey's theory of education, as it was already exemplary of what Dewey sought to theorize." Dewey performed the tasks of institutionalizing and theorizing the lessons that Addams shared with him. What inspired him to do so was her "legacy of exhaustive service, empowerment of the immigrant poor, and cooperative problem solving" (Seigfried 1996: 74). Addams and Dewey remained friends and colleagues throughout their lives and, through her pacifism and her practice of democracy "both as a process and institution," she continually helped Dewey to avoid "prejudice and convention." Her "perspectivism and her pluralism were concretely grounded" (1996: 75–6).

Most importantly, Addams and Hull House taught Dewey to "not sentimentalize democracy." It takes effort and patience to live and learn across cultural and class divisions. Without these virtues, even liminal spaces such as Hull House and the Laboratory School can "breed misunderstanding and deepen prejudice" (1996: 76–7). Jay Martin corroborates Seigfried's account: she suggests that Addams turned Dewey away from his growing anarchistic sympathies and back toward democracy because Hull House "perfectly matched Dewey's changing mind and emotional needs and filled in the spaces left empty by the withering away of his old allegiances" (Martin 2002: 164). Either way, Pullman and Hull House both left a lasting legacy on Dewey's philosophy, specifically on his pedagogy, and nourished his belief that the purpose of education is to capture the students' interest and to teach them the skills and habits needed for democracy and inquiry; this way they can be life-long learners who are politically active and socially engaged.

It is after leaving Chicago, too, that Dewey begins to compose his most important philosophical and critical works, which gradually unfold a thesis of *cultural naturalism*—the metaphysical position that experience emerges from an organism's transactions with its natural and cultural environment. As mentioned before, Dewey never turned away from the transactionalism he first sketched in "The Reflex Arc"; there were, however, critical moments at which he significantly revised and clarified his pragmatism. The most illuminating example occurs in the 1909 essay "The Influence of Darwinism on Philosophy," where he combines the insights of pragmatism and those of natural selection to vanquish any remnants of absolutism in his thought. As a young scholar, Dewey deeply appreciated the absolute idealism of the German philosopher G. W. F. Hegel. Indeed, most critics of Dewey dismiss his work as a folksy, watered-down version of Hegelianism. While this attitude is unwarranted, the association was real. Even late in his life, Dewey admitted to the "permanent Hegelian deposit" in his work (Dewey 1984: 155). However, understanding the distinctions between Hegel's dialectic and Dewey's pattern of inquiry is crucial not only to avoiding this mischaracterization, but to understanding the full significance of all the themes I will discuss in this book: fallibilism, meliorism, pluralism, verification, and hope.

Dewey begins the essay on Darwinism by claiming that the magnitude of Darwin's contribution to philosophy and culture has not been fully appreciated. Indeed, if taken seriously, the idea of evolution invalidates the theoretical foundations of western philosophy and civilization. According to Hegel, history is a gradual unfolding of reason, as humanity attempts to explain the world through a *dialectical* process. In brief, the human subject encounters the objective world and uses her reason to explain what she experiences. This explanation becomes a tentative thesis in the dialectical process and inevitably proves insufficient as the dialectical cycle begins to turn—through conversation with other rational human subjects and through further observation of the objective world. The insufficiencies of the subject's thesis are revealed in this dialectical process, and eventually an antithesis emerges. Next, the thesis and the antithesis conflict, until a revolution occurs: both positions collapse and merge to form a third—a synthesis of their best aspects. But this synthesis becomes a new thesis, and the dialectic of thesis–antithesis–synthesis begins again. On the grand scale, Hegel believes that history results from this dialectical process, as theologians, philosophers, and artists battle in the world of ideas while groups and societies fight physically to defend and advance these ideas. However, in Hegel's view this history of spiritual and physical conflict is not for nothing: despite the destruction involved, the ideas and the societies that emerge from the dialectical process are more advanced than those that preceded them. Thus thought and society improve through conflict as they advance toward absolute reason; and "absolute reason" is a perfect and complete unfolding of reason that awaits us at the end of history and where our subjective descriptions are identical with objective reality.

Owing to its future-oriented nature, Hegel's absolute idealism—in which dialectic pursues and achieves the ultimate goal of absolute reason—has been described as a teleology. Teleologies are philosophical systems that evaluate present beings, concepts, and actions in relation to how they contribute to some goal. For the western mind, this is a fairly common way of thinking, and at least our language and metaphors betray it. Many people believe that the purpose of philosophy is to clarify what our proper moral, social, and epistemological goals should be. Like Hegel, they assume that the purpose of philosophy, or of any kind of inquiry, is to discover eventually the truth, or some kind of "absolute reason." They believe that the existence of this universal truth is necessary if we want to decide whether our actions are moral, whether our beliefs are correct, or whether we have progressed as a society. And, if there is no ultimate truth, they imagine nihilistic anarchy to be the only alternative. Indeed, this is the reason why some religious fundamentalists reject the theory of evolution: they fear that it describes a hopeless nihilistic universe where life has no meaning because there is no ultimate purpose. However, fallibilism and pluralism function as a middle ground between absolutism and nihilism and, as we shall see, meliorism, verification, and hope enable us not only to cope with this reality but to thrive under it.

Hegel's absolute idealism served as the most pervasive philosophical teleology of Dewey's era, but the concept of *telos*, like the word itself, goes back to Greek antiquity. This is why, in "The Influence of Darwinism on Philosophy," Dewey's criticism of this concept that has guided the West for two millennia focuses on its articulation by Aristotle; however, if

Dewey successfully refutes this style of thinking at its source, the refutation implicitly applies to Hegel's teleology as well. Dewey describes the philosophical repercussions of Darwin's theory as follows:

> The conceptions that had reigned in the philosophy of nature and knowledge for two thousand years, the conceptions that had become the familiar furniture of the mind; rested on the assumption of the superiority of the fixed and final; they rested upon treating change and origin as signs of defect and unreality. In laying hands upon the sacred ark of absolute permanency, in treating the forms that had been regarded as types of fixity and perfection as originating and passing away, the "Origin of the Species" introduced a mode of thinking that in the end was bound to transform the logic of knowledge, and hence the treatment of morals, politics, and religion. (Dewey 1981: 32)

The most important consequence of this view is that we live in a universe of perpetual change with no clear origin, boundaries, or destiny. Dewey next explains how the reality of a universe of ceaseless change and novelty destabilizes the arsenal of Aristotelian concepts at the roots of western culture—and especially *eidos* (species, form) and *telos* (goal, purpose).

Readers may not be aware that biology and zoology—the fields of enquiry that Darwin writes about—are inherited, at several removes, from Aristotle, who did extensive research on all forms of life. But Aristotle also investigated any subject by determining its essential properties or "form" (*eidos*)—that which distinguished one type of being from any other. His method for determining a being's essence was to ask four questions that could be answered through observation: What is its matter, what is it made of? What is its origin, how did it come into the world? What is its form or essence? What is its purpose? These questions map out Aristotle's theory of causation—his famous four causes: by answering them one can determine the essential properties that cause any being to be unique. Take the statue of a horse: its material cause is the marble it is made of; its formal cause is the horse it represents

or imitates; its efficient cause is the artist who modeled the
marble into a statue—just as a father is the efficient cause of
the son; and its final cause is its purpose, the competition for
which the statue was ordered—just as health is the final cause
of walking, or hearing the final cause of the ear. Further along
the line, the Aristotelian four causes are bound up with the
classification of substances and with the concepts of genus
and species. Roughly speaking, the Aristotelian assumption
that there is one single essence that all members of one species
share and that makes them distinct from all other species of
beings has prevailed until Darwin.

Darwin's key insight is that species do not have a single and
unique essence; evolutionary biology postulates that populations of organisms change gradually across generations,
either through the recombination of traits in reproduction or
through random mutations. Each generation of a species is
slightly different from the preceding one, and across several
generations these incremental changes accumulate. Over time,
environmental conditions change and natural selection favors
the traits of some organisms over others, until eventually a
new species emerges—or even more; and they are different
from their common ancestors. Contemporary biologists still
use the term "species" to differentiate between populations of
organisms, but they admit that the boundaries between species with common ancestry are subtle, porous, different case
by case, and gradually changing. Indeed, one philosophical
conundrum is the disagreement between liberal "splitters"—
zoologists who assign species or subspecies status on the basis
of any significant difference between populations—and the
more conservative "lumpers," who are reluctant to classify
an organism or a population as a new species. Either way,
this philosophical difference illustrates the fact that, just as
the genetic difference between populations of common ancestry is vague, the concept of species is equally vague. There
is no consistent definition or criterion for species, yet the
term remains in use for pragmatic reasons. Again, we would
be committing the fallacy of misplaced concreteness if we
insisted that species exist in nature. In nature there are only
organisms and populations with similar traits that we call

species, but there are no species. The concept of species is just a map we use to describe features of the territory; it is not the territory itself.

However, the concept of species is merely the biological application of a more fundamental concept of essence, and much of western philosophy has been a search for the essences that define concepts, ideas, processes, human nature, justice, even reality. Thus the history of philosophical inquiry assumes, like Aristotle, Descartes, and Hegel, that the subjects of inquiry must have a clear, fixed, and essential property that differentiates them from all other types of beings. By revealing that species and organisms do not have essential properties because they change gradually across generations, the theory of evolution challenges the assumption that the subjects of philosophical inquiry have a fixed essential nature, which is there to be discovered. While some subjects *may* possess a single essential property, such as the circumference of a circle, that necessarily distinguishes them from other subjects, after Darwin there is no reason to assume, at the beginning of an inquiry, that all subjects *must* possess a single essential property. Furthermore, our understanding of the natural world has improved not because we have found the essences of more beings than our ancestors, but because many sciences are gradually relinquishing their demands for certainty or clarity. It is far more useful to accept Peirce's insight that some concepts or methods benefit from accepting the utility of the vague and fallible. And Dewey, too, insists that philosophy will improve dramatically once it abandons this quest for certainty.

This first implication alone is monumental, but Dewey recognizes that it is not as significant as the destabilization of the notion of *telos*. If, historically, beings have undergone perpetual change and continue to experience change in the present, it follows that perpetual change is likely to continue indefinitely. This second implication undermines not only Aristotle's teleology but also Hegel's. This universe that Darwin describes is a universe of continuous change in all spatial and temporal directions. If we look back on the history of the universe, we notice certain thresholds where local

or cosmic environmental conditions changed dramatically—
for example the ratification of the 13th Amendment in
America or, in the world, the invention of the printing press,
the invention of agriculture, the birth of modern humans, the
Pleistocene extinction event, the birth of the sun, or the Big
Bang; but these are merely locations of *contingent* events in
time to which human minds assign meaning. We could ascribe
landmark status to different historical events; or, in another
universe, time, location, or culture, events could unfold in
different sequence.

Likewise, the future is completely unwritten. There is no
end of history to be reached and no ultimate fate for humanity
or the universe. Our species may survive for eons, even avoiding or delaying the entropic heat death of the universe—that
is, the moment when all the stars finally burn out; or, as we
sleep tonight, the US DEFCON warning system may glitch,
triggering a chain of events that lead to a nuclear holocaust
before we rise. Dewey recognizes the seriousness of this possibility and diagnoses two possible responses:

> We must either find the appropriate objects and organs of
> knowledge in the mutual interaction of changing things; or
> else, to escape the infection of change, we *must* seek them in
> some transcendent and supernal region. The human mind,
> deliberately as it were, exhausted the logic of the changeless,
> the final, and the transcendent, before it essayed adventure on
> the pathless wastes of generation and transformation. (Dewey
> 1981: 34)

In other words, we can either continue to deny change by
insisting that there must be a fixed and final foundation,
concept, measure, or goal to which we can anchor or steer
our destiny, or embrace the reality of change and learn how
to adapt to it or shape it to our own ends. Clearly Dewey's
concepts of habituation, accommodation, and intelligence
prepare us for the latter; they prepare us to greet uncertainty
with hope rather than to flee in despair. Indeed, he claims
that Darwin has "conquered the phenomena of life for the
principle of transition, and thereby freed the new logic for
application to mind and morals and life ... he emancipated,

once for all, genetic and experimental ideas as an organon of asking questions and looking for explanations" (1981: 35). This is Dewey's summary of Darwin's achievements. This statement liberates Dewey from the fetters of Hegel's dialectic, because our transaction with our culture and nature does not reveal our goal or purpose. The purpose of life is to live, and we create meaning by altering our environment and through our various forms of cultural expression. Furthermore, since there are no fixed essences, the purpose of inquiry is not to describe reality precisely. Through inquiry we develop instead new tools, material or conceptual, that allow us to understand, shape, and adapt to the perpetual transitions within our experience and environment. Harkening back to Dewey's *Democracy and Education*, published in 1916, "education" became both the process and the goal, the means and the end of inquiry, because it was through it, in his judgment, that we continually reorganize, reconstruct, and transform experience within our own lives, cooperatively, and across generations and democracy, as a way of life provides the optimal cultural environment for inquiry.

These views culminate in the first major work of Dewey's late career: *Experience and Nature*, published in 1925. In the chapter titled "Existence as Precarious and Stable," Dewey describes how experience emerges through the living creature's transaction with an environment that permanently oscillates between periods of stability and precariousness. At the purely metaphysical level, experience remains stable for prolonged periods, until it is punctuated by moments of instability. This tendency toward stability makes experience intelligible, because we recognize patterns—that is, habits of nature—if they repeat themselves frequently enough for the living creature to adapt to problems when they arise. Usually these moments of precariousness are minor and short-lived, either owing to their own nature or as a result of the living creatures' abilities to resolve them. However, there are no guarantees that experience will remain stable, or that moments of precariousness will occur as anticipated, or that the living creatures' habits can successfully meliorate them. There are exceptions to *every* rule, and crises can strike without warning and with devastating consequences.

As Dewey alluded in his Darwin essay, the prospect of uncertainty terrifies most humans and, while inquiry should certainly be used in advance, in the hope of anticipating a crisis or adapting to it, it cannot eliminate that crisis, and nothing can guarantee our security. Thus we develop various *denials of uncertainty*, popular and philosophical, whereby we pretend either that uncertainty does not exist or that certain fetishes will protect us when a crisis does occur. At the popular level, such denials include superstition (e.g. astrology), forms of scientism that treat science as certain rather than fallible, the hope that advances in technology will prevail, reliance on the infallible authority of professionals, and the expectation that wealth can buy you out of any jam. At the philosophical level, the western canon is a history of the dualisms proposed for the purpose of eliminating uncertainty by putting down one opposite in favor of the other in pairs such as absolutism versus relativism, transcendentalism versus positivism, idealism versus realism, subjectivism versus objectivism, or universalism versus nominalism. Again, Dewey acknowledges that, while in the course of history these dualisms were proposed as pragmatic aids to inquiry, in time they created entrenched barriers between polarized extremes that blocked and still block the inquiry, for the sake of comfort in the face of uncertainties that we cannot control.

Thus we should not only embrace cultural naturalism, but recognize that fallibilism requires us to be meliorist. The precarious cannot and should not be eliminated, because it enables growth. At the biological level, the old generation must die so that the young may thrive; and natural catastrophes such as floods, volcanic eruptions, and forest fires renew and replenish the land. At the cultural level, ideas come into fashion and fall out of it, novel technologies create new industries as older ones become obsolete, new nations are born as empires fall, and even tyrants are mortal. Thus stability and precariousness, creation and destruction, are necessary phases of existence that must be accepted rather than denied. However, this does not mean we should harden ourselves to the precarity of others or nihilistically abandon the hope of a better way of life for ourselves or our descendants. Social intelligence demands that each of us becomes a creator in the acts of meaning-making that determine our present and future. This requires only that we acknowledge our fallibilism and admit that all our "habits," from the small gestures of the living creature through the fate of the species, are experiments and not guarantees—hence we must be open to constant revision. Likewise, precariousness is not a mistake to be eliminated, but a property of events that can be improved through intelligence and imagination.

Furthermore, this emphasis on meliorism contributes to pragmatism's most enduring legacy: its influence on the development of the emerging social sciences. Just as scholars recognize James as a founder of American philosophy and psychology, Addams and Dewey should be considered foundational figures in social work and education, respectively. Besides, their ideas and meliorism in general also influenced their friend and colleague George Herbert Mead (1863–1931). Well steeped in pragmatism, Mead studied with Royce at Harvard and worked with Dewey at the University of Michigan from 1891 until 1894, when Dewey invited him to teach at the University of Chicago. Mead played an equal role in helping Addams and Dewey to relieve the social problems in Chicago and expanded the scope of pragmatism.

In his posthumously published book *Mind, Self, and Society* (1934), Mead developed *symbolic interactionism* by combining Peirce's semiotics with Royce's social philosophy in order to explain with greater precision than Dewey how we develop our identities through transactions with our cultural and natural environments. As one of the first social psychologists, Mead proposed symbolic interactionism as an alternative to the research paradigm of behaviorism, which attempted to understand human behavior only by observing and quantifying people's actions in response to stimuli. While the pioneers of behaviorism were partly inspired by James's efforts to make psychological research more empirical, they did so by forsaking any research into our internal psychological states. In their view, our lived experience and stream of consciousness were better explored by poets and artists than by serious scientists.

By contrast, symbolic interactionism explains how our subjective experience—the mind and the sense of self, our identity—develops through our attempts both to interpret the behavior of others and to respond to our social context. Given the complexity of this reciprocal and constant interplay between the self and the social context, we develop, adapt, or inherit various social roles as efficient ways of organizing our experience. Thus our personality emerges from this process of organization; and it desires unity, belonging, self-realization, and social control. But, as we fashion our own identities, we also modify the roles we adopt by becoming *role models* for others, who will in turn adopt these same roles.

Sociology was not the only social science influenced by pragmatism's emphasis on verification, meliorism, and community. In an essay from 2012 titled "Dewey's Pragmatism from an Anthropological Point of View," Loren Goldman explains the profound mutual influence between Dewey and his Columbia colleague and friend Franz Boas, who is widely regarded as the founder of American anthropology; and Gabriel Alejandro Torres Colón and Charles Hobbs explore Dewey's influence on several of Boas's most illustrious students, specifically Margaret Mead and Ruth Benedict, in an article published in 2015 and suggestively titled "The Intertwining of Culture and Nature." Ironically, this interdisciplinary influence of pragmatism and its emphasis on meliorism would inspire many students to commit themselves to careers outside philosophy.

It should also be said here that this generation of anthropologists marshaled the findings of their research to defeat the widely accepted forms of scientific racism prevalent at the beginning of the twentieth century. In fact the following chapter will reveal how the next generation of Harvard pragmatists used the findings, theories, and tools of their socially conscious mentor to resist and repair the effects of the utter destructiveness of two absolutist ideologies: white supremacy at home and totalitarianism abroad.

— 3 —

Pluralism and the Harvard Pragmatists

With a base at Harvard and an outpost in Chicago, pragmatism established itself as a nascent philosophical movement before the turn of the century. This momentum was perpetuated by James's and Royce's instruction of a generation of America's finest students, who would apply pragmatism in their professional careers or would advance the movement through their own philosophy. Their high-profile alumni include the poets T. S. Eliot and Gertrude Stein, President Theodore Roosevelt, and the journalist Walter Lippmann, as well as scores of professional philosophers. Among the latter, the most notable are W. E. B. DuBois, Alain Locke, and C. I. Lewis. An examination of Lewis's work will initiate my survey of analytic pragmatism in chapter 4. For now, I will focus on the other Harvard pragmatists and examine how their own lived experience informed their modification of pluralism and helped them to resist racism at home and totalitarianism abroad.

In *Pragmatic Encounters*, Richard Bernstein (2015) contextualizes how pluralism emerged amid the waves of immigration at the turn of the century. According to him, "there is probably no other time in history when a country was so welcoming to immigrants" as the United States welcomed approximately 27 million immigrants, predominantly from Southern and Eastern Europe, between the years of 1870 and 1920. By 1910 "40 per cent of the population of New

York City was foreign born"; however, we are reminded that "it is a myth that this wave of immigration was a smooth and welcoming process" and cites a long list of policies and practices as evidence for the "widespread discrimination and fear of the 'pernicious' influence of foreigners" (Bernstein 2015: 76). Bernstein also reviews various forms of scientific theories, all popular and influential, that justified social divisions and that "proved" the alleged superiority of specific races. His examples include Herbert Spencer's social Darwinism, which explained socioeconomic divisions as an appropriate consequence of natural selection, or the various theories of eugenics developed by Francis Galton and others—social projects that came up with various proposals of improving the human potential with the help of selective breeding, either by encouraging reproduction between the "fittest" individuals or by preventing "inferior" individuals and peoples from proliferating; and the latter was achieved through the application of darker methods such as segregation, sterilization, and ultimately, as in the case of the Holocaust, genocide.

Although some scientists, especially anthropologists like Franz Boas, debunked such theories and the evidence or arguments used to support them, the theories were widely accepted at the time. For example, they were highlighted during Chicago's World Fair of 1893, which intended to celebrate America's "material progress" by sharing the "wonderful achievements of the new age in science, literature, education, government, jurisprudence, morals, charity, religion ... as the most effective means of increasing the fraternity, progress, prosperity and peace of mankind." Even the layout of the Fair's midway cohered with the logic of social Darwinism and eugenics. European villages were located at the entrance, the Germans first and the Irish last, after which came a "series of more 'barbarous' villages until [visitors] reached the most primitive, including the American Indians and Africans" (McKenna & Pratt 2015: 18).

Against this background, several of James's students began to appreciate how pragmatism, specifically pluralism, could be used to resist ideologies that supported discriminatory practices. Bernstein (2005: 77) reveals how James introduced the term "pluralism" in 1890, in his *Principles of Psychology*, when he emphasized the "flow and dynamic quality of all experience" in his critique of Hegel's absolute idealism. James developed this theme thoroughly in a series of Hibbert lectures titled *A Pluralistic Universe* (1909); as its most concise summary, Bernstein quotes the following passage from "The Will to Believe," a lecture from 1896:

> *Prima facie* the world is a pluralism, as we find it, its unity seems to be that of any collection; and our higher thinking consists chiefly of an effort to redeem it from the first crude form. Postulating more unity than the first experiences yield, we also discover more. But absolute unity, in spite of brilliant dashes in its direction, still remains undiscoverable. (Bernstein 2005: 77–78)

Pragmatism as a method of experience begins to diverge from pragmatism as a theory of truth as several students who attended James's lectures, specifically Horace Kallen and Alain Locke, came to see that they could enrich and extend his philosophical pluralism by letting the content of their own living experiences inform it and by using it to challenge absolutist ideologies. However, there were earlier members of the Harvard community, specifically George Santayana and W. E. B. DuBois, who developed their own critical concepts of cosmopolitanism and double consciousness to express and ameliorate their experience of alienation and racism. I shall begin with the latter, then explain how Kallen's cultural pluralism functions as an alternative to the more popular visions of Americanization that favored assimilation and were often chauvinistic. The chapter will conclude by examining how Alain Locke's democratic pluralism performs a similar function by providing an alternative vision and strategy to confront the forms of authoritarianism that appeared before World War II.

George Santayana (1863–1952) and Cosmopolitanism

Unlike the founders of pragmatism discussed in the two previous chapters, George Santayana, or more precisely

Jorge Agustín Nicholás Ruiz de Santayana y Borrás, who immigrated to the United States as a child, in 1872, was not born in Spain, namely in Madrid. His philosophy remains unmistakably American and pragmatic due to his subjects, themes, and approach, but his immigrant experience and his Spanish heritage blend to create a unique philosophical perspective fluent in and fascinated by American culture, yet slightly aloof as a result of a subtle international distance. Nevertheless, Santayana also resisted the pragmatist label and frequently critiqued James, Royce, and Dewey, even though he shared many of their assumptions and aims. Also, like several of the other progenitors of pragmatism, Santayana studied at Harvard (1882–1886) and returned there to teach (1889–1912); but he had the good fortune to be young enough to learn from James and to complete his dissertation under Royce, yet old enough to instruct DuBois, Locke, and other important American philosophers and intellectuals. Thus Santayana serves as an important bridge between the founding of pragmatism at the end of the nineteenth century and what it would become in the twentieth century.

More importantly, he writes from the perspective of the immigrant and the exile. He yearns to belong, struggles to create a place for himself in his new country, but never quite feels at home. He eventually retires from Harvard and returns to Europe in 1912, then settles in Rome in 1920 and remains there until his death in 1952. However, during his four decades abroad, which began before World War I and lasted until well after World War II, he was no less productive than during his American period. In fact while living in Europe he would write two major works of philosophy, *Skepticism and Animal Faith* (1923) and *The Realms of Being* (1927), and a Pulitzer Prize-winning bildungsroman, *The Last Puritan: A Memoir in the Form of a Novel* (1935). He based this last work on his own coming of age and education in New England, while the first two are heavily informed by and engaged with the authors and subjects of pragmatism.

In *The Last Puritan* Santayana dramatizes how the protagonist, Oliver Alden, inherits New England Puritanism from his stern and moralistic uncle, Nathaniel. Unfortunately for

Oliver, this Puritanism only reinforces his sense of duty and obligation rather than filling him with passion or purpose. In the Prologue, Santayana presents a character sketch of Oliver. At first he is critical, writing: "His puritanism had never been mere timidity or fanaticism or calculated hardness: it was a deep and speculative thing: hatred of all shams, scorn of all mummeries, a bitter merciless pleasure in the hard facts." Then he relaxes and claims that Oliver's "passion for reality was beautiful in him, because there was so much in his gifts and in his surroundings to allure him and muffle up his mind in worldly conventions" (Santayana 1949: 7). Sensitive readers realize that Santayana's ambiguous feelings for Oliver and for his Puritanism mirror his ambiguous relationship with America—a place he loved, but where he never belonged. Scholars note that this ambiguity also parallels Santayana's relationship with the pragmatists, in that he shared their commitments to naturalism, fallibilism, and aesthetics even as he found their fascination with science and social problems to be too serious and vulgar (Skowroński 2007: 9).

According to Skowroński, this ironic and ambiguous perspective forms the core of Santayana's cosmopolitanism and is informed by his complicated binational identity. Much like Royce, he insisted that one should be proud of one's heritage, but one should not identify with this heritage uncritically. Indeed, his teacher's overt displays of loyalty made him uncomfortable for two reasons. Aesthetically, he found Royce's philosophy to be obsessive and sentimental; ethically, he worried that "loyalty degrades an individual in relation to an external idea" rather than empowering him to use his reason in pursuit of his passions (2007: 10–11). Santayana advocated travel, not loyalty to a beloved community, as the best means for appreciating one's heritage:

[The traveler] must be somebody and come from somewhere, so that his definite character and moral traditions may supply an organ and a point of comparison for his observations ... He must not go nosing about like a peddlar for profit or like an emigrant for a vacant lot. Everywhere he should show the discretion and maintain the dignity of a guest. Everywhere he

should remain a stranger no matter how benevolent, and a
critic no matter how appreciative. (Santayana 1946: 449)

Through travel we earn not only a deeper sense of what we
love about our own culture, but also a deeper appreciation
and respect for other cultures, even ones with which we may
have significant moral or aesthetic disagreements. This process occurs through an initial form of humility or fallibilism
about one's culture and gets reinforced through travel, which
overcomes our "moral and ideal provinciality" and makes
us "see that every form of life had its own perfection, which
it was stupid and cruel to condemn for differing from some
other form, by chance one's own" (Santayana 1986: 170).

The cosmopolitan learns how to feel comfortable anywhere
by learning to enjoy the diversity that makes cultures unique,
while also learning, through absence, what it is that one loves
most about one's own culture—or, to quote Dorothy Gale
from *The Wizard of Oz* (1900), one learns that "there's no
place like home." Santayana presents cosmopolitanism as a
remedy for living in the increasingly diverse nations of the
twentieth century, but undoubtedly it originated as a remedy
for the alienation he felt as a Spanish American, especially
during the Spanish–American War of 1898.

Although Santayana never spoke publicly or wrote about
his feelings during this war, Bertrand Russell claimed that
he was "passionately on the Spanish side" and "whenever
his Spanish patriotism was involved, his usual air of detach-
ment disappeared" (Russell 1958: 86). By contrast, Krzysztof
Skowroński (2007: 9) reminds us that in his published work
Santayana clearly favored cosmopolitanism over traditional
versions of patriotism. While the Spanish–American War
undoubtedly troubled Santayana, he seemed to accept the
"American imperialism of the period" as a natural response
to Spain's meager foreign policy. He expressed a similar resignation about the inevitability of the Spanish Civil War of
1936 and (in Skowroński's words) a preference for "strong,
genuine, distinct, even militaristic regimes" such as the
"Italian Fascists and Russian Bolsheviks in the pre-World
War II period," which he considers necessary for maintain-

ing a nation's cultural integrity (2007: 10). On the whole, Santayana remained conservative until his death; but he did become more critical of authoritarian regimes as he witnessed and even experienced their oppression.

Santayana's genius lies in his pluralism, specifically in his comfort with ambiguity and in his ability to balance themes often perceived as antagonistic, specifically reason and spirit. Like previous pragmatists, he is fully committed to a Darwinian understanding of nature, but does not see naturalism as hostile to spirituality or to religious traditions. In fact religious traditions are to him extensions of rationality and help individuals to experience the sublime, or the moments of harmony between nature and spirit. Santayana's philosophy has been labeled aesthetic religious naturalism because of its emphasis on beauty as a bridge between the rational and the spiritual. The most succinct articulation of this ontology can be found in *The Realms of Being*, a book published in 1942 where Santayana guides the reader from the basic embodied states of matter, such as living organisms and sentient animals, to increasingly sublime states of mind, and here from conscious thinking to self-consciousness, concluding with spiritual awareness. Focusing on the relevance of this ontology to humans, he begins by saying that "[e]verything that exists is confined to a specific character at a particular place and time; if it escaped from those bonds it would cease to be itself" (Santayana 1942: 555).

Like the other pragmatists, he begins with our concrete, situated, and embodied experience as natural organisms but shows how our mental faculties make us suspect that there is more to the world than our contingent biological and social processes. He admits that the spiritual realm is intangible, but believes that it does not lie outside physical reality. We access it with the mind, through imagination, inspiration, legends, art, dreams, and even science, as we marvel at how the apparently random motion of atoms in the void gradually leads to the life and rich experiences we enjoy: "What is this life in me but vital oxygen drawn into my lungs; what is this warm breath exhaled but my very spirit and will?" (Santayana, quoted in Stuhr 2000: 410). Because there is no dualism between the natural and the spiritual realms, scientific inquiry is no threat to faith, and the discoveries it provides enhance our understanding of, awe for, and connection with the physical world, thereby broadening the majesty of our aesthetic and spiritual experience. On the other hand scientism or the demystification of the world through the belief that all phenomena can be reduced to matter and mechanistic laws should be avoided, as it blinds science as an institution to important lines of inquiry and shortens scientists' patience for people sensitive to the spiritual, numbs their respect for the faithful, and risks dulling their aesthetic appreciation of life.

Indeed, Santayana sees nature and spirit as inseparable, nature providing the contents of inquiry and spirit generating the curiosity that motivates it. This insight echoes a theme he develops throughout his work: that reason and passion are not antagonists, therefore neither the rational nor the spiritual individual needs to commit to reason at the expense of passion or the other way round; rather the individual must find the harmony between the two if she hopes to live a fully aesthetic life. Santayana explores this insight most thoroughly in *The Life of Reason* (1905), where he says: "Whatever forces may govern human life, if they are to be recognised by man, must betray themselves in human experience." Thus all "[p]rogress in science or religion, no less than in morals and art, is a dramatic episode in man's career"; and the value of these domains is confirmed by their "function and utility ... in his life" (Santayana 2009: 282). Reason functions as a form of reflection that "gathers the experiences together and perceives their relative worth; which is as much as to say that it expresses a new attitude of will[,] the presence of a world better understood and turned to some purpose" (2009: 283). This last sentence alludes to the fact that Santayana does not see reason as being opposed to passion. In fact they are inseparable, because "[r]eason requires the fusion of two types of life, commonly led in the world in well-nigh total separation, one a life of impulse expressed in affairs and social passions, the other a life of reflection expressed in religion, science, and the imitative arts." Thus the "Life of Reason is the happy marriage of two elements—impulse and ideation—which if wholly divorced would reduce man to a brute or to a maniac" (2009: 284).

In conclusion, Santayana's aesthetic religious naturalism provides yet another rich example of how the pragmatists incorporated the religious experience into their understanding of the natural world. Like James, Santayana neither reduces the spiritual dimensions of existence to mere material explanations nor hides them behind obscurantist apologies that cynically dismiss clear evidence. Likewise, Santayana joins Royce as a socially conservative voice who balances the cultural preferences of the individual with the reality of a pluralistic world. Indeed, he provides a glossary of the various stages through which the spirit develops through nature; and he does this in order to allow the "reader to criticize his favourite modes of expression and to be patient with those of other people" (Stuhr 2000: 413). Here Santayana acknowledges that aesthetic preferences are not only inherently pluralistic but personal. He accepts that others do not share his yearning for the sublime and may find fulfillment in their social relationships or in more pedestrian forms of aestheticism. In fact Santayana's preference for individual spiritual experiences, and also his cosmopolitanism, contrast with Royce's devotion to religious communities and to their right to maintain their provincial identity. However, there is one pragmatic concern that spans his career and distinguishes him from all his Harvard colleagues. How should I live my life, if I wish to live it to the fullest? His cosmopolitanism and his aesthetic religious naturalism remain the most elaborate answers to that question in the American canon.

W. E. B. DuBois (1868–1963) and Double Consciousness

Just as Santayana bridges two eras of pragmatism at Harvard, DuBois bridges multiple eras in African American history thanks to his longevity. His birth in 1868 coincides with the date of the ratification of the 14th Amendment; and his death, on August 27, 1963, occurred one day before Martin Luther King, Jr.'s delivery of his famous "I Have a Dream"

speech from the steps of the Lincoln Memorial. While the
latter event has been proudly canonized as a watershed in
American democratic history, the significance of the former
has often been occluded, yet studying its legacy explains how
DuBois's philosophy enabled activists such as King himself
to succeed during the civil rights era of the 1960s and 1970s.
Ratified soon after the end of the American Civil War, the
14th Amendment granted citizenship as well as equal protec-
tion under the law to all persons born in the United States.
The former states of the Confederacy deeply resented that
they must ratify the amendment to regain representation in
Congress and immediately began undermining it through the
passage of the Jim Crow Laws throughout the South. These
laws were designed to protect white supremacy by instituting
segregation between whites and people of color.

In its infamous ruling on *Plessy vs. Ferguson* in 1896,
the Supreme Court upheld the constitutionality of these laws
by a 7 to 1 majority. Justice Henry B. Brown summarized
the majority opinion in reasoning that, as long as "separate
but equal" facilities and accommodations were provided,
the mandate of the amendment had been fulfilled. Thus the
"color line" (as Frederick Douglas famously called it) that
DuBois would devote his career to understand and overcome
was reinscribed into American law. Slavery had ended and
black Americans were gaining cultural and political power,
but white supremacy continued to thrive and would not be
dealt another significant legal blow until the Supreme Court
finally ruled against segregation, nearly sixty years later, in
Brown vs. Board of Education of Topeka (1954). Sadly,
recent history confirms what DuBois predicted almost a century ago: that a significant portion of white Americans will
feel threatened by any progress in US race relations and will
work to repress and undermine it.

DuBois devoted his long and prolific career to developing
a wide array of conceptual tools for analysing the theoretical
and social causes of race problems, together with creative
strategies for ameliorating them. In *The American Evasion
of Philosophy*, Cornell West (1989: 140–141) highlights
three early philosophical influences on DuBois: his studies of

pragmatism with James, Royce, and Santayana at Harvard; his studies with German sociologists at the University of Berlin; and his introduction to pan-Africanism by Alexander Crummel. West also suggests that DuBois's relatively privileged upbringing in a family of free black activists resulted in a greater sensitivity to class discrimination than the experience of racial discrimination alone would produce. On the one hand, this fortunate upbringing shielded him from the violent excesses of the Jim Crow South, occasioning positive experiences with members of the white local community and access to educational opportunities. On the other, it disconnected him from the "kinetic orality, emotional physicality, and combative spirituality of black music, language, and customs"—a disconnection that would occasionally manifest itself as aloofness or elitism (West 1989: 138–139).

These paradoxes both aided and complicated his early attempts to represent the black community. For example, in "The Talented Tenth" (1903), he argues that the fate of black Americans rests in the hands of its most talented individuals, people like himself, who should culturally empower themselves through a classical education and the production of a unique and authentic black culture. This position countered the Atlanta compromise struck by Booker T. Washington, which encouraged black Americans to seek economic empowerment through vocational training and conformism to the mainstream political and cultural expectations of white folks. In retrospect, history proves that both economic security and cultural independence are necessary for the empowerment that any marginalized group requires; but DuBois's emphasis on exceptional talent discounted the contributions of most black folk, who did not enjoy his gifts and opportunities. By contrast, DuBois's call for resistance to white culture through authenticity and independence marks the beginning of an important theme in his work.

Some scholars, however, question West's genealogy of DuBois's philosophical and biographical influence, specifically the inclusion of this figure in the canon of American pragmatists. In "What's the Use of Calling DuBois a Pragmatist?" Paul Taylor (2004) answers his own question by arguing that

DuBois is certainly a pragmatist in a very broad sense, but the specific continuities are complex. He defends reading DuBois as a pragmatist because doing this adds a deeper understanding of DuBois's meliorism as a middle ground between optimism and pessimism. Even though DuBois's youthful enthusiasm for improving race relations was routinely dashed by successive setbacks and indignities throughout his long life, he refused to despair and redoubled his efforts to fight for equality. Most importantly, Taylor argues that DuBois's philosophy of race is inherently pragmatic, particularly in his later work *Dusk of Dawn* (1940), where he revises the biological essentialism of an earlier period in favor of viewing race as a cultural and historical phenomenon, constructed to either disenfranchise or empower particular groups of people. In a nutshell, Taylor encourages the inclusion of DuBois in the pragmatist canon, but not without qualifications.

Likewise, Kenneth Stikkers (2008) favors the inclusion of DuBois among the pragmatists, but worries that most attempts will be Eurocentric and will minimize the influence of black and African sources upon the development of DuBois's thought. Stikkers reminds us that modern western philosophy is entangled with Europe's colonization of the globe and, as result, most comparative works risk "colonizing" black and African thought and presenting it as subordinate to Euro-American traditions such as pragmatism. In fact he cites West's reading of DuBois as a paradigmatic example of this kind of failure, because it begins with DuBois's connection with pragmatism and focuses on his earlier work, "when he still believed that he could appeal to white America's conscience by reference to its own political ideals," unlike "the later DuBois, who turned his back, in disillusionment and anger, on white America and her hypocrisy" (Stikkers 2008: 46). Stikkers suggests instead that, with DuBois and other black philosophers, scholars should employ a methodological Afrocentrism as a "counterforce" that would not deny European influences but would "contextualize DuBois's thought strictly within Africana traditions and would take seriously and emphasize such features of and influences on DuBois's thought" (2008: 47). He also gives a few examples of how to do this—such as by emphasizing DuBois's extensive reading of African anthropology and slave narratives, or his familiarity and dialogue with more polemic black nationalists like David Walker and Marcus Garvey.

Finally, Jacoby Adeshei Carter (2017) issues several crucial warnings about canon construction in general, particularly when attempting to incorporate race into a preexisting canon, and definitely when attempting to racialize pragmatism, given the complications of the United States' racist history and its contemporary legacies. He agrees with Taylor's argument that interpreting DuBois as a pragmatist illuminates several important aspects of his thought; however, readers from outside philosophy rarely see him from this perspective, and "his thought on race is fairly well understandable without it" (2017: 85). Furthermore, the benefits of incorporating DuBois or other historical philosophers of race into the pragmatist canon are lopsided toward pragmatism. First, doing so "intentionally or inadvertently situate[s] pragmatism in the privileged epistemological position of legitimizing African American thought and thinkers in the United States" (ibid.). Such an approach would re-create colonialism, because it implies that any neophyte and her work were illegitimate until admitted by the larger tradition. Second, retroactively including non-white philosophers into the pragmatist canon "gives pragmatism a legitimacy that it does not merit" by allowing pragmatists to "advertise themselves as more pluralistic in their philosophic methodology and orientation" (2017: 86–87). Carter concludes that it is better to see DuBois and the African American intellectual tradition as standing on their own: this perspective allows us to appreciate "the novelty and expertise of persons outside the traditional canon in their own right and as uniquely situated to contribute much needed perspectives" (2017: 86).

All these warnings merit attention. Stikkers and Carter rightly remind us not to overstate the influence of pragmatism on DuBois and to focus on the greater significance of his sources from the African American intellectual tradition; yet it cannot be denied that pragmatism was an important early influence. Likewise, Taylor correctly observes that the inclusion of DuBois enriches our discussions of meliorism, pluralism, and aesthetics. Consequently, West's original mandate for including DuBois in the pragmatist canon still rings true:

> DuBois provides American pragmatism with what it sorely lacks: an international perspective on the impetus and impediments to individuality and radical democracy, a perspective that highlights the plight of the wretched of the earth, namely, the majority of humanity who own no property or wealth, participate in no democratic arrangements, and whose individualities are crushed by hard labor and harsh living conditions. James possessed the ingredients for such a view, but he did not see social structures, only individuals. Dewey indeed saw social structures and individuals yet primarily through an American lens ... DuBois goes beyond them all in scope and depth of vision: creative powers reside among the wretched of the earth even in their subjugation, and the fragile structures of democracy in the world depend, in large part, on how these powers are ultimately exercised. (West 1989: 147–148)

Clearly pragmatism needs DuBois more than DuBois needed pragmatism; but including DuBois in the pragmatist canon, albeit with qualifications, enriches many themes and broadens the pragmatist community of inquiry by offering a critical perspective, informed by his personal experience of segregation and white supremacy.

DuBois provides another example, along with the ones mentioned by Taylor, of how pragmatists used the theories, methods, and data of social sciences to ameliorate concrete situations and solve practical problems. His first major work, *The Philadelphia Negro* (DuBois & Eaton 1967), was published in 1899 and quickly became a landmark in American sociology. DuBois carefully gathered an exhaustive amount of statistical data to give an accurate description of the living conditions of blacks in Philadelphia. This evidence conclusively debunked the racist notion that the "Negro problem," or the slow economic and political advancement of newly freed black folk after the Civil War, was due to an alleged inherent intellectual or moral inferiority. Instead, DuBois reveals how the Negro problem resulted from the inability of white folks to extend the rights of citizenship as well as basic economic and educational opportunities to the large population of people whom they had enslaved for centuries. While white critics—and even some black ones—continued to blame racial inequality and other social problems on the moral failures of black communities, DuBois was the first one to use sociological methods and data to demonstrate that these racist assumptions have no empirical or statistical basis.

Most importantly, including DuBois in the pragmatist canon introduces his theories of race to readers who may not otherwise study critical race theory. *The Souls of Black Folk* (1903) ranks among the most illuminating critiques of race relations in the United States and its first chapter, "Of Our Spiritual Strivings," should be required reading for all Americans. As mentioned previously, DuBois prophetically states there that the problem of the twentieth century is the color line; and he speaks of "the veil" that shrouds not only the plight of those on the one side of the color line, but also the existence of the color line itself. This metaphor prefigures the contemporary notion of an epistemology of ignorance, as the veil represents the ways in which white supremacy conceals itself from those whom it benefits, causing them either to minimize the extent of race prejudice in America or to ignore it altogether. Indeed, the veil still remains, as most white Americans and even many people of color are ignorant about the country's history of racism, as well as about the racist origins and outcomes of its institutions and practices.

Numerous contemporary writers dedicate their work to lifting the veil for their readers. In *White Like Me: Reflections on Race from a Privileged Son*, Tim Wise (2011) carefully explains how the concept of whiteness was created in late seventeenth-century colonial America with the aim of breaking the solidarity between European and African indentured servants. Previously these people had recognized their mutual interests and would cooperate against wealthy landowners, until the colonies constructed the identities of white and black people by extending minor social and economic privileges to poor Europeans and by shifting to chattel slavery, which was based exclusively on race; this way they enlisted the newly created white working class in the oppression of black slaves. Wise then explains how poor and middle-class white people incrementally gained privileges throughout US history and reviews the occasional, reluctant extension of whiteness to other marginalized groups, such as Irish and Italian immigrants—all designed to maintain white supremacy. Thus white Americans continue to enjoy privileges in education, employment, housing, criminal justice, and beyond, even as they deny that these race-based privileges exist. Most importantly, Wise wants his white readers to realize that the benefits of white privilege are meager by comparison to the exploitation that its recipients endure as instruments of maintaining a racially segregated society. Thus the color line traps and harms them as well, albeit nowhere near as severely as it traps the targets of racist beliefs, acts, and institutions.

Meanwhile, Ta-Nehisi Coates thoroughly chronicles the history of racial privilege from the other side of the veil. In *We Were Eight Years in Power* (Coates 2017), an anthology of articles published in *The Atlantic* during the presidency of Barack Obama, to which the title refers, he bears witness to the continued injustices against black Americans and other people of color in "post-racial" America. While all the articles gathered in this anthology contain crucial insights, "The Case for Reparations" (originally published in 2014) has emerged as the most succinct yet comprehensive primer on the systemic discrimination faced by black Americans throughout the twentieth century. In this piece Coates explains how a variety of predatory techniques such as restrictive covenants, redlining, racial steering, sunset laws, racial profiling, segregated work places, and racist hiring practices were employed throughout the United States to maintain segregation and to exploit black Americans economically still further, even after the centuries of intergenerational theft represented by chattel slavery.

Likewise, Coates's (2015) book *Between the World and Me* serves not only as a letter to his teenage son about the racist history of the United States but also as an example of "the talk" that black parents must have with their chil-

dren about the reality of racially motivated violence and
about how to survive the increased possibility of their being
harassed, abused, or executed by representatives of law
enforcement owing to the color of their skin. Coates wrote
this book in the midst of a cascade of high-profile cases of
black youths murdered predominantly by police in which
most of the perpetrators were later acquitted despite clear
video evidence of their crimes. Not only do these incidents of
extreme racial prejudice support the continued reality of the
color line in the United States, but the social media backlash
to the #BlackLivesMatter movement through counterslogans
such as #AllLivesMatter or #BlueLivesMatter, which either
discount the severity of increased violence against people of
color or reflexively defend police officers against the possibility of false accusations of wrongdoing, demonstrates the
continued reality of the veil that blinds white Americans.
Coates acknowledges that the book was inspired by James
Baldwin's *The Fire Next Time* (published in 1963), which
established this genre of memoir and continues to be relevant
today; however, unlike Baldwin, Coates concludes that white
supremacy will never subside because it is essential to the
fabric of US history and American culture. Black Americans
and their allies will always need to confront and resist white
supremacy, as it mutates with each passing generation.

Even the title *Between the World and Me* evokes the first
sentence from DuBois's chapter "Of Our Spiritual Strivings,"
proving the continued relevance of DuBois in the twenty-first
century, which initiates his explanation of *double consciousness* or the ability to see beyond the veil by learning to view
society from both sides of the color line:

> Between me and the other world there is ever an unasked ques-
> tion: unasked by some through feelings of delicacy; by others
> through the difficulty of rightly framing it. All, nevertheless,
> flutter round it. They approach me in a half-hesitant sort of
> way, eye me curiously or compassionately, and then, instead
> of saying directly, How does it feel to be a problem? they say,
> I know an excellent colored man in my town; or, I fought at
> Mechanicsville; or, Do not these Southern outrages make your
> blood boil? At these I smile, or am interested, or reduce the

boiling to a simmer, as the occasion may require. To the real
question, How does it feel to be a problem? I answer seldom a
word. (DuBois 1996: 101)

What DuBois dramatizes superbly in this opening passage
is the meeting of black and white people at the color line. A
curious white person awkwardly attempts to see beyond the
veil by indirectly asking a black person about race. This act
uncomfortably reminds the black person of his problematic
identity in a culture defined and divided by race. Assuming
that the white person's motivations are pure (often they are
not), this interrogation unfairly shifts her responsibility to
learn about race relations upon the testimony of a black
person who has no responsibility for educating someone
who benefits from his oppression. Yet, despite this indignity,
DuBois feels compelled to respond, because he recognizes the
glimmer of constructive racial dialogue even as he feels guilty
about his lack of patience or interest to engage or frustrated
when he feels that the conversation is most likely to be superficial and fruitless.

This scene also demonstrates that in the United States black
people possess double consciousness almost natively, because,
in order to survive, any oppressed person must spend her
entire life imagining and understanding the view you get from
the dominant side of the color line. Meanwhile the privileged,
in this case white Americans, can spend their lives blissfully
ignorant of what their neighbors experience; indeed, this is
the purpose of the veil and the greatest privilege of white
supremacy—an untroubled conscience. DuBois dramatizes
this tragedy further by retelling his first encounter with racism
in elementary school, when a white girl refused to accept his
calling card. Until that moment he had never experienced
himself as different, but from that moment on he felt the veil
descend and realized that a world exists on the other side of
the color line and that his attempts to cross it will be resisted,
because of the color of his skin. This dawning awareness led
to an identity crisis. Will he internalize the color line and
police himself by conforming to the expectations of white
America and living in resignation on the black side of the

country? Will he transgress the color line through acts of political or criminal rebellion? Or will he earn a small place on the white side by proving himself useful through exceptional talent and accomplishments?

Fortunately, DuBois funnels the pain and frustration of his youth into excelling academically and athletically rather than contenting himself with mediocrity or surrendering to a life of delinquency; but he soon realizes that, as an apocryphal African American aphorism has it, a black person in America must work twice as hard for half as much. More importantly, he recognizes this path as one of assimilation, which will require him to surrender those parts of his black identity that make white folk uncomfortable. He also realizes that this bifurcation exists within his own body and soul, famously proclaiming: "One ever feels his twoness—an American, a Negro; two souls, two thoughts, two unreconciled strivings; two warring ideals in one dark body, whose dogged strength alone keeps it from being torn asunder" (DuBois 1996: 102). Thus the color line is embodied and spiritual as well as social and political, and all persons, black and white, must decide where their soul resides in relation to it. Because of the veil, white folk may remain blissfully ignorant of its existence whereas black folk are permanently aware of this struggle.

Astutely, DuBois recognizes that all three options are dead ends because none of them leads to a union or harmony of his competing identities, thereby fulfilling his deep yearning to participate fully in American culture and society without sacrificing his blackness (ibid.):

The history of the American Negro is the history of this strife—this longing to attain self-conscious manhood, to merge his double self into a better and truer self. In this merging he wishes neither of the older selves to be lost. He would not Africanize America, for America has too much to teach the world and Africa. He would not bleach his Negro soul in a flood of white Americanism, for he knows that Negro blood has a message for the world. He simply wishes to make it possible for a man to be both a Negro and an American, without being cursed and spit upon by his fellows, without having the doors of Opportunity closed roughly in his face.

Here and elsewhere, DuBois realizes that he and other black folk must create a fourth path through pan-Africanism, which involves the creation of black identities by black people according to their shared history and culture. These are consistent with the best parts of American history and culture, which they share with white folk; but they are not determined by white folk.

Historically, the relationship between African Americans and the American media and entertainment has been incredibly complicated. On the one hand, these venues serve as one of the most accessible means of black economic empowerment and as opportunities for black cultural development. For example, nearly all of America's unique musical genres originated in black culture, until the latter was appropriated by mainstream white culture. The most beloved gospel hymns were originally Negro spirituals; the blues gave birth to country music and rock n' roll; funk spawned disco; and most of the contemporary pop songs are sanitized versions of rap or hip-hop. Even bluegrass music, whose melodies, content, and structure are primarily of Celtic origin, relies heavily on the banjo, a derivative of the West African kora, which was brought first to the Caribbean, then to New Orleans, and on to the Appalachian plateau by both free and enslaved black folk. But, as this musical genealogy implies, the black originators of these genres rarely received economic and cultural rewards comparable to those of their white imitators.

On the other hand, while these examples of cultural appropriation are unjust, some forms of entertainment were explicitly harmful. DuBois was aware of the fact that the most popular form of entertainment in America before, during, and far too long after the Civil War was the minstrel show, which generated and popularized most of the vicious racial stereotypes; and these still linger. Minstrel shows were traveling variety shows that relied heavily on comedic skits that amused predominantly white audiences by pandering to their presumed racial superiority through the presentation of black people as impulsive, ignorant, bumbling, and lazy child-like persons. At first these dehumanizing skits were performed by white actors wearing blackface, but gradually black actors joined the troupes, until in many companies the whole cast was black under white direction. Not only did this arrangement re-create the economic dynamic of black labor for white profit, but it further demeaned the individual actors and made them complicit in perpetuating the racist political myth that black people either enjoyed their subordination or required the management of whites. Furthermore, it reinforced the veil by presenting fabricated racial identities to white and black Americans; and it excused white guilt, since the black actors were assumed to play these roles of their own free will.

Thus DuBois, Alain Locke, and other black leaders recognized that the present task for black folk who have secured access to education and economic opportunities was to create their own cultural products and identities, separate from these caricatures. Strategies included reconnecting and reconstructing their African roots, which had been severed through the slave trade, and celebrating black cultural movements such as the Harlem Renaissance through the publication of journals, for example *The Crisis* (in 1910), through novels that dramatized the experiences of black protagonists, for example DuBois's *Dark Princess* (in 1928), of anthologies, for example Alain Locke's *The New Negro* (in 1925), which included samples from black visual artists as well as essays, and through the founding of the National Association for the Advancement of Colored People (in 1910). Thanks to these efforts by DuBois and others, black Americans successfully created and established their own authentic cultural identities over a century ago; but, as long as the color line remains a reality, black artists will continue to share their double consciousness with those who wish to see beyond the veil.

The best recent example is the song and video "This Is America?" (2018) by the multitalented prodigy Donald Glover, known as Childish Gambino. First he disarms his audience with a pleasant opening of light vocalizations supported by a guitar that plays African folk rhythm. We feel uplifted, unless (or until) we realize that the song's hypnotic refrain is actually "Yeah, yeah, yeah, go, go away." This immediately, but subtly, invokes the double standard of mainstream audiences, who want to enjoy the fruits of black culture without being troubled by the reality of black lives. In the video, the setting is a vast but empty industrial warehouse, first occupied by the middle-aged black man who is playing the guitar. Soon our gaze drifts to Glover, who is standing still, naked from the waist up, but wearing white pants reminiscent of those worn by slaves. Just before we consciously notice that there are no scars from the master's whip on the black skin of his statuesque back, Glover distracts us again, now with his first jerky dance moves, as he sings "We just wanna party, Party just for you, We just want the money, Money just for you." These lines suggest that he is playing the role of the happy Negro, either to survive or for his own profit; and he reinforces this ambiguity as he begins dancing in a style reminiscent of the old minstrel shows.

A contemporary dance beat kicks in and we find ourselves compelled to mimic Glover's eccentric movements, until he violently shatters our trance by pulling a handgun from nowhere and executing the guitar player with a shot to the back of the head. The beat drops with the gunshot and settles into a paranoid, droning groove, like a police siren slowed down and pitch-shifted. Glover looks directly into the camera and says: "This is America, Don't catch you slippin' now." In a visually, sonically, and lyrically perfect instant, he symbolically rips apart the veil, to reveal the reality of life on the black side of the color line in twenty-first-century America. For the remainder of the song and video we experience double consciousness, as Glover oscillates between the superficial fantasies of racial progress Americans want to believe and the brutal realities they wish to forget. During this time, the formerly austere warehouse quickly becomes populated with disturbing vignettes of urban violence, rich in powerful symbolism but far too numerous to list, let alone explicate. Four symbols that cannot be ignored, however, are the gold chains on Glover's neck, the omnipresence of guns and the fact that they are treated with more reverence than the black bodies they destroy, the black youths dancing in Glover's footsteps, and the joint Glover lights at the end, as the camera zooms out and fades into black.

As with any great work of art, there is no single authoritative interpretation; but, given the prevalence of intergenerational symbols, the fact that Glover finds himself caught between the older black folk he murders and the black youth following in his footsteps suggests that black communities and artists still face the same problems as during the Reconstruction era, but in different forms. Even though meager material progress and political freedom have been achieved, as evidenced by Glover's gold chains and the absence of physical marks of slavery on his body, might these symbols not suggest that material success also represents a new, subtle but still destructive, form of psychological enslavement to the idols of wealth and fame? Likewise, Glover's execution of the folk guitarist and gospel choir probably symbolizes the displacement of the older and gentle genres of folk and gospel music by the confrontational cultural criticism of gangster rap. But does rap represent more authentically the black experience in America, or has it, too, devolved into a new form of minstrelsy? Is turning to intoxicants the most rational way to survive and endure racism in America, or does it maintain systems of oppression by legitimizing overpolicing as part of the war on drugs? Why does America value guns more than human lives? Why do guns magically appear in black neighborhoods and in black hands? Where do they come from and where do they go?

Ultimately Glover's genius is his ability to capture the complexity and ambiguities of America's racial and moral divisions. By exposing our naivety, he leaves his audience with more questions than answers, revealing, like DuBois, that there are no simple solutions to America's racial problems. These problems have a long and painful past; therefore no one should expect their resolution to be quick or easy. Also, these problems can be no more than ameliorated, for how can any nation undo five centuries of colonization or slavery? A violent counterrevolution may reverse the social hierarchy, but it would invalidate the sacrifice of those who sought more peaceful paths and would create new wounds without healing those of the past.

This leaves us with DuBois's most important insight, with which he concludes "Of Our Spiritual Strivings": *the sober realization of progress.* While progress in race relations is possible and does occur, and while each success should be celebrated, these victories are but a respite on the long journey to true human brotherhood, that is, to racial equality. Furthermore, each success reveals new challenges, which either could not be imagined until then or were minor in comparison to past problems. Likewise, opponents to racial progress will survive defeat and redouble their efforts. For example, when slavery was legal, only abolition could be imagined; but, once independence was achieved, the need to secure for blacks equal access to education, equal voting rights, and equal economic opportunities in order to achieve racial progress became obvious. Meanwhile new forms of racial oppression arose to hamper this progress: lynching, the Klu Klux Klan (KKK), segregation, redlining, sunset laws, and the like. Thus victories must be celebrated to restore hope, but one must soberly acknowledge that more work remains to be done, future success is not guaranteed, and yesterday's advances can be undone.

Horace Kallen (1882–1974) and Cultural Pluralism

DuBois would not be the only student at Harvard to be inspired by the pragmatism of James, Royce, and Santayana. As mentioned previously, James prioritized the philosophical, specifically epistemological and metaphysical, dimensions of pluralism, but he was also alert to its moral and social relevance. As discussed in chapter 1, in "The Moral Philosopher and the Moral Life" (1891) James explains that, if we live in a pluralistic universe, ethics becomes a process of articulating our unique perspective and values, of sharing and comparing those ideas with those of a community of inquiry, and of experimenting with solutions in the hope of satisfying as many concrete demands as possible. James expands on these ideas in "On a Certain Blindness in Human Beings" (1899) and "What Makes Life Significant" (1900), where he shows how our fallible perspectives limit moral inquiry and requires the participation of interlocutors who do not share our assumptions or conclusions. Bernstein describes his insight as follows:

> James argues that frequently we are blind and insensitive to other human beings who are genuinely different from us. We are too quick to scorn and condemn them. We fail to make the effort to see how the world looks and feels from the perspective of those whose life experiences are radically different from ours. James's pluralism is not flabby or sentimental. He calls for both understanding and critical engagement with other points of views and with other visions. (Bernstein 2015: 78)

Although James does not fully develop the implications of this moral pluralism, it clearly inspired his students Horace Kallen and Alain Locke, who "were to play critical roles in developing the religious, ethnic and racial consequences of James's pluralism" (ibid.). Indeed, the two men would remain lifelong friends, and one of the best summaries of Locke's value theory or aesthetics can be found in Kallen's memorial remarks, which reveal both the continuity of this theory with Kallen's cultural pluralism and its function as the foundation of Locke's own democratic pluralism.

After completing his dissertation with Santayana in 1908, Kallen articulates his cultural pluralism for the first time in 1915, in an essay titled "Democracy versus the Melting Pot," as an alternative to both Edward Alsworth Ross's position of chauvinistic cultural exclusion and Israel Zangwill's dream of romantic assimilation. Kallen begins his article with a careful summary of Ross's (1914) popular book *The Old World in the New: The Significance of Past and Present Immigration to the American People*. Ross was a Stanford sociologist who had been dismissed in 1900 for the controversial opinions he expressed in numerous public speeches. These opinions were related to his commitment to eugenics and to the fear that the American people was committing "race suicide" by allowing too many foreigners to enter the country, specifically immigrant laborers from East Asian countries. When his academic career ended, Ross embraced his new role as a public intellectual and his book summarizes his racialized genealogy of the American people. The first half of the book presents the

Puritans, the Northern Europeans, and the Scotch Irish as the original core of the populace, then devotes separate chapters to other waves of immigrants, explaining both the strengths and the weaknesses they brought with them, and concludes with a chapter titled "The Lesser Immigrant Groups." The second half resurrects discussions about the economic, political, and genetic consequences of immigration, suggesting that the "pioneering breed" must be protected by incorporating only immigrants who can contribute to its vitality. All of Ross's claims have since been debunked, but the book remains emblematic of how the pseudoscientific theories and evidence of eugenics were used to rationalize widespread racist, anti-Semitic, and xenophobic fears of white Americans; yet, sadly, echoes of Ross's arguments continue to resound in political discourse in the United States.

By contrast, *voluntary assimilation* rivaled Ross's position of cultural and genetic exclusion as the more compassionate response to immigration. It is during this period—the 1910s—that the trope of the United States as a "melting pot" of immigrants where anyone can be successful if they are willing to adapt to the host culture and work hard becomes entrenched in the American mind. First coined by J. Hector St. John de Crevecoeur in his *Letters from an American Farmer* (1782), this metaphor is popularized in 1908, through Israel Zangwill's musical of the same name. As a Russian Jewish immigrant to Britain, Zangwill drew largely on his family's experience to spin an uplifting love story about his Jewish protagonist, David, who flees the Kishinev pogrom and, ironically, falls in love with a Russian immigrant, Vera, whose father was responsible for the execution of David's entire family. Despite this complication, the love between David and Vera has a cathartic effect on the tragic past and America becomes the stage where the intergenerational prejudices and feuds of the Old World can be shed, allowing the creation of a new generation of people in a New World of limitless opportunity. The musical soon became a hit both with immigrants and with natural-born citizens, because it presents a vision of America that gave newcomers hope while ameliorating the anxieties of the residents through the celebration of a shared national identity and destiny.

But, while this metaphor sustained generations of immigrants and continues to inspire, it assumes that assimilation is desirable, beneficial, and necessary for the success of immigrants and of the nation. It also distracts from that fact that, while many immigrants willingly choose to assimilate, others did not enjoy that privilege, even when their migration was due to desperation. First, the economic and social integration of African Americans continued to be actively thwarted. Furthermore, while the love of David and Vera was celebrated for its power to erase ethnic and religious divisions, romance across the color line continued to be violently suppressed. Racist whites justified most lynches by alleging that a black man looked inappropriately at or spoke inappropriately to a white woman; and interracial relationships were criminalized through laws against miscegenation (i.e. race mixing) in a majority of states, until these laws were ruled unconstitutional by the Supreme Court in *Loving vs. Virginia* (1967).

The Wounded Knee Massacre of December 29, 1890—in which 356 Miniconjou and Hunkpapa Lakota men, women, and children of the Pine Ridge Indian Reservation were slaughtered by the 7th US Army cavalry—signaled the overt end of extermination policies and marked the beginning of a new era, of *forced assimilation*: American Indians were forcibly assimilated either through policies of the US government or through private institutions such as the Carlisle Indian Boarding School. This controversial Pennsylvania school would become a model of "Americanization" of Indian children, which it achieved by removing them from their communities, giving them settler names, cutting their hair, requiring them to wear modern clothing, forbidding the use of their first languages, and emphasizing vocational over academic education. While some graduates of Carlisle, such as Charles Eastman and Luther Standing Bear, would benefit from the experience and become important leaders and activists of their nations, many survivors reported rampant physical and sexual abuse on top of the psychological harms inherent to this method of assimilation.

In "Impressions of an Indian Childhood" (1900), the Lakota author Zitkala-Sa describes her excitement when missionaries from the Indiana Manual Labor Institute first arrived in her village on the Yankton Reservation. Dazzled by their stories, the eight-year-old begs her mother for permission to leave with the school. Initially her mother resists and an empathetic reader can easily imagine her inner turmoil: Do I risk my child's future by keeping her here and maintaining her connection to her culture, or do I sacrifice her culture, so she can survive in the white man's future? Eventually she relents, and Zitkala-Sa quickly realizes that the promises of the missionaries were false. The scene culminates with the administrators forcibly cutting her hair:

> I cried aloud, shaking my head all the while until I felt the cold blades of the scissors against my neck, and heard them gnaw off one of my thick braids. Then I lost my spirit. Since the day I was taken from my mother I had suffered extreme indignities. People had stared at me. I had been tossed about in the air like a wooden puppet. And now my long hair was shingled like a coward's! In my anguish I moaned for my mother, but no one came to comfort me. Not a soul reasoned quietly with me, as my own mother used to do; for now I was only one of many little animals driven by a herder. (Zitkala-Sa 1921: 56)

The young, innocent, and vulnerable Zitkala-Sa endures not only the physical indignity of being arrested and restrained: the cutting of her hair represents the inherent violence of severing persons from their culture. Nevertheless, enrollment in Indian boarding schools continued to climb throughout the twentieth century until reaching its peak in the 1970s; after that it declined, in the wake of the pan-Indian activism that led to the passing of the Indian Self-Determination and Education Assistance Act (1975), the Indian Child Welfare Act (1978), and other pro-Indian policies.

It is in this context that Kallen defines his cultural pluralism. After summarizing Ross's argument, he not only provides counterexamples to specific claims, but highlights how these anxieties are largely fueled by the *yellow journalism* of the time, which deliberately pandered to fears and biases in order to sell more copies. He then engages the problematic assumptions at the heart of Ross's view, specifically the belief that languages, cultures, or races can remain static or pure. Kallen explains that there is no singular American culture, people, or minds. America, like all other nations, is a collection of cultures and emerges from their interaction:

> It is the fundamental fact of American life to-day, and in the light of it Mr. Wilson's resentment of the "hyphenated" American is both righteous and pathetic. But a hyphen attaches, in things of the spirit, also to the "pure" English American. His cultural mastery tends to be retrospective rather than prospective. At the present time there is no dominant American mind. Our spirit is inarticulate, not a voice, but a chorus of many voices each singing a rather different tune. (Kallen 1915b: 217)

In this passage, Kallen reveals that all forms of chauvinism are literally versions of the "appeal to purity" fallacy, in which one asserts a generalization about a group and creates ad hoc rationalizations for counterexamples. Indeed, the fallacy is often called the "no true Scotsman" appeal, because claims of cultural, national, or racial purity are the ones most likely to commit it. Ross conveniently presents the core of American identity as emerging from the interaction among the Puritans, Huguenots, Germans, and Scotch Irish colonists, but it is well known that, for many generations, those groups did not see one another as possessing a shared identity.

Consequently the franchise of any identity group fluctuates according to popular whim or the political agenda of the day, and Tim Wise rightfully reminds us that skin color has consistently influenced the construction of American identity more than any other factor. Kallen also acknowledges this trend when he mentions that even assimilationists like Zangwill, who promote the mingling of diverse peoples, conveniently avoid the "difference of opinion as to whether negroes also should constitute an element in this blend" (Kallen 1915a: 193). Yet the problem of working across differences still remains, and Kallen asks: "How to get order out of this cacophony is the question for all those who are concerned about those things which alone justify wealth and power, concerned about justice, the arts, literature, philosophy, science. What must, what *shall* this cacophony become—a unison or a harmony?" (1915b: 217). If Ross advocates the silencing of alien voices and Zangwill recommends unison by mimicking the dominant voice, Kallen envisions a choir where distinct voices contrast and complement one another in order to achieve a harmony that is otherwise unattainable. Pluralism creates this diverse body politic by offering the "conditions under which each may attain the perfection that is proper to its kind" (1915b: 219). Furthermore, Kallen asserts that cultural pluralism is the necessary condition of any democracy and that, if there is a unique "Americanism," it consists in the understanding "that democracy means self-realization through self-control, self-government, and that one is impossible without the other" (ibid.).

Alain Locke (1885–1954) and Democratic Pluralism

Kallen devotes his career to articulating cultural pluralism and does so in parallel with Alain Locke (1885–1954), who develops an aesthetic theory to support it and articulates its political implications by giving his own vision of democratic pluralism. Kallen makes one of the best summaries of Locke's aesthetics in remarks at a memorial meeting, one year after Locke's death in 1954. The two men enjoyed a lifelong personal and professional friendship, which started since they first met at Harvard. In his memorial remarks, Kallen describes their shared concern for "the meaning and the future of freedom, alike as a philosophical conception and as a working idea," and explains how the US State Department and the United Nations Security Council had adopted their versions of pluralism for improved "intercultural relations" and as a bulwark against various "totalitarian creeds." Thus, in the fifty years since the two first coined the term, pluralism had become a recurring idea in public as well as in academic discourse (Kallen 1957: 119).

Kallen also recapitulates the two criteria for his mature

version of *cultural pluralism*: it must function as a "working hypothesis concerning human nature and human relations" and as an "ethical ideal—an article of faith which challenges certain prevailing philosophical conceptions about both." As a hypothesis and as an ideal, it stands in opposition to "fundamentally monistic" views on science and politics that "assert and somehow establish the primacy of totalitarian unity at the beginning, and its supremacy in the consummation, of all existence." Not only are these totalitarian monisms examples of circular reasoning, but they require a perpetual denial of the fact that "multitude and variety seem pervasive, always and everywhere" (1954: 119–120). Therefore cultural pluralism aspires to establish "friendship by people who are different from each other but who, as different, hold themselves equal to each other" by postulating "that individuality is indefeasible, that differences are primary, and that consequently human beings have an indefeasible right to their differences and should not be penalized for their differences, however they may be constituted, whatever they may consist in: color, faith, sex, occupation, possession, or what have you." By contrast, many "continually penalize one another for their differences" and demand the other to surrender their "different being to be digested into identification with mine. You must replace your purpose with mine, your ways and means with mine. Unless you do this you refuse brotherhood" (1954: 120). This approach is not only unethical but foolish, because it assumes the superiority of one's own culture and experience, thus cutting one off from learning something new—as well as from mutual friendship.

At this point Kallen describes the acts of racism that Locke endured while they were students at Harvard and Oxford and tells us how this informed his commitment to pluralism. These experiences undoubtedly "left scars" on Locke's "philosophic spirit" and impressed upon him how the assumption of *totalitarian monism* among philosophers coerces the "many and somehow argue[s] away the actualities of penalization for one's being oneself into unimportant appearances, without in any way relieving the feelings of dehumanization, the pain and the suffering; and without lessening the desire never again to expose oneself to them" (1954: 122). Locke would not be cowed, but rather asserted his right to self-acquiescence or the "unalienable right to his difference," which "became the core of his value-system" (1954: 123). Kallen elaborates as follows (ibid.):

> This acquiescence is not primarily defensive, not a struggle for political or economic or other form of equalization. It expresses itself in affirming the integral individuality of one's person, of taking freely the obligations that go with it; of insisting not on becoming *like* anybody else, but on having one's singularity recognized and acknowledged as possessing a title equal with any other's to live and grow.

Most importantly, self-acquiescence is not opposed to cultural pluralism; rather it is the pretext that enables it. This realization converted Locke from monism and universalism to pluralism and particularism, because it allowed him to see that "difference is no mere appearance, but *the* valid, vital force in human communication and in human creation" (ibid.).

At this point Kallen mentions an essay from later on in Locke's career, "Pluralism and Ideological Peace" (1947), which makes an important distinction between unity and union. Unity requires "liquidation of difference and diversity, either by way of an identification of the different, or by way of a subordination and subjection of the different to the point where it makes no difference." Today, these two forms of unity would be either assimilation to the dominant culture or a superficial form of diversity where some aspects of minority cultures (e.g. food, dress, music, holidays, etc.) are allowed to express themselves as long as they do not make members of the mainstream culture uncomfortable. By contrast, "[u]nion resides in the uncoërced, the voluntary commitment of the different to one another in free coöperation." It does not require either the suppression of culture or the submission of each person's individual identity, as both partners must first "self-acquiesce" in what it is that makes them unique and then develop mutual respect and appreciation not only for their similarities but also for their differences. Doing so leads to ideological peace or to a "free intercommunication of diversities—denoting the cultivation of those diversities for the purpose of free and fruitful intercommunication between equals" (Kallen 1954: 124).

Thus Locke's cultural works, such as *The New Negro* (1925), present an "authentic Negro cultural community sensitive not only to the positive values of all the present, but aware also of the immemorial African past and rendering it presently a living past" (Kallen 1954: 125). All peoples must reconstruct their history and art as a "complete culture," in order to invigorate their identity in the present and preserve it for future generations. Likewise, every individual should, through "exploration and study," develop an identification with her culture and participate in its expression for the sake of her own integrity and the integrity of her community. If individuals reject "such an identification because they perceive themselves to be penalized on account" of their differences, they have chosen to identify as penalized members of society by default. Kallen concludes his memorial with these stirring remarks (1954: 124–125):

> The Negro, Locke held, is not a problem. The Negro is a fact, and American fact, but not merely because he has lived and labored in America since Colonial times. He is American in virtue of his commitment, in common with non-Negro Americans, to the essential American Idea, the idea that human beings, all different from each other, are equal to each other in their inalienable rights to life, liberty, and the pursuit of happiness, and owe each other participation in the joint endeavor "to secure these rights" on which the institution of government rests in free societies. All "these rights" may be comprehended as the right to be different without penalty, without privilege, and with each of the different maturing its own excellence, the excellence expressive of its individual or associative singularity in willing coöperation with all. Believing this, Alain Locke gave expression to his own commitment to the Negro fact by undertaking to disclose to Americans, especially to Negro Americans, the Negro, not the problem. He made himself the philosophical midwife to a generation of younger Negro poets, writers, artists.

As inspiring as Locke's fulfillment of his personal and philosophical project may be, Kallen admits that challenges remain, perhaps perpetually, because other people and communities, regardless of their race or identity, may face greater prejudice or may lack self-awareness or the courage to admit who they are and foster union.

Furthermore, these challenges are active not only at home but also abroad, and Locke astutely realizes that, until the US resolves its racism, attempts at international leadership will be undermined. To quote Charles Molesworth's words in his edition of Locke, the latter "knew that the greatest threat to democracy came from its two most persistent opposing forces: racism and imperialism" (Locke 2012: xxxii). Consequently his most important legacy may be his thorough explanation of the necessity of pluralism to democracy, which he articulates in a series of articles written and published on the eve of the United States' entrance into World War II. In "Color: Unfinished Business of Democracy" (1942), Locke describes the imminent global crisis as a choice between the "alternatives of world chaos, world tyranny or world order, and democracy must take serious stock of that" (Locke 2012: 534). Locke saw that the future of democracy was imperiled by the rise of totalitarian regimes: Soviet communism, Japanese imperialism, national socialism in Germany, and fascism in Italy and Spain. Most of these regimes had already successfully invaded and occupied neighboring nations, many of which had been capitalist democracies.

Consequently critics across the globe, but also within the United States, argued that democracy as a political ideal had failed and must be reformed or replaced by more authoritarian forms of government. Chief among the institutions they promoted was the American First Committee, founded in 1940. Although this committee began as a public group lobbying against US intervention in any European conflicts, it soon became increasingly nationalistic and started to use the forum to express sympathies for the Nazis and fascism, as well as anti-Semitic views. It most high-profile member, the famous aviator and US Colonel Charles Lindbergh, best represents this shift in attitude. From the spring of 1941 on, he served as headline speaker at rallies and delivered a stock speech against intervention, claiming that it would be logistically impractical to muster and transport the necessary troops across the Atlantic and that Britain and France were in conflict with Germany because of the inordinate influence of a minority of "interventionists." Then he concluded with an appeal to America's history of isolationism. Later on, in September, he added a section that disclosed the identity of the "interventionists": Jews, specifically those in media and government.

Although Lindbergh carefully parses his statements—he laments Jews' current and historical persecution and praises Jews who oppose intervention—only one year earlier, in 1939, he penned for *Reader's Digest* an essay titled "Aviation, Geography, and Race" in which he confesses his true opinions to a popular audience:

> We, the heirs of European culture, are on the verge of a disastrous war, a war within our own family of nations, a war which will reduce the strength and destroy the treasures of the White race, a war which may even lead to the end of our civilization ... It is time to turn from our quarrels and to build our White ramparts again ... We can have peace and security only so long as we band together to preserve that most priceless possession, our inheritance of European blood, only so long as we guard ourselves against attack by foreign armies and dilution by foreign races ... With all the world around our borders, let us not commit racial suicide by internal conflict. (Lindberg 1939: 66)

Surprisingly, Lindbergh does not make any explicitly anti-Semitic statements in this essay; but he clearly hopes to rally popular support for an authoritarian American ethnocracy, sees common cause with Nazi Germany against foreign invaders, and sprinkles the essay with warnings against America's further decline through the actions of materialistic people of lesser character, who wish to divide the populace and are unwilling to make sacrifices for their country. Clearly these warnings are anti-Semitic dog whistles.

Locke agrees with Lindbergh that racial animus critically

influences the impending crisis, but he does not think that the imminent war will be a "war of races." He admits that the current democratic world order was established through colonialism and that the hypocrisy of the racial oppression exerted by these democracies has led to internal strife, for example to the American Civil War, which allows totalitarian critics to question its "moral fitness." Indeed, authoritarian regimes continue to use the propaganda technique of *whataboutism* to deflect attention from their clear use of systemic brutal oppression and onto the troubling history of their more democratic rivals. Therefore Locke asserts that the "crucial issue is whether or not our vision of democracy can clear-sightedly cross the color line, and whether we can break through the barriers of color and cultural racialism to reach the necessary goal of world democracy" (Locke 2012: 534–535). Doing so would require the United States and other democratic nations to engage in a "drastic self-reform of social practice and cooperative realignment of political policy" to "totalize democracy if we would stave off and effectively counter totalitarian tyranny" (2012: 538–539).

Locke insists that this totalization of democracy must be founded on a *democratic pluralism* that relinquishes white supremacy at home and abroad, thereby allowing the full participation of individuals, regardless of their racial or cultural identity. First he argues in "Cultural Relativism and Ideological Peace" (published in 1942) that democracies must embrace "three working principles"—specifically cultural equivalence, cultural reciprocity, and limited cultural convertibility—which are "derivable," "as corollaries," from the relativist approach and will lead to "a more objective and scientific understanding of human cultures and a more reasonable control of their interrelationships. These pragmatic (and not ideological) principles enable democratic populations to find, first, common ground through mutual respect and, then, common cause through cooperation, until new syncretic cultural identities emerge through these social and political transactions across differences (Locke 2012: 551). However, in "Pluralism and Ideological Peace" (published in the same year, 1942) Locke soon asserts that James's philo-

sophical pluralism can function as a "favorable foundation
for wide-scale ideological peace" because it is an inherently
"antiauthoritarian principle" that insists upon the "irreducible variety of human experience" (Locke 2012: 567).

Thus,
while democratic pluralism requires people to accept only
the superficial principle that "the affirmation of one's own
world of values does not of necessity involve the denial or
depreciation of someone else's," a deeper acceptance of pluralism leads to the realization that most, if not all, monistic,
absolutist, and orthodox creeds should be surrendered or
avoided (2012: 568).

While science, technology, and globalization support this
deep pluralism, Locke realizes that it will take time and
careful work to make this deeper shift towards it; those on
the side of democratic pluralism, much like the adepts of
Addams's concept of sympathetic knowledge, will have first
of all to maintain a proper mindset and patiently accept the
challenges that lie ahead:

> Of course, such intellectual tolerance and courtesy cannot be
> effectively arrived at by cynical indifference or by proclaim-
> ing value anarchy, but only through the recognition of the
> importance of value systems on a "live and let live" basis. For
> this we need a realistic but sympathetic understanding of the
> bases of our value differences, and their root causes—some of
> them temperamental, more of them experiential, still more, of
> cultural derivation. (Locke 2012: 568)

For democratic pluralism to be successful, its proponents must
avoid a naive relativism that makes no critical judgments just
as much as a zealous pluralism that makes diversity its own
oppressive cause. Some people may be incapable of accepting
the deeper implications of pluralism, but this does not mean
that they cannot become democratic allies. For true pluralism
to obtain, conservative people, communities, and values must
have respect for one another. Locke reminds us that we all
indulge the "[u]topian dream... that somehow a single faith,
a common culture, an all-embracing institutional life and its
confraternity should someday unite man by merging all his
loyalties and cultural values" (2012: 570). This hope inspires

us all and may someday be achieved, but Locke knows that will not happen if we assume that it can only be achieved through the rushed imposition of our own values on others. Locke identifies other challenges, too. Citing the comparative philosopher F. S. C. Northrop, he tells us that the democratic pluralist must not only accept the reality of difference but also realize that "the ideological beliefs to which any people has been conditioned by its traditional education, political propaganda, artistic creations, and religious ceremonies," therefore they are deeply entrenched and shape all areas of their lives and society (Locke 2012: 568; see also Northrop 1946: 479). Furthermore, these forms of conditioning are ongoing, and Locke offers important guidance on how to confront totalitarianism when it appears in what Jürgen Habermas will call the public sphere. Should members of a democratic society silence, tolerate, or confront authoritarian monism?

Locke answers this question by reminding us that democratic pluralism is a method of social practice, not a dogmatic political theory. Just as Dewey asserts that democracy is a way of life, so that the cure for the problems of democracy is more democracy, Locke could make the same statements about pluralism. Indeed, he identifies the impulse to abandon pluralism in times of discomfort, self-interest, or crisis as indicative of one's unrecognized "value-bigotry"; but he challenges us to view these moments as opportunities to perform the hardest work of democratic pluralism:

These principles call for promoting respect for difference, for safeguarding respect for the individual and preventing the submergence of the individual in enforced conformity, and for the promotion of commonality over above such differences. Finally, more on the intellectual side, additional motivation is generated for the reinforcement of all the traditional democratic freedoms, but most particularly for the freedom of the mind. For it is in the field of social thinking that freedom of the mind can be most practically established, and no more direct path to that exists than through the promotion of an unbiased scientific conception of the place of national culture in the world. (Locke 2012: 564–565)

In this passage, Locke hopes to rally democratic pluralists to go on the offensive, not by chauvinistically attacking the values of others or rationalizing how the current moment requires an exemption from our own values, but by passionately championing democratic values, by using science to discover and reassert the basic common values shared by all people, and by being inspired by the moments when America fulfilled its democratic hopes without denying the moments when it failed.

Thus, as individuals and as a nation, we must work daily to overcome our personal biases, find common democratic cause with others, especially with those who have troubling prejudices or are tempted by authoritarian politics, and work to ensure social justice at home by confronting and ameliorating racism and abroad by resisting the imperialistic act of other nations and our own. Performing this work robs critics of their greatest weapon, the accusation of hypocrisy, and helps Americans and their country to become compelling examples of the democratic values that have always made them great. Fortunately these commitments prevailed and contributed to the success of the United States and of the Allies in World War II; but one should not forget the failures of nerve during the war, such as the unwarranted racist policy of Japanese internment in the United States and Canada and the controversial decision to drop atomic bombs on the civilian populations of Hiroshima and Nagasaki. This act signaled the beginning of the nuclear age; and, in Molesworth's words, "the post-war period's slide into the cold war left many of these ideas underdeveloped and far from implemented" (Locke 2012: xxxiii). I will now consider how the consequences of the war and Cold War fears contributed to the decline of pragmatism during the mid-twentieth century, or at least to the eclipse of this pluralistic branch, committed to social inquiry.

– 4 –

Verification and the
Analytic Pragmatists

Despite pragmatism's contributions to progressive political reforms, influence on the emerging social sciences, and imprint on two generations of students from Harvard, Chicago, and Columbia, by the mid-twentieth century its earliest waves crested and pragmatism began to decline. The global philosophical scene changed dramatically when members of both the Vienna Circle and the Frankfurt School fled in response to the rise of fascism before World War II. Of the two, the members of the Vienna Circle fared better for at least two reasons. First, they scattered widely and became rooted enough to remain in American universities, whereas the Frankfurt School successfully transplanted to New York City and remained intact until its members' return to Germany in 1953. Second, the logical positivism of the Vienna Circle sprang in part from the thought of Anglo-American thinkers Bertrand Russell and Alfred North Whitehead, whereas the Frankfurt School had its origin in the critical thought of Austrian German theorists such as Sigmund Freud, Karl Marx, and Max Weber. Hence the former was welcomed and remained, while the latter was met with suspicion and returned.

As a result, pragmatism was displaced in America by the rise of analytic philosophy, introduced by the heirs of the Vienna Circle; and it was eclipsed globally by the more radical critical theories of continental philosophy. Yet, despite pragmatism's falling out of fashion, at least one strain of it remained active while the others lay dormant; and this was thanks to the work of C. I. Lewis. Lewis was one of James's last undergraduates (1902–1906) and would later write his dissertation under Royce's supervision, in 1910. He also studied Russell and Whitehead's recently published *Principia Mathematica* at Royce's suggestion and, while he was not the first pragmatist to engage with logical positivism, he was the first to merge the insight of its exponents so as to form his own *conceptual pragmatism*. Lewis's version of pragmatism embraced logical positivism's preference for analysing statements that can be cognitively verified through empirical evidence or logical implication (or both), but rejected its strict bifurcation between facts and values and retained an understanding of experience that was based on Peirce's pragmatic maxim. Following Peirce, Lewis argued that not only are all statements verifiable, since all beliefs inevitably have practical effects, but all judgments, even those based on logical implication, are affective, and therefore based on values. Thus he concluded that the positivist distinction between statements of fact and statements of value is a false dichotomy, since the two are continuous.

Lewis would not be the last analytic philosopher to mine pragmatism for insights or to drift toward its conclusions. W. V. O. Quine presents a similar critique of logical empiricism in his famous 1951 essay "Two Dogmas of Empiricism," where he argues that analytic truths must be supported by empirical confirmation and that, consequently, logical empiricism's preference for reductionism is itself an analytic preference that lacks empirical confirmation. His *pragmatic holism* describes the function of scientific inquiry better, because it acknowledges that the scientific method is a more efficient and reliable way to predict future experiences: it is pragmatic rather than claiming that its success stems from specific analytic truths such as reductionism. Likewise, Wilfrid Sellars pushes analytic philosophy even further toward pragmatism through *the myth of the given*, which argues that the first premise of Lewis's conceptual pragmatism—that sense data present themselves to the mind independently of conceptualization—is false, since all sense data must be conceptualized to be intelligible.

Ultimately this gradual process of using pragmatic insights to critique the assumptions of analytic philosophy reaches its zenith in Richard Rorty's (1979) *Philosophy and the Mirror of Nature*. While Rorty's (1967) earlier book *The Linguistic Turn* firmly supported analytic philosophy, Rorty began to see Quine's and Sellars's critiques not as attempts to rehabilitate analytic thought but as unknowingly laying the groundwork for its repudiation. If the dogmas of logical positivism are no more than preferences (Quine) and no sense data present themselves to the mind prior to conceptualization (Sellars), then any attempt to ground philosophical inquiry in foundational principles, whether conceptual or empirical, will prove impossible. Rorty's alternative, often labeled *neopragmatism*, retains the analytic preference for language; but, rather than seeking clarity or foundational principles (i.e. polishing the mirror of nature until it accurately represents reality), it focuses on how language functions and how meaning is created through use. Borrowing from Ludwig Wittgenstein, Martin Heidegger, and, most importantly, John Dewey, Rorty boldly asserts that any discipline, including philosophy and even science, is simply a sophisticated language game used to describe our experience and best evaluated by its pragmatic results. This hybridization of pragmatic and analytic thought has been praised and condemned, but it has not been ignored.

Was Pragmatism Eclipsed, Displaced, or Silenced?

The current descendants of the analytic pragmatists argue that pragmatism was not eclipsed but that its better ideas, the ones that are the subject of this chapter, contributed to and remain influential within mainstream philosophy. The most succinct criticism of the *eclipse narrative* can be found in Robert Talisse and Scott Aikin's (2011) introduction to their anthology of pragmatism. In brief, they suggest that the eclipse narrative is a "persecution story" told by frustrated philosophers who resent their professional displacement, scapegoat their analytic colleagues as "philosophical villains," and bask in their perceived "vindication," which followed the publication of Richard Rorty's *Philosophy and the Mirror of Nature*. While this psychoanalytic diagnosis seems suspicious, Talisse and Aikin also offer facts to corroborate it. First,

> several of the most influential figures in philosophy from the past sixty years—for example ... Ludwig Wittgenstein, Bertrand Russell, Karl Popper, John Rawls, John Searle, Daniel Dennett, Charles Taylor, Michael Dummett, and Jürgen Habermas ... either explicitly acknowledge a distinctively pragmatist inheritance or take themselves to be responding critically to identifiable pragmatist arguments.

Second, there were major analytic philosophers who defended, advanced, and modified pragmatism throughout the twentieth century (Talisse & Aikin 2011: 6–7)—the very ones who will be discussed in this chapter.

Finally, since the eclipse "coincides with Dewey's gradual withdrawal and death," it was only the pragmatism of James and Dewey that declined; and Talisse and Aikin argue that this decline was due to philosophical weaknesses rather than to contingent sociological reasons. In their view, "new articulations of the old positions that Dewey claimed to have undermined" were developed by philosophers—for example John Rawls's contractarianism, Roderick Chisholm's foundationalist, yet fallibilist epistemology, Jerrold Katz's and Jerry Fodor's philosophy of language, and John Searle's naturalist reformulation of mind–body dualism. These advances challenged Dewey's assumptions, undermined his "claim that Darwinism supplied a perspective from which centuries of philosophy could be swept away with a single gesture," and offered new, more modest versions of Dewey's metaphysical targets that were both naturalistic and pragmatic. Thus there was a crisis in pragmatism, but "[t]here was no eclipse or abandonment of pragmatism; rather ... pragmatism was forced to confront powerful challenges from opponents who had the opportunity to revise and rework their positions in light of pragmatist criticisms" (2011: 7–9).

Talisse and Aikin make a compelling argument and it is
healthy both to emphasize pragmatism's influence and successes in the twentieth century and to guard against potentially
pathological narratives and approaches rooted in personal
grievances, caricatures of rival positions, and apologies for
obsolete ideas. Peirce would certainly describe the latter as
unnecessary barriers to inquiry based on tenacity, authority, or a priori commitments and it is difficult to imagine
that Dewey would want his legacy to be at the center of a
philosophical cult unwilling to adapt to advances in science
or culture. However, others have suggested sociological reasons why analytic philosophy eclipses pragmatism around
the middle of the century: the synergy between positivism
and professionalization, the US Cold War politics, and the
takeover of institutions, journals, and professional societies
by Vienna Circle refugees and their disciples.

First, as higher education expanded dramatically at the
turn of the century, philosophy was undergoing a process
of *professionalization* designed to make this discipline more
amenable to the nascent university systems. William James
complained about this transition as early as 1905, although
it is certainly the focus of Emerson's ire much earlier, in
"The American Scholar" (1837). The historian Bruce Kuklick
describes the phenomenon as follows:

> The realists [Sellars and Lewis] came of age in the new uni-
> versity order and exhibited the standard characteristics of
> individuals in that order: their philosophizing began with a
> set of problems that their mentors and graduate training had
> bequeathed. As James put it, they regurgitated "what dusty-
> minded professors have written about what other previous
> professors have thought." His students gained preferment
> by earning a PhD and publishing about these problems. The
> professional system with a set of professorial grades culmi-
> nating in tenure and promotion to a full professorship, was
> established during this time. Professors not only moved up the
> ranks in a single institution, but also might move around the
> system, obtaining a coveted chaired professorship at a well
> known school. Finally, more complicated factors blocked or
> advanced the careers of these men—the perception of them as

solid citizens or otherwise; their personalities; and calculations
about the relation of their doctrines to their morals or politics.
(Kulik 1977: 201–202)

While philosophers have always been tempted to conform
their subjects and conclusion to local and broader politics at
least in order to secure their safety and livelihood, if not to
obtain grander luxuries and rewards, the university system
harnessed these motives in the name of credentialing, produc-
tivity, and progress by standardizing academic career paths.
Unfortunately this system often causes colleagues to become
rivals, as they compete among themselves to control the
research agenda for their programs and their departments'
criteria for hiring, promotion, tenure, and other forms of
funding and prestige.

Undoubtedly Dewey's decline and death, together with
the fact that many of his students pursued careers in the
other emerging social sciences, left a power vacuum within
professional philosophy. This vacuum was filled locally at
first, thanks to the scattering of eminent positivist refugees to
universities across the country, and then nationally, once the
influence of those refugees transformed these savvy students
into first waves of graduates. Subsequently a new generation
of PhDs established themselves in other programs, as well
as on the boards of scholarly journals and as officers of professional organizations. These advances not only influenced
the next generation of undergraduates but determined the
subject and agenda of mainstream philosophy—what candidates were to be accepted, hired, tenured, and promoted
by institutions—and the awarding of the "objective" metrics
upon which these career decisions are based: publications and
presentations at professional meetings.

In a recent article, Joel Katzav and Krist Vaesen (2017)
painstakingly compile publication data during the transitional period from the 1930s to the 1960s in order to depict
how this rapid shift occurred. They begin by focusing on
America's premier philosophical journal, the *Philosophical
Review*, then broaden their scope to reveal subsequent shifts
in the other major US journals. They conclude that the "speed

of the shift at *PR*, along with the absence of similar simultaneous shift in other publication venues, strongly suggests that its immediate cause is a change in editorial policy," specifically the way it parallels changes at the "Susan Linn Sage School of Philosophy at Cornell University, the school from which *PR*'s editors were drawn during the period being considered." Thus these "changes in editorial policy are not themselves primarily the result of the changing political climate in America or the passing away of rival approaches to philosophy" but the "replacement of editors who were open to a wide variety of approaches" with editors who supported a more exclusive and narrow view of philosophical subjects and methods (Katzav & Vaesen 2017: 773).

Furthermore, the values, methods, and subjects of logical positivism coincide with and support professionalization, whereas the values, methods, and subjects of pragmatism, especially the pluralistic strands descended from James, conflict with professionalization. Logical positivism postulates that all beliefs and positions should be reduced to precise definitions, statements, or arguments that can be empirically tested, which dovetails perfectly with academic professionalization because it clearly delineates the proper subject matter of philosophy through contrast with other disciplines and generates standardized metrics that can be cited as evidence of career progress or contributions to the field. By contrast, pluralism insists that there are no boundaries to philosophical inquiry and no single standard for progress. Thus the pragmatists' analytic colleagues could unashamedly claim to be impartial and objective in such philosophical and professional decisions because their own subjective and cultural biases remained hidden behind the screen of reductionism, precision, and progress.

The final sociological reason for the decline of pragmatisms is the US political climate after World War II. Professionalization made academics more vulnerable not only to intellectual trends, but also to actual political trends. First, the association of analytic philosophy with United States' allies cannot be ignored. The great analytic philosophers of the twentieth century were either coming from the allied countries (e.g.

Bertrand Russell and Alfred North Whitehead, from Britain) or, as mentioned before, fleeing the Nazi regime at home. Some were even war heroes, like A. J. Ayer, who served as an agent in MI6. The most famous example, Alan Turing, used his genius and expertise in philosophy of mathematics and logic to become the leading cryptanalyst at Bletchley Park and to crack the Enigma code. The American philosophers Willard Van Orman Quine and Wilfrid Sellars, whom I will soon discuss in depth, performed similar code-breaking and intelligence duties for the US Navy. Such work not only placed their patriotism above question, but gave analytic philosophy a practical value and justification: although esoteric and obscure even to professional philosophers, it could be relevant to engineering and scientific research, thanks to its focus on logic, mathematics, science, language, and the mind.

Furthermore, if the intellectual products of analytic philosophers did not contribute, even indirectly, to the success of espionage or to progress in the space race and in the nuclear arms race (the two main scientific fronts in the emerging Cold War with the Soviet Union), they were at least politically neutral. Analytic philosophers largely ignored ethical and political philosophy all throughout the first half of the twentieth century and, when they did approach those areas, they tended to be more abstract and less applied. Certainly some of them entered the political fray (and not only in high-profile ways), as did G. E. M. Anscombe, and occasionally engaged in criticism of western foreign policies, like Bertrand Russell, who actively opposed nuclearization in 1955 in *The Russell–Einstein Manifesto* and imperialism one decade later, in 1966, when he organized the International War Crimes Tribunal (also known as the Russell Tribunal). However, none of these ethical and political philosophers was American and no major work in these fields was produced by an American analytic philosopher right until 1971, when John Rawls published *A Theory of Ethics* amid a global resurgence of interest in applied ethics.

Now, if we ask why no American analytic philosophers pursued ethical or political topics in the mid-twentieth century, we will arrive at the darkest sociopolitical reason why pragmatism vanished: McCarthyism. As tensions between the United States and the Soviet Union rose, Americans experienced a second Red Scare, which lasted at least until the late 1950s and contributed not only to the animus against the countercultural revolution of the 1960s and 1970s but also to the ongoing culture wars that continue to shape US politics. The spirit of this period is best exemplified by the career of anticommunist firebrand Senator Joseph McCarthy, whose influence on the House Un-American Activities Committee, leadership of the Senate Permanent Subcommittee on Investigations in 1953 and 1954, and support of J. Edgar Hoover, the director of the Federal Bureau of Investigations, resulted in decades of outright political oppression for anyone suspected of socialist sympathies and created a general state of paranoia and guilt around any projects or positions critical of the United States. While McCarthy's blacklisting and persecution of media and entertainment figures such as Lucille Ball, Charlie Chaplin, Arthur Miller, and Orson Wells (among many others) are well known, less attention has been given in popular culture to McCarthyism's impact on academics.

John McCumber provides a thorough history of the influence of McCarthyism on professional philosophy and of lasting legacy in his books *Time in the Ditch* (published in 2001) and *The Philosophy Scare* (McCumber 2016). In an earlier essay he succinctly described how the discipline of philosophy faced greater scrutiny because it was considered at best unproductive and at worst subversive: "For what was Marxism, basically, but a kind of philosophy?" (McCumber 1996: 7). McCumber supports these serious claims by citing statistical evidence from the American Association of University Professors to the effect that in 1957 professional philosophers were overwhelmingly more likely to be disciplined than specialists in any other academic field and that, when it came to the total number of professors dismissed nationally according to discipline, philosophy departments were at the top, rivaling English and economics departments. He also investigates several dismissals as case studies, to reveal not only that some philosophers were being purged for political reasons but also that, sadly, "other philosophers were helping to purge them" (1996: 38). Philosophically, this situation resulted in a "crucial confrontation between certain logical positivists, who held that philosophy dealt with a priori (and hence timeless) truths of meaning," and the work of the analytic pragmatists, who insisted upon the pragmatic necessity for all propositions to be confirmed through some degree of empirical verification (1996: 44).

Fortunately the analytic pragmatists did win this philosophical debate, but their pluralistic colleagues were more likely to be among the political casualties. Thus Talisse and Aikin (2011) can earnestly claim that pragmatism was not eclipsed in the twentieth century, because the Peircean branch of pragmatism endured and continued to be influential. Unfortunately Talisse and Aikin's narrative is incomplete: it fails to explain why other versions of philosophy, including those developed by members of the Jamesian branch of pragmatism, were not allowed or not able to compete philosophically or chose not to because of the feedback loop of professional and political pressures against them. Established scholars who did not conform were purged and forced to resort to self-censorship, or they were gradually replaced as they retired. Some pragmatists, for instance William Barnett, Sidney Hook, and Arthur O. Lovejoy, even supported McCarthyism and contributed to these acts of political and professional suppression.

It may be that the next generations of graduate students could not find senior professors to support scholarship in these areas, or shrewdly chose not to pursue them for obvious reasons, or did not know about them as they were not widely taught, or disdained them as a result of caricatures inherited from critics of pragmatism. Sympathetic students took their meliorism seriously and pursued careers in the social sciences, or relocated outside the United States in order to study critical theories without fear of political reprisal. Thus these two populations of pragmatists underwent a process of speciation. The Jamesian branch either went dormant or found other venues for the work of its members, through correspondence with continential sources. The Peircean population more easily adapted to the changing habitat because these philosophers' earlier interest in scientific methodology, fallibilism, and empiricism enabled them to emphasize the necessity of *verification* as they critiqued the positivists and their heirs. Coincidentally, their sociopolitical context should remind us both that verification guards against false claims in our lived experience and that we should be suspicious of any narrative that reduces complicated historical shifts to some single cause or perspective.

Clarence Irving Lewis (1883–1964) and Conceptual Pragmatism

The genealogy of analytic pragmatism begins with Lewis's career and his lifelong interest in the philosophy of Immanuel Kant. However, Lewis was not the first pragmatist to develop a sustained response to Kant. In fact another way to describe pragmatism is to say that it emerged from Peirce's lifelong engagement with Kant's transcendental idealism. I must now take a moment to explain Kant's concept of the synthetic a priori, since this was the central concept inherited by the positivists that the analytic pragmatists critiqued. More importantly, this digression will not only introduce the theme of *verificationism*—the philosophical position that all statements must be verifiable through empirical evidence in order to be meaningful; it will also dramatize it as a process.

Although Kant was not an adept of fallibilism and was rather optimistic about rationality, his clarification of the limits of theoretical reasoning and advocacy for the use of practical reason to ground ethical and political philosophy do characterize him as a proto-pragmatic figure in the history of philosophy. While chapter 1 focused more on Peirce's deeper critique of modernity via his essays on Descartes, Peirce studied seriously *The Critique of Pure Reason* as a teenager and, while always critical of Kant, late in his career he would routinely make comments like the following one, which comes from a letter dated May 20, 1911 to Victoria, Lady Welby:

I show just how far Kant was right, even when twisted up on formalism. It is perfectly true that we can never attain knowledge of things as they are. We can only know their human aspect. But that is all the universe is for us. (Peirce, quoted in Burch 2014)

Thus there remained several interesting similarities between Kant and Peirce's late work, which contemporary analytic pragmatists such as Susan Haack and Cheryl Misak typically consider to be more authoritative. According to Robert Burch, Peirce admitted to reaching several of the same conclusions as Kant but consistently rejected Kant's foundationalism, specifically his "claim about the *a priori* status of space and time" (Burch 2014).

Kant founds his philosophical idealism on the notion that our experiences would be unintelligible without the categories of space and time. If we cannot organize our experiences in relation to space and time, we can neither differentiate among these experiences nor communicate them to others. But, since we must code our experiences according to the categories of space and time, Kant reasons that these categories must be a priori, in other words they must precede our experiences; they cannot be a posteriori or come after our experiences, at a later point in time. Space and time form the transcendental structures of experience that make knowledge possible. Because they precede experience they are best explored via conceptual–theoretical reasoning rather than through empirical scientific investigation. They can be known analytically, through conceptual reasoning alone, but they can function synthetically, since these categories imply conclusions about other phenomena. Consequently space and time constitute the synthetic a priori: they are concepts we can deduce analytically, prior to experience, but use synthetically, to reason about claims and subjects that arise from experience. Like Descartes' cogito, the categories of space and time found all other philosophical claims, because we can know them objectively without reference to our subjective experiences. Unlike Descartes' cogito, Kant's synthetic a priori does not risk solipsism and does not reinforce the mind–body dualism;

the reason is that we can know, by analogy, that time and space are both properties of the universe and categories present in other minds, since our phenomenological experience would be meaningless without them.

Peirce disagrees with Kant on three grounds. First, inquiry does not need foundations; it always begins within a context. We start from certain experiences or assumptions and reason with and about them. We can never know the proper foundations of an inquiry *before* that inquiry begins. This is why knowledge always remains fallibilistic. Although we may deduce interesting or useful criteria *after* inquiry and use them to initiate or guide *future* inquiries, we cannot know whether these criteria will remain useful when tested through *further* inquiry. Second, Peirce insisted that space and time, as well as other Kantian categories, might be more fruitfully investigated through empirical scientific research than through analytic conceptual reasoning. Most likely Peirce put together this critique by combining his familiarity with current astronomical research (acquired from his father, Benjamin), his own study of Carl Friedrich Gauss's non-Euclidean geometry, and his general experience as a field scientist.

Thus, while the transcendental nature of the categories of space and time could be deduced through analytic reasoning, astronomers and other physicists gain empirical knowledge about these categories every night when they look through their telescopes. Meanwhile, non-Euclidean geometry supported the possibility that the behavior of either space or time might not be consistent, depending on the point where they are measured on a given plane. In the context of such developments, Peirce suspected that space and time might not be truly universal; and this produced a third major disagreement with Kant's metaphysics. Kant expected the synthetic a priori and categories such as causation to function universally, just like Sir Isaac Newton's laws of thermodynamics. Peirce, on the other hand, admitted that the universe acquires certain habits or laws over time (synechism), but stipulated that random chance (tychism) and conscious intention (agapism) also contribute to the unfolding of the cosmos. Thus Peirce could not support Kant's conclusion that space, time, and causation behave consistently all throughout the universe and its evolution. Within a decade of his death, Albert Einstein's theory of relativity and Werner Heisenberg's uncertainty principle would contradict both Newton's physics and Kant's metaphysics, confirming Peirce's suspicion that analytic metaphysical categories can be empirically researched and supporting some elements of his cosmology.

This brief history shows not only how science and philosophy work in tandem but also how empirical and conceptual reasoning work in tandem. Drawing on his empirical knowledge, Newton developed a new physics in order to explain the motion of objects. Inspired by Newton's physics, Kant used its implications to speculate about the functions of the mind and what structures enable us to have reliable knowledge about the universe. Peirce admired Kant's epistemology but suspected that some of his metaphysical assumptions and conclusions either were not logically necessary or conflicted with new findings from empirical sciences. Those findings were unavailable to Newton and Kant, yet they resulted from research projects made possible by their conceptual schema. With further reasoning and research, Einstein and Heisenberg verify Peirce's cosmology. This sketch shows that inquiry is a historical and fallible process, with no foundations and no necessary end, and one that progresses through a permanent oscillation between conceptual analysis and empirical verification. New evidence invites new speculation, which prompts new research; but, no matter how logically consistent and sophisticated the new theoretical tools might be, they must always be confirmed through empirical verification in order to be considered knowledge.

In many respects, this Peircean view of inquiry as a non-linear historical process of speculation, verification, analysis, and revision anticipates the *paradigm shifts* described by the physicist and philosopher Thomas Kuhn. In his highly influential 1962 book *The Structure of Scientific Revolutions*, Kuhn claims that each branch of science operates under its own paradigm or set of theoretical axioms, assumptions, and problems that allow professionals to develop new research projects and experiments. During periods of normal science, the paradigm remains stable because it inspires a variety of programs and sufficiently explains most of the new evidence and data. Over time research begins to stagnate, or anomalous results begin to accumulate that the paradigm cannot explain. Eventually the established paradigm collapses and a period of revolutionary science follows, until a new paradigm emerges and becomes widely accepted. This new paradigm could completely replace the old one, or even become its own separate branch of scientific research. Although there are "no obvious historical lines of influence" between Kuhn and the analytic pragmatists, Kuhn's work emerges from the same philosophical context as theirs, and his conclusions strongly resemble those of his Harvard colleague Quine (Philström 2012: 82–84).

Like the figures discussed in the previous chapter, Lewis belonged in the last generation of scholars who studied with the classical pragmatists at Harvard. Although he took classes with James, his dissertation, titled "The Place of Intuition in Knowledge" and delivered in 1910, was supervised by Royce. During this phase of his career, Royce focused on logic and developing the implications of the semiotics he had inherited from Peirce. Through his service as Royce's research assistant on this project, Lewis encountered the *Principia Mathematica* co-authored by Bertrand Russell and Alfred North Whitehead and published between 1910 and 1913. In it Russell and Whitehead hoped—in Russell's own much quoted words—to "show that pure mathematics follows from purely logical premises and uses concepts definable in logical terms" by deriving the definitive set of axioms and logical rules that ground all mathematics (Russell 1959: 74). Ultimately Russell and Whitehead did not achieve their ambitious goal. Ludwig Wittgenstein, one of Russell's graduate students, immediately found problems with their distinction between pure and applied logic; but the conclusive criticism of their project arrived two decades later, when Kurt Gödel's two incompleteness theorems provided logical proofs that (1) any sufficiently expressive mathematical system must be either incomplete or inconsistent and (2) a consistent mathematical system cannot prove its own consistency. In other words, there must be some true statements that cannot be proved conclusively through any system of mathematics, and no such system can logically justify its own consistency. Any system of mathematics must chose consistency over completeness in order to yield valid conclusions, and something outside that system must verify its consistency.

Nevertheless, the *Principia* became the lodestone of professional philosophy in the early twentieth century, when the positivists were trying to preserve the project of a complete and consistent pure logic, while others, such as Gödel and the analytic pragmatists, challenged these assumptions and goals. The latter focused primarily on Russell and Whitehead's distinction between pure and applied logic, which depended on a modification of Kant's metaphysical categories—more specifically, on a modification of the distinction between a priori versus a posteriori claims and analytic versus synthetic claims. To be a proposition of pure logic, a statement must have four properties. First, it must be necessary, that is, true in all possible worlds. Second, it must be a priori, that is, known or knowable independently of experience. Third, it must express conceptual relationships, that is, contain only logical connectives, quantifiers, and the like and no non-logical constraints. Finally, it must be a purely abstract variable, with no content. Pure logical statements would be analytic a priori propositions, because they would be necessarily true propositions derived through conceptual reasoning alone, with no empirical restraints or content.

As we shall see, Lewis critiques this understanding of the a priori; and later on Quine will critique the analytic–synthetic distinction as well as Carnap's insistence on reductionism. Lewis begins a 1923 essay titled "A Pragmatic Conception of the *a priori*" with the following critique:

> The conception of the *a priori* points two problems which are perennial in philosophy: the part played in knowledge by the mind itself, and the possibility of "necessary truth" or knowledge "independent of experience." But traditional conceptions of the *a priori* have proved untenable. That the mind approaches the flux of immediacy with some godlike

foreknowledge of principles which are legislative for experience, that there is any natural light or any innate ideas, it is no longer possible to believe. (Lewis in Talisse & Aikin 2011: 166)

While Lewis does not refer directly to Peirce in this article, the final sentence unmistakably and beautifully reconstructs Peirce's first two "consequences," as given in an article titled "Some Consequences of Four Incapacities" (originally published in the *Journal of Speculative Philosophy* in 1868): "1. We have no power of Introspection, but all knowledge of the internal world is derived by hypothetical reasoning from our knowledge of external facts"; and "2. We have no power of Intuition, but every cognition is determined logically by previous cognitions" (Peirce 1992: 30).

Lewis's preceding argument explains, from a Peircean perspective, how these two incapacities lead to mistakes within Russell and Whitehead's conception of the a priori, according to which a priori statements are necessarily true and independent of experience. With regard to the first incapacity, Lewis distinguishes between two connotations of "necessary": necessary as the opposite of voluntary; and necessary as the opposite of contingent. Now, if a statement is necessarily true because it is not *voluntary*, then it must be believed; but if a statement is necessarily true because it is not *contingent*, then it could not be otherwise. An example of necessity of the first kind would be the statement "if you do not breathe, then you will necessarily die." An example of necessity of the second kind would be the statement "the interior angles of a triangle necessarily total 180 degrees." In the first example, an individual cannot doubt for long that breathing is necessary for life because, if he does and acts accordingly, "brute fact" will confirm the truth of that statement (Lewis in Talisse & Aikin 2011: 166). This is why belief in breath as necessary for life is involuntary. By contrast, the second statement is necessarily true because it is true by definition or by logical implication (or both). The statement describes a particular concept—a shape—that possesses certain properties—three sides and three interior angles (and in this statement those angles add up to 180 degrees). We could call shapes with those properties something else—we could give them any names we want—but the properties of those shapes could not change. They could not be otherwise because they are not contingent—they are necessary properties of those shapes.

From this distinction between voluntary and contingent, Lewis argues that Russell and Whitehead are guilty of assuming that a priori statements are involuntary because they cannot be contingent. These are two separate properties. Consider the previous examples: while breath is necessary (non-voluntary) for life, we could imagine its being otherwise (contingent). For example, fish do not need to breathe and perhaps a handful of yoga masters do not need to breathe either (doubtful, but imaginable). By contrast, triangles necessarily (non-contingently) possess those properties, yet our belief in those properties is voluntary. Granted, a statement is true independently of whether I believe it or not; but I can refuse to accept the truth of that statement, with limited consequences. This leads Lewis to write the following:

> What is *a priori* is necessary truth not because it compels the mind's acceptance, but precisely because it does not. It is given experience, *brute fact*, the *a posteriori* element in knowledge which the mind must accept willy-nilly. The *a priori* represents an attitude in some sense freely taken, a stipulation of the mind itself, and a stipulation which might be made in some other way if it suited our bent or need. (2011: 166, emphasis added)

Thus a priori statements can be necessarily true as opposed to contingently true, but they are not necessarily true as opposed to voluntarily true. This confusion undermines the significance of the first property that Russell and Whitehead claim all pure logical statements must possess: that they must be necessarily true in all possible worlds. An a priori statement may be necessary via contingency but, if so, then it cannot be involuntary, unless it has some connection to experience. Only a posteriori statements can be involuntary, because they pertain to features of experience that compel our assent. Thus we can refuse to believe in the Pythagorean theorem, but we cannot refuse to believe in the law of gravity, because the first describes the necessary conceptual properties of triangles and the second describes the necessary consequences of walking off high ledges.

Further, the reason for this confusion leads to Russell and Whitehead's second mistake, as expressed in the remaining three properties of pure logical statements: that they must be *independent* of experience, must express only *conceptual* relationships, and must be *abstract* in content. If a statement is independent, conceptual, and abstract, then it cannot be involuntary, because it would have no connection to experience. Lewis explains this as follows:

> And the *a priori* is independent of experience not because it prescribes a form which the data of sense must fit, or anticipates some preëstablished harmony of experience with the mind, but precisely because it prescribes nothing to experience. That is *a priori* which is true, *no matter what*. What it anticipates is not the given, but our attitude towards it: it concerns the uncompelled initiative of mind, or as Josiah Royce would say, our categorical way of acting. (2011: 166)

Although Lewis refers to Royce in this paragraph, notice the Peircean elements in his critique. Essentially Lewis recapitulates Peirce's pragmatic maxim that propositions are meaningless unless they have some observable consequence that can be evaluated (hence my emphasis on Lewis's reference to "brute fact" in the previous quotation). Purely logical statements that are independent, conceptual, and abstract are either impossible or meaningless.

From this critique, Lewis draws three consequences that pertain respectively to logic, mathematics, and science. First, there is no definitive separation between purely logical and applied logical statements: all logic must be pragmatic. Lewis does not deny that logic can and should aspire to be conceptual and abstract; rather he wants us to bear in mind that our preference for conceptual and abstract reasoning arises from our practical needs and must inevitably be applicable to experience. Therefore the distinction between pure and applied logic is relative to the degree of conceptualization and abstraction required by practical needs (2011: 166–167). Second, mathematics describes experience but does not affect it. No matter how sophisticated, abstract, or conceptual, its purpose is to count and measure the objects of our experience. Hence the truth or value of any mathematical system is not in the completeness or consistency of its axioms but in how accurately it allows us to describe our world numerically (2011: 168). We could further suggest that completeness and consistency are themselves pragmatic values, because Russell and Whitehead hope to derive the axioms that allow mathematics to work the same way in all situations; but Lewis does not make this claim.

Lewis devotes the remainder of the article to applying these consequences to science. While science is obviously more empirical than logic and mathematics and more likely to generate a posteriori statements from and about experience, Lewis carefully acknowledges the a priori elements of science and envisages how they should be reconceptualized. First, classification and definition are important scientific activities and do aim at describing essential features that objectively distinguish between phenomena. They must be determined prior to empirical investigation, which suggests that they should be evaluated conceptually or a priori (i.e. independently of experience). While it is wise to have clear definitions or to classify a subject carefully before investigation, conceptual reasoning only refines these definitions and classifications, whereas their truth or falsity depends on how well they "represent *some* uniformity in experience or it names nothing" (2011: 169).

Second, Lewis addresses how "the fundamental laws of any science—or those treated as fundamental—are *a priori* because they formulate just such definitive concepts or categorial tests by which alone investigation becomes possible." Like definitions and classifications, these "laws" must be clarified prior to inquiry; but they, too, are subject to revision in the light of experience:

> Such definitive laws are *a priori*; only so can we enter upon investigation by which further laws are sought. Yet it should also be pointed out that such *a priori* laws are subject to

abandonment if the structure which is built upon them does not succeed in simplifying our interpretation of phenomena. (2011: 170)

In many respects, this critique anticipates Kuhn's notion of paradigm shift by almost forty years: Lewis claims that, in order to initiate research, we must stipulate certain principles, which are gained through observation and refined through conceptual reasoning, but a long-term purpose of research is to test and gain evidence for revising these principles. He even gives the theory of relativity as an example.

The last a priori element of science that Lewis discusses is its goal, or that of any epistemological activity: to seek to know what "constitutes the criteria of the real as opposed to the unreal in experience." If we have knowledge, then we can recognize real things, because they conform to our awareness of uniformities in experience; thus "[a] mouse which disappears where no hole is, is no real mouse; a landscape which recedes as we approach is but an illusion." Unfortunately we cannot tell the real from the unreal, or which uniformities to use as principles, until after we have engaged in observation and research:

> This is one of the puzzles of empiricism. We deal with experience: what any reality may be which underlies experience, we have to learn. What we desire to discover is natural law, the formulation of those uniformities which obtain amongst the real. But experience as it comes to us contains not only the real but all the content of illusion, dream, hallucination, and mistake. The *given* contains both real and unreal, confusingly intermingled. If we ask for uniformities of this unsorted experience, we shall not find them. (Ibid.)

Apart from describing the challenge at the heart of empiricism (and, possibly, of epistemology itself), this passage articulates one of Lewis's concepts—the myth of the given—that Wilfrid Sellars will later critique, thereby pushing analytic pragmatism further from these Kantian and positivistic roots.

However, Lewis and Sellars would both agree that the

perennial philosophical desire to discover the perfect set of a priori principles for all future inquiry is a fool's errand despite admirable attempts by Plato, Descartes, Leibnitz, Kant, Russell, and Whitehead. These projects do refine the first principles of inquiry in valuable ways, but their application to experience verifies their accuracy and efficacy. Lewis summarizes as follows these reconceived relations between logic and science and between a priori and a posteriori claims:

> At the bottom of all science and all knowledge are categories and definitive concepts which represent fundamental habits of thought and deep-lying attitudes which the human mind has taken in the light of its total experience. But a new and wider experience may bring about some alteration of these attitudes, even though by themselves they dictate nothing as to the content of experience, and no experience can conceivably prove them invalid. ...
> Neither human experience nor the human mind has a character which is universal, fixed, and absolute ... Our categories and definitions are peculiar social products, reached in the light of experiences which have much in common, and beaten out, like other pathways, by the coincidence of human purposes and the exigencies of human coöperation. Concerning the *a priori* there need be neither universal agreement nor complete historical continuity. Conceptions, such as those of logic, which are least likely to be affected by the opening of new ranges of experience, represent the most stable of our categories; but none of them is beyond the possibility of alteration. (2011: 171–172)

Again, Lewis functions as a cable stretched between Peirce's understanding of inquiry and Kuhn's understanding of science. In order to understand our experience, we must flex between conceptual and empirical inquiry. Neither is superior to the other and each one yields its own forms of truth.

Logic helps science to be more efficient by simulating conceptual possibilities and probabilities, but science must eventually verify all theoretical speculations. For example, Einstein's general theory of relativity implied in 1915 the a priori necessity of gravitational waves, but the technology did not exist to confirm their existence. However, this logical implication warranted devotion of some resources to theorizing the most efficient means for gathering *indirect* evidence to corroborate it. Subsequently, Russell A. Hulse and Joseph H. Taylor, Jr. used this implication to focus on binary pulsars as the deep space objects most likely to exhibit indirect evidence of gravitational waves. The strength of the logical implication compelled enough gatekeepers to approve of Hulse and Taylor's research project, and their research successfully gathered enough traces to win the Nobel Prize in 1993. More importantly, this indirect evidence convinced the US National Science Foundation, the French National Centre for Scientific Research, and the Italian Institute for Nuclear Physics to grant in the following year the massive amounts of funding needed to construct laboratories (LIGO and the Virgo Interferometer) that could observe and measure *direct* evidence of gravitational waves. Then, on February 11, 2016, these laboratories announced that they had successfully observed and measured such evidence. Thus an a priori hypothesis, implied in 1915, was finally confirmed in 2016. A minor, but exciting scientific revolution occurred, and a new branch of astrophysics, gravitational wave astronomy, began with it. This new science has a research paradigm based on the a priori principles of general relativity theory, but as we gather radical new evidence, it will revise those principles and possibly warrant revision or even replacement of Einstein's physics.

   This anecdote further confirms the theme of chapter 2, that scientific knowledge and the scientific method, as well as their authority, arise from their fallibilism. Hulse and Taylor accept that all knowledge is conditional and should be revised through further inquiry and in light of new evidence. Peirce and James initiate classical pragmatism by incorporating this insight into philosophical inquiry. Philosophical speculation is always tentative and must be verified by applying it to experience and studying its effects. Yet the history of philosophy and current professional philosophy, as represented by the analytic tradition, remain nervous and suspicious of this approach. Lewis addresses these criticisms in the final paragraph of his article in the Talisse and Aikin volume:

Pragmatism has sometimes been charged with oscillating between two contrary notions; the one, that experience is "through and through malleable to our purpose" [James] the other, that facts are "hard" and uncreated by the mind [Peirce]. We here offer a mediating concept: through all our knowledge runs the element of the *a priori*, which is indeed malleable to our purpose and responsive to our need. But throughout, there is also that other element of experience which is "hard," "independent," and unalterable to our will. (2011: 173)

This essay not only provides an important pragmatic critique of logical positivism but also prefigures the conceptual pragmatism that Lewis articulates in 1929, in his masterwork *Mind and the World Order*. Lewis reformulates pragmatic empiricism by insisting that inquiry and knowledge begin with the *sensations* given in our experience. While these sense data are immediately perceived by the mind, they do not become intelligible until the mind provides an interpretation. Finally, these interpretations are distilled further, until they generate abstract concepts that we can discuss and use as theoretical tools; and we can also take them on board when we interpret future sensations. As we have seen, mathematics is a set of sophisticated abstract concepts that emerged from a historical process of interpreting sense data given in experience. Thus it appears to be purely conceptual and theoretic, but Lewis reminds us that mathematical concepts originated from empirical experience. Consequently, if we wish to take seriously any theoretical concept—mathematical, logical, or of any other kind—we must verify it empirically at some point. No truth can be determined through conceptual analysis alone; the truth of all statements should be empirically verified.

Willard Van Orman Quine (1908–2000) and Pragmatic Holism

Quine's academic career, like Lewis's, begins with the *Principia*, but he, unlike Lewis, focuses more on applying pragmatism to the philosophy of science rather than to logic.

What explains this preference is his work with Alfred North Whitehead at Harvard and with Rudolf Carnap in Vienna. When Quine arrived at Harvard in 1930, with a BA in mathematics from Oberlin College, Whitehead was the obvious choice of supervisor to a dissertation in philosophy of mathematics. However, it had been decades since the publication of the *Principia*, and in that time Whitehead turned from logic, mathematics, and positivism towards science, metaphysics, and pragmatism.

During the period when Quine was his student, Whitehead published three books on these subjects—*The Concept of Nature* in 1920 (Whitehead 1964), *Science and the Modern World* in 1926 (Whitehead 1967), and *Process and Reality* in 1929 (Whitehead 1978)—and was working on two more— *Adventures of Ideas* (Whitehead 1933) and *Nature and Life* (Whitehead 1968), to be published in 1933 and 1934 respectively. These works established what is now known as process philosophy: the ontological position that the fundamental nature of reality is change. On this view, the universe is not composed of disparate particles that accidentally interact, but rather a vast and intricate bundle of continuous processes, intertwined with one another. In at least one key respect, this turn marks a volte-face from the *Principia*, because the project of deriving a complete set of logical axioms for mathematics assumes that there must be at least some features of the universe, namely the axioms, that do not change.

A variety of factors influenced this turn, such as the early criticisms of the *Principia*; but chief among them was Whitehead's growing awareness of the incongruity between what rapid scientific breakthroughs were revealing about the universe and philosophy of science's unwillingness to revise its outdated ontology in light of these revelations. In brief, contemporary science continued to assume, uncritically, the authority of Isaac Newton's materialism, which reduced the universe to bits of matter in the void. Whitehead rejected this assumption not only on the grounds that new scientific evidence was available, but also because this ontology described a universe devoid of ethical purpose and of aesthetic beauty. He felt that professional philosophy risked being reduced to the narrow epistemological concerns (logic, language, and mathematics) that fall within the boundaries of skepticism and reductionism and fit in. The cause of this bad ontology and the problems that flow from it result from "the fallacy of misplaced concreteness" or treating these heuristic abstractions originally imagined as features to aid inquiry as concrete necessary features of the universe (Whitehead 1967: 51).

By this stage Whitehead's emerging pragmatic affinities should be obvious, and it should be no surprise that he stated in his preface to *Process and Reality* that he was "greatly indebted to Bergson, William James, and John Dewey" and that his new mission was to "rescue their type of thought from the charge of anti-intellectualism, which rightly or wrongly has been associated with it" (Whitehead 1978: xii). Basically Whitehead creates a metaphysical system that uses the epistemological insights of the pragmatists to present a new ontology, which describes reality as a continuous process in which the objective world of facts and the subjective world of values are reunited. The universe itself is a grand organic process, in which elementary processes constantly overlap, interact, and progress toward concrescence (i.e. growing together) in order to form an undifferentiated whole. Thus the cosmos is a living process, not dead matter, and the abstractions created not only by the sciences but also by art, religion, and ethics are not mental entities separate from the material world but representations of real relations between these processes.

Although Quine ultimately avoided Whitehead's process philosophy, he followed his mentor's turn away from logical positivism and toward a pragmatic philosophy of science. Likewise, he inherited his mentor's preference for holism over reductionism, even though his dissertation ("The Logic of Sequences: A Generalization of *Principia Mathematica*," published in 1934 under the title *A System of Logistic*) was largely a rejection of Whitehead's early ontology via criticism of the role of properties in the *Principia*'s propositional logic. Quine worried that Russell and Whitehead's treatment of "properties in the same manner as individuals by including them in quantifiers" was problematic because "one

does not properly quantify over attributes or properties";
he preferred identification through classes over identification
through properties, and would continue to refine his "well-
defined criteria for classes" throughout his career (McHenry
& Shields 2017: 487). Otherwise he seems to have respected
Whitehead's later process philosophy and its metaphysics,
though he never bothered to engage with it, on the grounds it
was too obscure (2017: 489).

However, Whitehead was not the only influence on Quine
at this time. In 1933, one year after completing his dissertation, Quine traveled to Europe to study with members of the
Vienna Circle and of the Polish School. Chief among them
was Rudolf Carnap, who intended to revise logical positivism by placing "truth and meaning on a proper scientific
footing by countenancing only *a priori* analytic and *a posteriori* empirically testable statements as properly significant."
Although initially a "devoted Carnap acolyte," Quine "soon
developed reservations about the dichotomy between analytic
truth by definition and empirically testable synthetic truth."
He would argue that all scientific truths "rely upon both at
once, and both are revisable under sufficient theoretical pressure" (Janssen-Lauret 2018: xviii). Also, Quine did not share
the "anti-metaphysical attitudes" (2018: xvi) of Carnap and
the logical positivists.

This hostility toward metaphysics sprang from philosophical and political concerns. Philosophically, Carnap felt
that logical positivism's epistemological project of deriving
logical axioms required only an acceptance of naturalism,
which rendered further metaphysical speculation obsolete.
Politically, he rightly feared that European philosophers in
the "neo-Thomist, Heideggerian, and Hegelian style" were
joining and "fueling the rise of fascist ideologies" (2018:
xxi). Conversely, Quine "admired Carnap's attempts to put
logic and mathematics on a naturalistically solid footing"
but, given the more sober and naturalistic metaphysics of his
democratic culture, that is, the various naturalisms of Peirce,
James, and Whitehead, "he did not have cause to associ-
ate metaphysics with dangerous political authoritarianism"
(ibid.). Thus he never shared the political concerns of these

philosophers and grew increasingly critical of their agenda throughout his career.

In his first major article, "Truth by Convention," published in 1936, Quine rejects "Carnap's linguistic theory of the apriori" (Soames 2014: 106), arguing that, while "the bearers of analyticity are sentences ... the bearers of apriority and necessity seem not to be"; for example, "[w]hen one says that *it is necessary, and knowable apriori, that all squares are rectangles*, what is said to be necessary and known apriori is not the sentence 'All squares are rectangles,' or any other" (ibid.). It is not the sentence that is necessarily true a priori, but the shape it describes. While this critique was "powerful, for many years it didn't attract much attention or change many minds" (ibid.). Quine spent the first decades of his career "attack[ing the] quantified modal logic as developed in the 1940s by Ruth Marcus and Rudolf Carnap" (2014: 109). Although he still shared their presuppositions that "[n]ecessity is apriority" and that "both are defensible only if they are reducible to analyticity," his refusal to reduce the a priori to analytic statements would eventually lead him to conclude that "there is no apriori knowledge and no necessary truths" (ibid.).

Thus the matter lay dormant until Quine revisited and extended his critique of Carnap's understanding of the connection between analyticity and necessity in his most important essay, "Two Dogmas of Empiricism" (1951). This essay revised analytic philosophy in two ways. First, "[b]y undermining the analytic/synthetic distinction ... [Quine] decisively challenged the picture of philosophy as conceptual analysis" because even the truth of analytic statements must eventually be empirically verified (Soames 2014: 114). Second, "by embracing a holistic view of empirical confirmation, it drove the final nail in the coffin of the logical empiricists' verificationist criterion of meaning" and replaced it with a form of pragmatic verification (ibid.). Quine begins the article as follows:

> Modern empiricism has been conditioned in large part by two dogmas. One is a belief in some fundamental cleavage between

truths which are *analytic*, or grounded in meanings independently of matters of fact, and truths which are *synthetic*, or
grounded in fact. The other dogma is *reductionism*: the belief
that each meaningful statement is equivalent to some logical
construction upon terms which refer to immediate experience.
Both dogmas, I shall argue, are ill founded. One effect of
abandoning them is, as we shall see, a blurring of the supposed
boundary between speculative metaphysics and natural science. Another effect is a shift toward pragmatism. (Quine in
Talisse & Aikin 2011: 202)

Just as Lewis's earlier critique of Russell and Whitehead's
modification of Kant's a priori–a posteriori distinction
revealed that it is a posteriori brute fact, not a priori statements, that must be involuntarily accepted as necessarily
true, Quine's critique of the first dogma, Carnap's modification of Kant's analytic–synthetic distinction, reveals how a
similar confusion again obscures the necessity of empirical
verification.

Let us follow Quine's argument in this classic article (my
quotations are from the reprint in the 2011 Talisse & Aikin
volume). First, if one understands an analytic statement
in the original Kantian sense, as "one that attributes to its
subject no more than is already conceptually contained in
the subject" and is "true by virtue of meanings and independently of fact," then analytic truth can only be a property of
"subject–predicate" statements and only at a "metaphorical"
or conceptual level (2011: 202). In other words, analysis can
demonstrate the truth of certain statements; but, even if those
statements are true, analysis may or may not give information
about the material world of experience. Quine gives several
examples that illustrate this problem, beginning with one of
Frege's identity puzzles. In the famous 1892 essay "On Sense
and Reference," Frege had demonstrated how, even though
the names Phosphorus (Morning Star) and Hesperus (Evening
Star) function as two signs that refer to the same heavenly
body, namely the planet Venus, they are not identical signs
because they do not share the same properties with each other
or with Venus. Notice how all the following statements are
true, both with regard to reference and with regard to identity:

Table 4.1 Set 1

#	STATEMENT (SET 1: PURE ANALYTIC)	REFER	ID
1	Phosphorus is the Morning Star.	T	T
2	Hesperus is the Evening Star.	T	T
3	Venus is either Phosphorus but not Hesperus or Hesperus but not Phosphorus.	T	T

Statements 1 and 2 are identity statements because their subjects and predicates contain the same properties. Therefore their respective subjects and predicates can be interchanged without any loss or gain of information. Likewise, Venus can be either Phosphorus or Hesperus, but not both at the same time. Now notice how reference and identity diverge in the next series of statements:

Table 4.2 Set 2

#	STATEMENT (SET 2: ANALYTIC–SYNTHETIC)	REFER	ID
4	Venus is the Morning Star.	T	F
5	Venus is the Evening Star.	T	F
6	Phosphorus is Hesperus.	T	F
7	Phosphorus is not Hesperus.	F	T

While Statements 4 and 5 are factually correct, they do not express identity. Venus cannot be identical with the Morning Star because the conceptual identity of Venus includes the property of not being the Morning Star (Statement 3). More significant is the tension between Statements 6 and 7 where Statement 6 expresses a true reference but a false identity and Statement 7 expresses a false reference but a true identity.

This tension between reference and identity becomes even more problematic if applied to a person's propositional attitude or to whether a person's *belief* about the statement is true. Notice how all the following statements are true beliefs even though they may be false in terms of either reference or identity:

Table 4.3 Set 3

#	STATEMENT (SET 3: ATTITUDE)	BELIEF	REFER	ID
7	Joyce believes that Venus is the Morning Star.	T	T	F
8	Joyce believes that Venus is both Phosphorus and Hesperus.	T	T	F
9	Joyce believes that Phosphorus is Hesperus.	T	T	F
10	Joyce believes that Phosphorus is not Hesperus.	T	F	T

Set 3 illustrates why this example is puzzling. First, both Statements 9 and 10 are true beliefs even though they contain contradictory predicates (Hesperus and not Hesperus). Second, the truth of these beliefs does not appear to depend on whether or not the statements are true or false in terms of reference or identity. Therefore, if Joyce believed either Statement 9 or Statement 10 separately, her belief would be only partially true, whereas, if she first observes the movement of Phosphorus every morning until it's no longer visible, then notices that Hesperus becomes visible in the evening sky, she would learn the whole truth: that Phosphorus and Hesperus refer to the same planet, Venus, but the separate names are used to identify whether Venus can be seen at dawn or at night. Through observation and verification, one not only learns the complete truth but realizes the relevant pragmatic distinction between reference and identity.

These truth tables prove Quine's dismissal of the analytic–synthetic distinction to be legitimate and further corroborate Lewis's claim that nothing can be known a priori because the only way for a statement to be purely analytic would be for it to make claims only about identity, not reference. Unfortunately such a claim would tell us nothing about the world, since Statement 10 expresses a true belief about identity even though it is clearly false with regard to reference. Thus it is ultimately verification that allows us to know whether we should evaluate a belief on the basis of its referential truth or on the basis of its identity truth. This supports Quine's dismissal of the second dogma, the preference for reductionism, because that dogma rests on the assumption that identity claims are more authoritative than reference claims. As the example of Venus shows, it is only through the process of verification that we learn the practical conditions that reveal when and why theory (identity) should trump experience (reference), or vice versa. Thus pragmatism emerges as the victor again, because it insists that we must always remember that our theories are fallible, hence must be verified and revised in the course of an inquiry.

As we have seen, the history of analytic philosophy during the first half of the twentieth century revolves around how best to solve this dilemma. Russell and Whitehead wrote the *Principia* in an attempt to find a complete and consistent set of a priori analytic statements (axioms) that will allow the truth of a belief to depend only on the truth of the relevant identity statements. Unfortunately, Gödel proves logically that any set of axioms can be either complete or consistent, but not both. Furthermore, Lewis explains how all a priori statements are derived from a posteriori experience, in other words all identity statements must refer to something, otherwise they tell us nothing about our experience. Thus Carnap proposes that philosophers should isolate statements whose truth and falsity with regard to identity corresponds consistently to their truth and falsity with regard to reference. These a priori analytic statements could then be confirmed or falsified through empirical science. Like Lewis and Carnap, Quine demonstrates once more that, while logical analysis remains an important tool of inquiry, the creation of new knowledge requires a complementary system of empirical investigation to confirm or falsify our speculations. As a result of the criticisms mounted by Lewis and Quine, the foundations of logical positivism began to crack and mainstream philosophers gradually recognized the significance of this process.

Lewis's and Quine's pragmatic critiques of logical positivism gained even greater momentum in 1956, when Wilfrid Sellars published "Empiricism and Philosophy of Mind." In this essay Sellars convincingly disproves Lewis's notion of sensation, which he calls "the myth of the given," by contending that there is no basic and distinct cognitive state (the given) prior to conceptualization. In order to recognize any object (sensation), let alone to identify it (interpretation), our minds immediately conceptualize the sense data we perceive. For example, when we notice a stop sign, what do we *sense*? We may be tempted to follow Lewis and claim that we sense specific colors, shapes, and words before we *interpret* those sense data as a stop sign. Using resources from psychological research and philosophy of mind, Sellars argues that the moment we become aware of the sign our mind immediately interprets it, using conceptual frameworks such as language or any other knowledge we already possess. We do not receive raw sense data, because our mind instantly labels the properties of any object, and these labels originate from the concepts present in the mind. Thus we have no sensation without conceptualization.

Likewise, Donald Davidson provides an important parallel critique of his teacher, Quine. In "On the Very Idea of a Conceptual Scheme" (an article first published in 1974), he suggests that Quine's pragmatic holism depends on an unrecognized "third dogma of empiricism" that introduces the "dualism of scheme and content, of organizing system and something waiting to be organized" (Donaldson in Talisse & Aikin 2011: 291). This dualism becomes problematic when two schemes describe the same content. While it may be practical to allow multiple schemes to function independently rather than reducing one to the other, Quine's holism implies that translation from one scheme into another either is theoretically impossible, since no scheme can be reduced to another, or cannot explain how we recognize obvious translation errors in practice. Davidson reminds us that this sort of translation occurs all the time when we translate the same content across human languages.

For example, if an English-speaking person visits Mexico and urgently asks a Spanish-speaking local, *¿Dónde está la biblioteca?*, most likely the local will direct the traveler to the nearest bathroom, not to the nearest library. If Quine's holism is correct, then Davidson asks: How is this error of recognition possible? He sees Quine as allowing only two possibilities: either a new scheme emerges to fill in the gap when people attempt to communicate across schemes; or the occurrence of error depends on what Quine elsewhere calls the "principle of charity," according to which speakers will refer to an object that will "make the largest possible number of statements true" (Quine 1960: 59, n. 2). According to Davidson, these options are insufficient. First, while hybrid languages are created when two people with different languages meet, it takes time for this scheme to develop; thus it seems absurd to suggest a new language scheme is created every time two new people meet. Second, our ability to select referents likely to be successful would imply that the principle of charity requires that both speakers already possess a third scheme, which they share and which allows each one to anticipate referents that the other is likely to recognize.

If this explanation is true, then there is no essential difference between languages or schemes; then some schemes are reducible to other schemes, and this possibility would contradict Quine's holism. Thus Davidson concludes that we must abandon this third dogma of empiricism—the dogma that separates between schemes and content. This means that communication is possible without any empirical verification and that we enter a purely linguistic territory, where truth is determined by the interplay of various language games. Truth is, then, relative to these language games, and a property of sentences rather than of the claims they represent.

Standing on the shoulders of these criticisms, adduced by the likes of Kuhn, Lewis, Quine, Wittgenstein, Sellars, and Davidson, Richard Rorty will announce the end of analytic philosophy in his infamous masterpiece *Philosophy and the Mirror of Nature*; and it is to him that I now turn.

Richard Rorty (1931–2007) and Metaphilosophy

In many respects, Richard Rorty's career symbolizes the process of academic professionalization discussed at the beginning of this chapter. Just before his fifteenth birthday in 1946, he enrolled in the Great Books program developed by

Robert Maynard Hutchins (1899–1977) at the University of Chicago. This program educated precocious youths through an interdisciplinary curriculum centered around the master-works of the western canon. Rather than studying history or science as separate subjects, the students would read important historical works on the subjects, like Tocqueville's *Democracy in America* (1835) or Newton's *Principia* (1687). Rorty excelled in this environment and would continue to employ Hutchins's method of understanding texts in their historical contexts; he will do so throughout his life, but particularly in his later works. After earning his BA, Rorty remained at Chicago, where he studied philosophy with Richard McKeon and Charles Hartshorne. McKeon owed his interest in ancient philosophy and pluralism to his mentors at Columbia, Frederick J. E. Woodbridge and John Dewey. Hartshorne directed Rorty's master's thesis, which was on Whitehead's metaphysics (Voparil 2010: 7).

Rorty's early training in contextualism and pragma-tism would continue at Yale, where he went next. There he prepared a doctoral dissertation titled "The Concept of Potentiality" (1956) under the supervision of Paul Weiss, yet another student of Whitehead's. More importantly, he encountered analytic philosophy for the first time. Many faculty members were Harvard graduates and former stu-dents of Lewis and Quine, and insisted on symbolic logic as "indispensable for philosophical reasoning" (Voparil 2010: 8). Rorty was intrigued by this approach, even though it clashed with his historical interests and literary style of argu-ment. This tension increased when he received his first major posting at Princeton in 1961. Unlike Yale, Princeton was a place where analytic philosophy had a firm foothold, even though the department chair, Gregory Vlastos (1907–1991), was an ancient philosopher, in fact one of the top Plato scholars of the era. Furthermore, Rorty's position there was only for one year and initially not part of a tenure-track line. Fortunately he obtained a tenure-track appointment the following year, and eventually received full professorship in 1970. Nevertheless, he adapted to the precariousness of the situation by "desperately" learning "what was going on in analytic philosophy" (Rorty, quoted in Gross 2008: 17). Ironically, he would prevail at Princeton and became one of the most well-regarded experts in analytic philosophy. Yet he never felt free to follow his own muse, a state of mind best expressed in the following statement he made to the president of Princeton University: "Roughly speaking, I tell historical stories and everybody else in the department analyses arguments" (Rorty, quoted in Gross 2008: 231).

During this time Rorty engaged many of the subjects common to analytic philosophy, but his early literary interests made him incline more toward philosophy of language, and he became increasingly interested in the work of Ludwig Wittgenstein (1885–1951). Much like Rorty, Wittgenstein would earn the status of exemplary philosopher twice over: first for his early work in analytic philosophy and then for his later work, which predominantly criticized the tradition. In the first section I discussed how, even as a graduate student, Wittgenstein recognized the fatal flaws in Russell and Whitehead's *Principia*; and his own genius would culminate in his early masterpiece, *Tractatus Logico-Philosophicus* (1921). Whereas Russell and Whitehead sought to solve the problems of philosophy by deducing the foundational axioms of mathematics, Wittgenstein understood logic to be a form of language. Consequently he begins the *Tractatus* by stating that the problem of philosophy "rests on the misunderstanding of the logic of our language," therefore the book intends to "draw a limit to thinking, or rather—not to thinking, but to the expression of thoughts; for, in order to draw a limit to thinking we should have to be able to think both sides of this limit (we should therefore have to be able to think what cannot be thought)" (Wittgenstein 1922: 23). This work becomes the foundational text of the Vienna Circle and, by extension, one of the major texts of analytic philosophy to date. In the same passage Wittgenstein also asserts that, since "[t]he limit can ... only be drawn in language," then "what lies on the other side of the limit will be simply nonsense" (ibid.). The authority of this statement accounts for much of the rivalry and even hostility between analytic philosophy and pragmatism, because the statement itself invalidates several themes and subjects valued by the pragmatists—especially the primacy of experience and the appreciation of pluralism and holism. Indeed, Rorty himself eventually runs afoul of many pragmatists for saying that Dewey's primary mistake was to use the term "experience" rather than "language."

However, Wittgenstein would recant or redefine these assertions in his 1953 *Philosophical Investigations* and repudiate the foundational assumptions of the philosophy of language. Specifically, he moves away from clarifying the logic of language, to exploring how words obtain meaning through their use. At the basic level, we use words to represent and describe objects in our environment. However, the meaning of words does not remain stable and the structure of our language emerges from the way we use words to communicate with others. No word has a definitive meaning, and the logic of language undergoes constant modifications. The late Wittgenstein prefers to think of *language as a game*. Although any language has an underlying logic, this logic functions more like the rules of a game. Such rules determine what "moves" are permissible, but they are not exhaustive and can be changed. Thus situations arise where the rules must be interpreted by the players, or where new rules may be proposed. Players may even break rules, depending on the situation or on the outcome, or simply for the sake of novelty.

Consider the popular board game Monopoly. While every box from the same edition should contain identical copies of the "official rules," the rulebook also contains alternative "official short game rules," in case time is limited. Furthermore, almost everyone plays by "house rules" rather than following the "official rules." Some of these house rules are more common than others (e.g. the Free Parking Jackpot, Double Salary, No Mortgages, etc.), but any variation is possible and permissible, provided that the players explicitly agree on it before the game begins. The biggest arguments occur not when someone cheats (i.e. intentionally breaks an explicitly agreed-upon rule), but either when players play according to conflicting house rules that were assumed rather than agreed upon in advance or when a crafty player exploits a lacuna or loophole not explicitly addressed by the rules (e.g. creates a housing shortage by never upgrading to hotels). Ultimately there is no supreme authority as to what rules we select or create, or how we resolve conflicts. If we are training for a tournament, we should follow the official rules, as they are the ones more likely to be adopted by that institution (though this is not necessarily so). If not, we may adopt whatever rules we like, according to the occasion and the preferences of the players involved. Language functions similarly, except that its rules are more complex; we rarely formally discuss the rules we choose to follow, and there are no authorities who create the official rules. However, there are language games where participants do discuss the rules: professional fields such as medicine and law, the sciences, the religions, and, of course, academic subjects like philosophy.

Essentially the late Wittgenstein pivots away from analytic philosophy and toward pragmatism: he emphasizes that the use of language and the meaning of words are determined more by context, use, and outcome than by syntax or conceptual definitions. Two experiences led to this U-turn in the interval between the *Tractatus* and the *Philosophical Investigations*: he taught in elementary school (1920–1926); and he read Peirce. Rorty recognized Wittgenstein as a kindred spirit and used his insights to express his growing professional and philosophical angst toward analytic philosophy, in an essay titled "Recent Metaphilosophy" and published in 1961. There he defined *metaphilosophy* as "the result of reflection upon the following inconsistent triad":

1 A game in which each player is at liberty to change the rules whenever he wishes can neither be won nor lost.
2 In philosophical controversy, the terms used to state criteria for the resolution of arguments mean different things to different philosophers; thus each side can take the rules of the game of controversy in a sense which will guarantee its own success (thus, in effect, changing the rules).
3 Philosophical arguments are, in fact, won and lost, for some philosophical positions do, in fact, prove weaker than others. (Rorty 1961: 299)

He then suggests there are three obvious ways of resolving this inconsistency. First, one insists that (3) is false by emphasizing (2). This *metaphilosophical skepticism* basically asserts that it is impossible for philosophy to make progress toward the truth. But, an individual can be pessimistic about this conclusion and abandon philosophy altogether, as a useless enterprise (i.e. "nailing Jell-O to the wall"); or one could be optimistic and, like Santayana, see inspiration rather than truth as the goal of philosophy (1961: 299–300). Second, one could say that (3) is obviously true and (2) is plausible but false. These *metaphilosophical realists* insist that "something external" to philosophical reasoning provides a check for claims and arguments, whether that "something" is common sense, history, or an eschatological goal at which inquiry aims (1961: 300–301). Throughout time, most philosophers have committed themselves to either skepticism or realism, the majority embracing some form of the latter.

Finally, one can "deny the truth of (1), and say that, on the contrary, philosophy is the greatest game of all precisely because it is the game of 'changing the rules'" (1961: 301). These philosophers see the function of philosophy as "making communication possible," therefore their role is to "make possible communication between competing metaphysicians and epistemologists" (ibid.). From this perspective, progress is not measured according to a specific standard but by either making communication intelligible between contrasting position, provocatively reframing conflicts, or by yielding novel but practical concepts. Naturally, Rorty calls this approach *metaphilosophical pragmatism*; and, although he links it explicitly to Dewey, it also fulfills Peirce's mandate of never blocking the path of inquiry.

Essentially Rorty applies Dewey's notion of inquiry as a congenial and constant pursuit to Wittgenstein's understanding of language games and family resemblances: philosophical inquiry is one among many language games that people play and, while its vocabulary, subjects, and methods may at times resemble some language games more than others, it possesses no qualities that make it necessarily distinct from the language games of science, art, baking, Monopoly, and so on.

He concludes by thanking analytic philosophy for "making us self-conscious about metaphilosophical issues," but chides it for continuing to insist upon reductionism. He notes that returning to reductionism continually gives analytic projects a "new lease on life," by reducing their critics to absurdity. Unfortunately, "they have lacked the courage to apply these analyses to themselves" (1961: 317).

Although he does not liberate himself from analytic philosophy for another twenty years, Rorty spends the remainder of his career clarifying the implication of this Deweyan–Wittgensteinian insight: analytic philosophy perceptively reveals philosophy to be the language game that talks about language games; but, rather than admitting philosophy's status as one language game among many, analytic philosophers uphold the authority of philosophy and of their tradition by reducing philosophy to *their preferred style of play*, thereby excluding and dismissing other styles of play as absurd or not philosophical. He explores the first half of this insight in 1965 in *The Linguistic Turn*, a survey of twentieth-century Anglo-American analytic thought in which he announces that linguistic philosophy is "the most recent philosophical revolution" because it promises that "philosophical problems are problems which may be solved (or dissolved) either by reforming language, or by understanding more about the language we presently use" (Rorty 1967: 60). Instructors widely adopted the book as an authoritative textbook on the subject, owing to Rorty's skill, insight, and genuine praise of linguistic philosophy, even though Rorty's conclusion reformulates his metaphilosophical criticisms.

In this iteration, analytic philosophy fails to live up to its promise because it cannot offer "either a presupposition-less method or agreed-upon criteria for success in dissolving philosophical problems" (Voparil 2010: 15). The history of philosophy shows that every time a philosopher successfully proposes a new start, direction, or method in philosophy, inevitably a future critic reveals the problematic assumptions at the heart of their revolution. As Voparil points out, Rorty cites several examples of this dialectic, but the best is also the most recent: Wittgenstein, who starts and ends his own philosophical revolution. This pattern repeats itself because no philosopher, no player in any language game, is neutral. All games occur within an exterior (historical) and interior (psychological) context, therefore the needs, content, and agenda of any revolution or revolutionary are conditioned by place.

There is no end to this cycle, because there is no "presuppositionless starting point" and no rationally agreed-upon criterion for success. Rorty cites Nietzsche and James as the first philosophers to recognize that, "[t]o know what method to adopt, one must already have arrived at some metaphysical and some epistemological conclusions" (Rorty, quoted in Voparil 2010: 16). Of course, they respond to this reality differently. Nietzsche infers that the methods we adopt are purely in our interest, the *will to power*, whereas James concludes that we should select methods according to the demands of our context, in other words he recommends *pragmatism*. In *Contingency, Irony, and Solidarity*, Rorty (1989) will split the difference, saying that we must create new methods of discourse to fulfill both the private, Nietzschean need for self-creation and the public, Deweyan good of sustaining democratic societies, but that these are two *incommensurate* projects. They are separate language games, adopted for separate but equally important ends.

True, the vocabulary and topics of these language games often overlap or conflict, but the history of philosophy from Plato through Kant has been founded on the fallacy that one of them is reducible to the other or that there is a third thing, like the Platonic Forms or Kant's synthetic a priori, in other words a *skyhook*, which can lift us to a point outside our contingent language games, to a *view from nowhere*. The best we can do is accept the fallibility of these games and use them to develop either new vocabularies to describe our personal identities better or conceptual tools for solving practical problems. Furthermore, when private interests and the public good conflict in practice, there is again no method or standard to determine when or why we should favor one over the other. Our choices will be relative to the situation and to our personal preferences, as determined by our idiosyncratic experiences and the contingent values of our culture.

Consequently, democratic societies must develop creative means for advancing both private needs and the public good without unfairly compromising one or the other, and democratic citizens should become *liberal ironists* who continue to advance their private interest while remaining sensitive to the contingency of their beliefs and to how their worldview and actions negatively impact or exclude the interests of others. The best resource we possess for self-creation, creative democracy, and solidarity with people who do not share our commitments is literature, broadly construed to include everything, from philosophy to novels, to films, even to comic books. Such texts broaden our experience, help us understand the world from the perspectives of others, and fund our imagination.

Readers familiar with Rorty may notice that I have skipped over his most important work, *Philosophy and the Mirror of Nature*. Rorty's work can easily be divided into his early analytic phase and his late pragmatic phase, just like that of Wittgenstein, his hero. Thus *Contingency, Irony, and Solidarity* can be viewed as the first major work of his late career, and *Philosophy and the Mirror of Nature* as the last major work of his early career. However, it is important to note that, while Rorty's constructive contributions to analytic pragmatism end with the latter, it becomes the foundational text of the movement's latest phase. Just as the *Principia* or the *Tractatus* reconstructed logical positivism to establish the problems and methods of analytic philosophy, *Mirror* establishes the problems and methods of what has been called neopragmatism. Ironically, this label has been applied both to critics of Rorty's critique of representationalism and to those who have attempted to defend or extend it. Their criticisms and contributions will be the focus of the next chapter. For now, I must turn to the central thesis of *Mirror*: that science is (or at least realist epistemologies of science are), like philosophy, merely one language game among many. This *antirealism* is a much harder sell, and for deeply pragmatic reasons. For example, while there may be theoretical ambiguities in science or assumptions that are socially constructed, when I board my return flight to Portland this afternoon, my confidence suggests that I believe the science of aerodynamics to be more than merely a sophisticated language game. It seems that aerodynamics *must* represent brute reality better than, or in a different way from, philosophy or literature, otherwise I would not place my life in its hands.

Rorty is reluctant to assign this privileged status to science, or at least not to the leading epistemologies of his day that share this bias, specifically *the correspondence theory of truth* and *representationalism*. The correspondence theory of truth, or direct realism, is the classic dualistic assumption that reality exists independently of our perception of it and that we know it either through careful observation and classification (Aristotle—Locke—Lewis) or through the derivation of fundamental logical principles (Plato—Descartes—Russell). Representationalism, or indirect realism, agrees with Sellars, his rejection of the given, and the view that we do not sense reality directly, but argues that we can develop linguistic concepts that describe our perceptions more accurately. Thus we can evaluate claims to be true or false on the basis of their precision. I need not describe Rorty's critique in detail, as this entire chapter has been a prelude. Basically, he uses the insights of Lewis, Quine, and Sellars to show that neither mathematics and logic nor sensation can be used to support direct realism. He then uses Wittgenstein, Kuhn, and Davidson to critique indirect realism and to assert that even science is one language game among many. It does not have a special franchise on reality, because Kuhn teaches us that multiple paradigms could pragmatically explain causal occurrences and Davidson teaches us that language games can function through their own internal semantics, without either being reduced to an authoritative scheme such as science or requiring empirical verification—as long as the inquirers reach consensus.

Thus Rorty declares *the end of philosophy*, or at least the end of analytic epistemology and of the Platonic and Kantian project to represent reality accurately through an authoritative description. He argues that we must turn to Dewey and the pragmatists, because they recognized, one century before us, that the purpose of philosophical inquiry is to develop not an absolute ideology but creative conceptual tools designed to ameliorate the concrete problems of lived experience. Thus philosophers should recognize tradition as a form of comparative literature, which analyses a text using the interpretative tools of continential philosophers such as Martin Heidegger, Jacques Derrida, or Michel Foucault, to deconstruct problematic ideas, while turning to the pragmatists to discover more social goods that should join the plurality of those already enjoyed by democratic societies. Meanwhile Rorty expects scientific discoveries to continue unabated, as science has not significantly needed the help of epistemology since the standardization of the scientific method. In a nutshell, the title of Eduardo Mendieta's anthology, *Take Care of Freedom and Truth Will Take Care of Itself*, captures Rorty's position succinctly and well. It is a title taken from one of the interviews with Rorty contained in that book.

– 5 –

Hope and the
Contemporary Pragmatists

During the period when pragmatism was eclipsed by analytic philosophy, the pragmatists found new venues for their work by engaging other philosophers and other traditions that were also largely excluded from participation in mainstream conferences and from publication in academic journals. These engagements resulted not only in interesting new applications of pragmatism but also in new professional alliances.

In *A Fashionable Nihilism* (2002), Bruce Wilshire describes how, during this exile, many philosophers developed their own societies to discuss and publicize their work. The Society for the Advancement of American Philosophy (SAAP), founded in 1972, became the leading venue for pragmatists. Soon the SAAP and other groups began to convene during the annual meetings of the American Philosophical Association (APA), after the official program concluded. Eventually these groups reached critical mass, called themselves "the committee on pluralism," and conspired to organize a revolt against the elected leadership of the APA. They unexpectedly launched their coup during the officer nominations meeting of 1979. The APA leadership stopped the elections, but not before several pragmatists were elected to administrative positions. Coincidentally, Richard Rorty was president of the APA and decided to let the vote stand.

Outrage ensued and set in for months, but the result was

reforms intended to prevent another takeover and protocols for ensuring a more equitable representation on the APA program and in leadership positions. John Lachs, one of the pragmatists involved in the "pluralist revolt," claimed at a later stage that the revolt had achieved its goals, since its purpose was never vindictive: all it intended was to "introduce a wholesome pluralism into the profession" (McKenna & Pratt 2015: 196). Despite these concessions, some animosity remains, but one may hope that the efforts of future generations of philosophers will dispel it.

In the spirit of the "pluralist revolt," this chapter surveys how pragmatism engaged with a variety of traditions in order to enrich and apply its generative themes and find hope in the twentieth and twenty-first centuries.

Jürgen Habermas (1929–) and the Public Sphere

Like John Rawls in the United States in the late twentieth century, Jürgen Habermas continues to be the most illustrious political philosopher of Europe. His work focuses on developing a "democratic politics beyond the nation-state" through the "process of European unification as a potential model for the transition from international law to cosmopolitan society which he advocates" (Cronin 2006: vii). This project arose from several sources. First and foremost, Habermas's long life and career span the painful history of Germany in the twentieth and twenty-first centuries, a history he witnessed firsthand: from the horrors and madness of national socialism (1933–1945), through Germany's difficult reconstruction and tragic division during the Cold War (1961–1989), to its reunification and emergence as the economic and political leader of the European Union (1992–) and to the more recent cascade of crises it suffered, such as the aggressive foreign policy of the United States during the Bush administration (2000–2008), the deep and uneven economic recessions (2007–2016), the massive migration of refugees after the Arab Spring (2010–2012), and various xenophobic returns to nationalistic and authoritarian policies or political candidates both within and

202 American Pragmatism

outside the Union, for example Brexit (2016–) and the US presidential election of 2016.

This tremendous experience justifies Habermas's hope that a peaceful global democratic political order inspired by Kant's cosmopolitanism can be achieved, as an alternative to the brutal and competitive national regimes of the previous centuries. Now in his nineties, Habermas continues to write and bear witness to our times. Thus, given his influence on Rorty and his prior embrace of pragmatism as a method of fostering the democratic systems, norms, practices, and habits that are needed if we want to counter the ills of neoliberalism or the global expansion of free market capitalism and democratic institutions, his work is the best example of the global impact of pragmatism nowadays. Also, through Habermas's studies at the Frankfurt School, pragmatism entered the orbit of European critical theory; and an examination of historical parallels highlights the strengths and weaknesses of pragmatic social inquiry in the twentieth century. Against this background, the current chapter presents the ideas of the Frankfurt School and its criticism of pragmatism, then compares them with the social philosophy of Dewey and C. Wright Mills, and from there proceeds to an examination of Habermas's synthesis of Marxism and pragmatism.

The critical theory of the Frankfurt School centers on two modifications related to Marxism. First, the Frankfurt School was "not vulgarly deterministic about economic issues but took a complex view of them"; and, second, it "condemned capitalist society, whose ills could not easily be meliorated" (Kuklick 1977: 231). These modifications allowed the School to critique "not just the economically exploitative aspects of the social order but also the dreariness of cultural and personal life under capitalism"; thus it incorporated insights from aesthetics, existentialism, and psychoanalysis into their analysis of social problems, as well as economics (ibid.). Fleeing the rise of national socialism and remaining in exile throughout World War II (1933–1939), the School relocated to Greenwich Village through the assistance of Columbia University, where Dewey still worked, just a few blocks away from the New School for Social Research. Co-founded by

Dewey along with Thorstein Veblen, Kallen, and others in 1919, the New School intended to continue the fruitful inter-action between pragmatism and the social sciences and to develop new theories, concepts, and methods for ameliorating social problems. Despite these opportunities for collaboration on similar concerns, the members of the Frankfurt School did not feel comfortable in the United States, and the country itself quickly became the subject of their social critiques. Above all, they worried that "American mass culture, indeed, was fascistic." According to Kuklick, these philosophers "could only imagine that a healthy cultural life was determined from above; culture for them was aristocratic and was degraded and degenerate if it were not" (ibid.). Their best work on this subject appears in *The Authoritarian Personality* (1950), a collective volume that analyses the relationship between "authoritarianism and family structure" in the United States and concludes that there is a high probability of fascism aris-ing there (ibid.).

The members of the Frankfurt School were equally critical of pragmatism. Philip Deen (2010) provides the best summary of the misunderstandings and missed opportunities between the two schools. Basically, the Frankfurt School dismissed pragmatism as "the manifestation of the worst of America's national culture—the crude utilitarianism of success, profit, and anti-intellectualism" (2010: 243). Their most sustained criticism of pragmatism appears in Horkheimer's *The Eclipse of Reason*, originally a series of public lectures delivered at Columbia in 1944 in which Horkheimer accuses pragmatism of putting the ends above the means rather than defending objective reason as "the abstract functioning of the thinking mechanism," which includes the faculties of "classification, inference, and deduction, no matter what the specific content" (Horkheimer 1974: 3). Thus, as Deen explains, pragmatism becomes "incorporated into the dominant cultural logic of its day," because it cannot realize that "the objects of everyday perception are socially constituted." Inevitably, this "reduc-tion of thought to instrument opens the door to domination" and "subjective reason becomes the process of rationaliza-tion whereby all of existence is demythologized, that is, evaluated by efficiency alone, then wrapped in the mythology of the enlightenment. " Pragmatism has "no critical potential" because it abandons "issues of value" and "collapses into the cultural logic of late capitalism" (Deen 2010: 246).

Unsurprisingly, the entire Frankfurt School soon returned to Germany after the war; but one important member, Herbert Marcuse, remained in the United States until his retirement in 1965. Unlike Horkheimer and the others, Marcuse enjoyed American culture, even though his best works, *Eros and Civilization* (1955) and *One-Dimensional Man* (1964), remain astute explorations and criticisms of the American psyche. Deen is of the view that Marcuse had a better, though flawed, understanding of pragmatism and adduces Marcuse's 1941 review of Dewey's 1938 book *Logic: The Theory of Inquiry* as an example. Deen claims that, while Marcuse still agrees with Horkheimer's inaccurate assumption that Dewey's "material logic, is actually idealistic" and "robs inquiry of its critical capacity" (Deen 2010: 247–8), he makes three other distinctions that his German colleagues missed: he accurately separates pragmatism from positivism; realizes that, for the pragmatists, inquiry begins with problematic situations, not with hypothetical conceptual problems; and admits that their naturalism supports an engagement with social problems. However, Marcuse still insists that Dewey's contextualism and naturalism collapse into predetermined scientistic solutions to social problems, and that his "[i]nstrumentalism possesses no standpoint of critique that does not already presuppose the dominant cultural commitments" (ibid.). Deen argues that ultimately Marcuse failed to notice several advantages of Dewey's approach, such as the active experimental character of inquiry, or to take stock of the fact that Dewey's fallibilism and value pluralism resist mere submission to capitalistic motives, or to see that Dewey's Darwinian naturalism connects his political commentary both to culture and to economics (2010: 251–254).

These advantages are on full display in several short books written against the backdrop of the Great Depression (1929–1939), in the years leading up to World War II. For example, in *The Public and Its Problems* (1927), Dewey warns about the eclipse of the public through the organization of special interest groups that use the new tools of mass communication to disseminate propaganda for the benefit of corporate interests. In *Individualism Old and New* (1930), he laments the identity crises experienced by the multitudes of lost individuals, who cope with the destruction of their lives and communities through the mechanisms of capitalism and industrialization. He also warns about the modified version of pioneer individualism on offer, namely the problematic entanglement of liberty with entrepreneurialism that prefigures contemporary libertarianism. This modification only makes matters worse, because it further isolates the lost individual from her community by reducing citizenship to the pursuit of personal economic interests and rationalizes the creation of a predatory political economy, which caters to the private profit of an industrial and corporate oligarchy. In fact we should acknowledge that, during this period between the era of the common man and the Cold War, the term "American exceptionalism" was used primarily by political Marxists, for example by Jay Lovestone, the general secretary of the Communist Party in America, in 1927 and by Joseph Stalin in 1929, to label the United States' historical and inexplicable resistance to socialist ideas in general and to a communist revolution in particular (see Fried 1997; Pease 2009).

As indicated by this genealogy of American individualism, Dewey also considers how culture shapes US political life. In *A Common Faith* (1934) he defends religious communities against the aggressive forms of atheism, political and scientific, that undermine the bonds of faith which sustain such communities, especially during a crisis like the Great Depression, and also against authoritarian forms of religious fundamentalism that intend to mobilize the faithful for political movements that undermine democracy by governing and legislating on the authority of supernatural claims. All these critiques reach their apogee in *Freedom and Culture* (1939), where Dewey argues that the complexity of human behavior should humble theorists and encourage them to avoid the reduction of political shifts to a single, determinate cultural value or material cause. In his view, totalitarianism results when the vast power of the state responds to a crisis by embracing an absolutist ideology, whether religious, political, economic, racial, philosophical, or otherwise and uses violence and oppression to enforce its monistic vision at home or abroad. Dewey admits that theory enables us to understand, recognize, and anticipate potential threats to democracy, but the best defense is to guard the institutions that enable democracy: public education, social welfare programs, freedom of the press, scientific research, protocols, and political norms.

Furthermore, Marxist critics of pragmatism often forget the work of the sociologist C. Wright Mills (1916–1962). As an undergraduate of Texas A&M, Mills encountered pragmatism through his studies with George Gentry and David L. Miller, who had been a student of Mead at the University of Chicago. Building on their insights, he developed a theory of the sociological imagination. This theory was meant to resist the positivistic assumptions of Talbot Parson's social action theory, which hypothesized that social behavior can be reduced to discrete units, namely acts made up of an actor, a goal, a situation, and the values that regulate these components. Just like logical positivism, Parson's research paradigm synergized with the professionalization of sociology, because it claimed that through accurate observation and recording sociology could progress incrementally, as other objective sciences do (Dillon 2014: 161).

By contrast, Mills felt that sociology should be concerned with "all the social worlds in which men have lived, are living, and might live" (Mills 1959: 132), and therefore must return to the "empirical realities in individual lives, and their intersection with history and social structures" (Dillon 2014: 228). In other words sociology should describe our lived social experience, rather than reducing social behavior to data and theoretical explanations. More importantly, Mills turns the tables on the discipline of sociology by treating its professionalization as a subject of sociological inquiry and analysis. According to Cornell West, this reversal enabled Mills to explicate how, rather than being objective and apolitical, social action theory supported the "corporate liberal

establishment" by encouraging a "conformist and compla-
cent academy"; thus Mills's work focuses on "two basic
features of postwar America: the decreasing availability of
creative human powers in the populace and the stultifying
socio-economic circumstances that promoted this decrease"
(West 1989: 113 and 125).

Early suspicion about these features grew into a more
strident form of radical social criticism, which honed the
experimentalism of Dewey's social inquiry and mirrored the
acuity of Marcuse's critical analysis of American culture. West
describes Mills's first major work, *Sociology and Pragmatism*
(1964), as aspiring to "awaken the Promethean energies of
the masses by means of critical intelligence and social action,"
through the "critical intelligence" of the public intellectual
(West 1989: 125). It also admitted that Dewey was unable
to fashion the sharper critical tools and methods needed to
challenge the oppressive political–economic strategies of the
corporate liberal elite during the rise of mass society. Thus
Mills supplied these devices in his popular trilogy *The New
Men of Power* (1948), *White Collar* (1951), and *The Power
Elite* (1956). In these critical works he identifies (in West's
words) "three basic intellectual fronts" on which public intellectuals must use social inquiry:

> First, it must expose corporate liberalism as an elitist ideology
> that pays lip service to the ideas of democracy and freedom
> and conceals gross inequality and people's powerlessness and
> lack of control over their lives. Second, it has to contend with
> Marxism by critically appropriating its powerful insights
> regarding class inequality and the power of capital while dis-
> carding its rather grand expectations of the working class.
> Third, Mills must hold at arm's length the pervasive "tragic-
> sense-of-life" perspectives that either foreclose social action or
> limit it to piecemeal social engineering. (West 1989: 128)

Consequently, Mills recognizes Dewey's "nostalgia for
small-town American life," as West (1989: 125) puts it, as a
genuine liability; but, unlike the Frankfurt School, whose critique is based on caricature, he displays a more accurate and
charitable awareness of the merits and flaws of pragmatism.

This enables him to reconstruct pragmatic social inquiry by giving it a more radical form, less vulnerable to supporting the status quo and more sensitive to how the American political economy manipulates the economic interests of the professional classes and of the working classes while minimizing, hiding, or excusing the exclusion and oppression of minorities at home and rationalizing the necessity of an aggressive interventionist foreign policy during the Cold War. Furthermore, these tools would not be idle, as both Mills and Marcuse, through their activism and the popularity of their books, profoundly influenced the politics of the New Left and the countercultural movement of the 1960s and 1970s.

Ultimately Habermas is the best demonstration of pragmatism's potential when compared with critical theory during the Cold War. Although a student of Horkheimer, Habermas dramatically breaks ties with his mentor, using pragmatism to reconstruct the reductive dialectical materialism of the Frankfurt School. By the mid-twentieth century, most modern democracies possessed effective socialist programs (e.g. universal healthcare, collective bargaining rights, social security, and other welfare programs) and supported socialist political parties and politicians (e.g. in France and Canada); and a few prosperous democratic socialist nation-states existed (e.g. in Scandinavia). However, there were also multiple nation-states organized around various authoritarian forms of socialism: the Soviet Union, its satellite states in Eastern Europe, East Germany, China, and North Korea. By contrast, nation-states tended in increasing numbers to be organized according to free market capitalism in theory, but in practice to be governed by authoritarian dictators or military regimes.

Habermas recognizes that these historical paradoxes pose a serious problem for Marxist critical theory because they demonstrate that neither socialism nor capitalism inevitably leads to democracy or to authoritarianism. A nation's economy heavily influences its politics and culture; but these are not determined by it. Therefore Habermas turns to the pragmatism of Peirce, Dewey, and Mead to uncover the specific practices and institutions that enable and maintain democracy at home and peaceful international cooperation abroad. Through this research he develops a theory of universal pragmatics, which conceives of democracy as an extended public political conversation carried out among citizens for the purpose of controlling state power and of maintaining a productive economy, social policies that support equal political participation and economic opportunity, a just legal system, and national defense. For this public dialogue to be successful, its participants require the skills, knowledge, information, and venues needed to practice *communicative rationality*, which is the process of developing a shared understanding of political differences and mutual trust so as to reduce social conflict by establishing shared democratic norms to guide ethical governance and policies. Habermas's most thorough articulation of these concepts is to be found in his books *Communication and the Evolution of Society* (1976) and *The Theory of Communicative Action* (1981).

But Habermas is an exceptionally technical and precise thinker, and the essays gathered in his 1989 book *The Structural Transformation of the Public Sphere* serve as the most concise and accessible introductions to these ideas for anyone who is not well versed in the vocabulary and nuances of political theory. He defines the public sphere as any "domain of our social life in which such a thing as public opinion can be formed" for the purpose of discussing "matters of general interest without being subject to coercion" (Habermas 1989: 231). Its existence depends more on the participants' ability to "assemble and unite freely" and to "express and publicize their opinions freely" than on the specific location of this conversation or the means by which it occurs. Political conversation takes place when "public discussions concern objects connected with the practice of the state" (ibid.). In a democracy, the state not only avoids coercion, but supports and protects its citizens' freedom to engage in public political conversation and is subordinate to public opinion or to the "functions of criticism and control of organized state authority that the public exercises informally, as well as formally during periodic elections" (ibid.). Thus the public sphere functions as an intermediary between the state and society.

Once these terms are defined, Habermas provides a genealogy of the public sphere's emergence and diversification
during the Enlightenment and attributes these processes to a
variety of factors such as the clarification and institution of
new political principles (e.g. freedom of speech, freedom of
assembly) and the opportunity for more citizens to participate
in the public sphere enabled by greater economic prosperity
and education, and through the development of a political
daily press (1989: 232–234). He concludes with a brief but
masterful survey of the mechanisms through which public
opinion is shaped, as well as an explanation of how they can
subvert communicative rationality, thereby undermining the
practice of democracy. In mass industrial democracies, the
primary ideological rift emerges between those who favor
the use of state power for the public good and those who
favor private interests; and the allegiances of citizens usually
(but not necessarily) correspond to their economic class.

This rift requires constant attention because, without the
economic security that public welfare programs provide,
either the poor and vulnerable will be unable to participate
in the public sphere or their attempts will be unsuccessful.
Success also depends on a citizen's access to an adequate
education, which allows her to access credible information,
evaluate its claims, construct her own view, and convincingly
communicate it in the public sphere.

Furthermore, the existence of propaganda and of special
interest groups actively thwarts communicative rationality,
because these deliberately try to misinform the citizens, to prevent the participation of those who disagree with the agenda
of such groups, or to overwhelm other opinions through the
strength of numbers. Without secure checks and balances on
state power or on private influence, the public sphere itself
eventually becomes subverted, social conflict increases, and
participation decreases, as citizens become cynical as a result
of witnessing the erosion of democratic norms. Consequently,
democracies end informally when the citizens stop participating in the public sphere, or the latter becomes merely a
forum for propaganda. They end formally when an organized interest group or enough frustrated citizens embrace an

authoritarian ideology, seize control over the state power, and use it to impose their ideology on society. Thus, political revolutions occur when citizens lack the will to continue democratic dialogue, no longer see one another as sincere, or legitimate public spheres no longer exist (Habermas 1989: 235–236). While not as polemic as Mills or as intriguing as Marcuse, Habermas provides a sophisticated theory of democracy as public discourse that merges the best insights of Marx and Dewey. His theory shows how material conditions influence political opinion and structure political processes more than other determining factors; but it does not reduce democracy to a system of government. Instead it presents democracy as a way of life that depends on the quality of each citizen's political participation and is reinforced through the vital social institutions that provide the necessary education, economic security, and credible information for democratic practice to be effective.

Huw Price (1953–) and Truth as a Normative Practice

Unfortunately, when Rorty announced the end of philosophy, few of his contemporaries appreciated the claim that their profession had ended, especially as his conclusions appeared to be a sophisticated form of relativism, if not a bourgeois nihilism. As happened to the Chicago pragmatists at the beginning of the century, in this case too non-philosophers embraced Rorty's insights, but mainstream analytic philosophy largely dismissed his work without reading it. However, given Rorty's clout and professional stature, he could not be ignored, and the controversy of *Mirror* renewed the interest in pragmatism, even though this interest was more critical than charitable.

While Rorty shifted his attention to literary and sociopolitical projects, he continued to engage his critics for the remainder of his career. The best introduction to these critiques and to Rorty's responses to them is *Rorty and His Critics* (Brandom 2000). This collection of articles on Rorty is edited by Rorty's student Robert Brandom, engages the most glaring loose ends in Rorty's pragmatist turn, and its contributors could make a "who's who" list of neopragmatists at the turn of the century. In his introduction, Brandom classifies the material into essays that are critical of Rorty's antirealism and require him to clarify his understanding of the distinctions between philosophy, science, and poetry and essays that worry about the political dangers of his antirealism (Brandom 2000: xx).

For example, Jürgen Habermas disagrees with Rorty's antirealism for pragmatic reasons. He finds no fault with Rorty's preference for practical epistemic concerns such as intelligibility, constructive discourse, or an interlocutor's responsibility toward his community of inquiry over classic epistemological obsessions with truth obtained through conceptual certainty or through accurate representation of reality, because this preference echoes his own criteria for communicative rationality (Brandom 2000: 32). Instead, he argues that Rorty's semantics conflicts with our lived experience—our lifeworld—and the everyday actions and activities where, much as in Dewey's version of the reflex arc, we continually adjust our actions in response to changes in our environment, a process comparable with maintaining balance on a bicycle.

By contrast, Jacques Bouveresse worries that Rorty's deflation of the dogmas of analytic realism has erased important disciplinary distinctions not only between philosophy and science, but also between philosophy and poetry. Consequently, "philosophy hasn't yet found a way of defending its identity against the threat of absorption coming from the sciences, except by moving closer to literature and art" (Brandom 2000: 130). Furthermore, this drift entangles Rorty more deeply both in the literary criticism of the new "academic left," which he dislikes on account of its obsession with identity politics, and in the thought of continental philosophers he admires, such as Derrida and Foucault, who have "no real place for refutation" as long as we can produce a "half-formed new vocabulary which vaguely promises great things" (2000: 143; see Rorty 1989: 9). Finally, James Conant argues that Rorty's sentimental plea to minimize cruelty in the hope of increasing solidarity cannot guard against totalitarian regimes and the cruelty that George Orwell dramatized in 1948, in his novel *1984*. While Orwell may or may not be an epistemological realist, Conant uses textual evidence from *1984* and other Orwellian writings to show that appreciation of truth is the most important bulwark against totalitarianism, since one of the main political objectives of these regimes is to control reality and the public by depriving "us of our hold on the concept of objective truth" through constant surveillance, through the destruction of language, through propaganda, and through the rewriting of history (Brandom 2000: 285).

In response, Rorty points out that it is not the epistemic stability of realism that Orwell's character Winston Smith requires because, even when Winston does cling to facts, they are impotent by comparison to the power of the totalitarian state. At best, facts sustain him in private moments; but no appeal to facts, arguments, or theories will prevent an authoritarian person or regime from causing harm.

Most of these critiques against Rorty persist, but remain unresolved; nevertheless, the most strident criticisms come from within pragmatism, specifically from those pragmatists who are committed to a Peircean theory of truth. In general, they see Rorty as the inevitable outcome of an overemphasis on Jamesian pluralism at the expense of a more robust theory of inquiry. Cheryl Misak leads this recent revival of Peirce's scientific realism; but her move is problematic for at least two reasons. First, her commentaries on Peirce's epistemology minimize the significance of his metaphysics, especially his reinstatement of the random and vague as ontological states. Second, even though this emphasis on scientific realism in Peirce and, to a lesser degree, in James and Dewey has defended pragmatism from the accusation that it lacks a substantial epistemology, it also reduces pragmatism to a theory of truth at the expense of the aesthetic, ethical, existential, and social content that most scholars of this tradition find invigorating.

This angle enables Misak in her later historical works (for example Misak 2013), and also others, such as Talisse and

Aikin (2011), to construct a narrow narrative of pragmatism, one that ignores the richness of the tradition, excludes the fascinating work of many figures, and dismisses or undermines the work of contemporary philosophers who are using pragmatism to engage in a wider variety of subjects. These Pericean pragmatists have successfully repopularized pragmatism for the twenty-first century, but did so through a one-dimensional interpretation of Peirce that, again, forces pragmatism to conform to analytic philosophy's obsession with epistemology. It can be said in their defense that their reconstruction is motivated by a sincere concern that Rorty's pragmatism is either philosophically problematic or politically dangerous for the reasons contained in the aforementioned criticisms. Admittedly, the most glaring problem with Rorty's antirealism is its inability to explain how inquiry functions. Fortunately, the Australian epistemologist Huw Price suggests the most interesting resolution of this tension between neopragmatism and science. His entire pragmatic naturalism coalesces around these issues and provides not only a robust theory of truth that should satisfy the Peirceans, but also a thorough defense of pluralism that does not invalidate the heirs of William James.

The most accessible version of this resolution can be found in Price's 1999 essay "Truth as Convenient Friction," which advocates for a humbler understanding of truth as a practical tool or as a byproduct of inquiry rather than as its determining *telos*. He begins with a claim advanced by Rorty in 1998, in a piece titled "Is Truth the Goal of Inquiry?," that there is no meaningful pragmatic distinction between truth and verification as normative commitments of inquiry. Price argues that Rorty's pragmatic evaluation of truth as norm of inquiry is an empirical claim that can be verified by examining human behavior and practice. Much like Habermas in his earlier appeal to the practical necessity of truth when we continuously adjust our actions through transactions with our perpetually changing lifeworld, Price claims that such an adjustment "is a behavioral pattern so central to what we presently regard as worthwhile human life that no reasonable person would knowingly condone the experiment," most likely out of fear we would be harmed through our neglect of brute reality (Price in Talisse & Aikin 2011: 451).

Price also explains the significance of truth within our linguistic practices, specifically what he calls assertoric dialogue or conversations through which we assert, defend, and evaluate propositions or claims that can be verified only empirically, not through their content (e.g. "The meteorologist expects rain this Saturday"). Propositions of this kind are crucial because they constitute the kind of claims that science investigates, as their truth value depends upon empirical verification. But Rorty's antirealism cannot explain how they function, since his rejects the notion that statements represent or correspond to reality. Therefore it is through these propositions, and through inquiries into their truth value, that Rorty's antirealism seems impractical, or even absurd. Returning to the example of whether it will rain on Saturday, it seems obvious that we can simply step outside on Saturday and check whether it is raining. If it is, the statement is true; if not, the statement is false. Simple enough? Maybe, but Rorty struggles to develop a compelling explanation, consistent with his antirealism.

In these cases, Price argues that all members of the community of inquiry must practice "three norms, in order of increasing strength, roughly: sincerity, justification, and truth itself," whereas Rorty's antirealism proposes that only sincerity and justification are needed for inquiry (Talisse & Aikin 2011: 452). Price insists that truth is needed as a norm and is the strongest, for several reasons. First, truth is the "automatic and quite unconscious sense of engagement" that we experience when we inquire together. Second, truth is the "grit that makes our individual opinions engage with one another." Third, it motivates inquiry. Finally, truth functions as the social glue that enables our shared inquiry as a group; it is the norm that governs this process (ibid.).

Thus truth is a practical, not a theoretical norm, and it enables the community of inquiry and the process of inquiry, regardless of any other metaphysical status. For example, when I play the board game Clue with my family, we all expect that there is a single "accusation," that is, an assertoric proposition that correctly matches the three cards (person, weapon, place) randomly placed in the "confidential" envelope before the game begins. This expectation demonstrates how the norm of truth enlists our participation and guides our actions and questions during the game. But let us suppose that, the next time we play, I fake the placement of the cards in the envelope and I pocket them through sleight of hand. Even though there are no cards in the envelope, the game can continue as long as the players remain committed to the norm of truth, that is, to the practical assumption that a true "accusation" exists and that our choices can help us uncover it. This second round of Clue seems to confirm Rorty's claim that truth is not an essential ontological feature of reality, while it still supports Price's view that, even if we cannot reach a final representation of truth (either because it does not exist, as in Rorty's antirealism, or because we lack the ability to know for certain that we have discovered it, which is Peirce's final opinion), as long as we postulate truth as a norm, inquiry can continue unaffected.

More importantly, Price doubts that "giving up truth," as antirealists do, is really an option open to us, particularly in our lived experience—but also in our linguistic practices, which in that case would be radically different from the style of discourse we are accustomed to. Returning to my own example of Clue, how would we play the game if we intentionally abandoned our inquiry to discover the correct accusation? How long for would such a bizarre style of play uphold our interest, before we either quitted or relapsed into the familiar habit of an inquiry that assumes truth as a norm? Finally, Price admits that Rorty is often ambiguous as to whether he thinks that we should reject the truth as norm or simply be "suspicious of the realist–antirealist debate itself" (Talisse & Aikin 2011: 453). Price agrees with the latter position and insists that the former is misguided. Instead, he thinks that we should reject this dualism "not by rejecting truth and representation, but by recognizing that in virtue of the most plausible story about the function and origins of these notions, they simply do not sustain that sort of metaphysical weight" (ibid.).

Price concludes by placing himself close to Rorty's minimalistic understanding of truth but explains why he prefers a normative rather than a semantic notion of truth. First, it maintains his connection to pragmatism rather than neopragmatism, by grounding truth in practice. However, when making truth a part of inquiry separate from the process of justification, Price admits: "This contrast reflects a deep tension within pragmatism"—namely a split between the Peircean theory of truth and the Jamesian method of experience. Although Price leans in the direction of Peirce, who could not avoid the "'ontological' or reductive question about truth," he laments that Rorty and the pragmatists in general do not appreciate "the range of possibilities for nonreductive pragmatism about the truth," for example "explanatory or genealogical approaches" (Talisse & Aikin 2011: 454).

Thus Price defends a genealogical approach that attempts to explain the function of truth as a norm of inquiry. In this regard he contrasts with Peirce, because he focuses on an "explanation of practices, rather than a reduction of their objects"; and he explains how understanding *truth as a convenient fiction* has several advantages in comparison to Peirce's notion of warranted assertibility:

> Without truth, the wheels of argument do not engage; disagreements slide past one another. This is true of disagreements about warranted assertibility. If we did not already have truth, in other words, we simply could not argue about warranted assertibility. For we could be aware that we have different opinions about what is warrantedly assertible, without that difference of opinion seeming to matter. What makes it matter is the fact that we subscribe to a practice according to which disagreement is an indication of culpable error, on one side or other; in another words, that we already take ourselves to be subject to the norms of truth and falsity … [thus] assertoric dialogue requires an intolerance of disagreement. This needs to be present already in the background, a pragmatic presupposition of judgment itself. I am not a maker of assertions, a judger, at all, unless I am already playing to win, in the sense defined by the third norm. (Talisse & Aikin 2011: 464)

In other words, truth is not located at the end of an inquiry but at the beginning. In order for the inquiry to occur, we must already possess an implicit understanding of the truth, which gives us both the motive for assertoric dialogue and possession of the means for evaluating a proposition prior to the beginning of inquiry. Much like Peircean doubt, truth functions as the irritation that occurs when we disagree with another's claim; at the same time truth provides the means for assuaging that irritation. Indeed, the reason why this irritation occurs is that we already possess the norm of truth: we used it almost reflexively, to judge an informal claim during a casual conversation.

In conclusion, Price reconstructs the most insightful concerns of Rorty's antirealism in order to avoid the pitfalls of Peirce's flirtation with realism and reductivism. Furthermore, seeing truth as the practical norm that motivates, unites, and guides inquirers in their attempts to uncover, clarify, critique, and resolve their differences reveals a richer understanding of inquiry, which is consistent with our lived experience and not too vulnerable to realist critiques. It explains how inquiry progresses; and it does so without seeing this process as an idle linguistic exercise, or its results as merely interesting semantic refinements of our vocabulary. Although Misak avoids a total endorsement of Price's notion of truth as "convenient friction," she speaks highly of it in her essay "Making Disagreements Matter," where she explains how this notion aids moral and political inquiry by revealing the significant and critical differences between interlocutors even as it provides an inclusive means of resolving conflict (Misak in Talisse & Aikin 2011: 477–478).

Further, Misak finds Price's appeal to normative practices to be more successful than the "stronger" but less "plausible" forms defended by Habermas and Apel, which are too "transcendental." She also views it as enriching Joseph Heath's more "modest" examination of normative practices as they unfold in real situations, for example in traffic court. She insists that what Price and Heath get right is the value of experiencing disagreement which motivates deliberative democratic debate (Talisse & Aikin 2011: 480–481). One therefore assumes that Price satisfies Misak's hopes not only for an improved theory of truth that should inform pragmatic inquiry but also for one that meets Talisse's call for a form of democratic political inquiry that can accommodate the problem of real pluralism.

Gloria Anzaldúa (1942–2004) and the Coyolxauhqui Imperative

Perhaps the most promising development among pragmatists results from their increasing engagement with American Indian philosophy and other philosophical traditions throughout the Americas. In *Native Pragmatism*, Scott Pratt (2002) explains the deep debt that American thought in general, but pragmatism in particular, owes to the contributions of various indigenous sources during the United States' transition from being a group of thirteen British colonies to beginning its own expansion westward, as an independent unitary state.

According to Pratt, three types of evidence confirm the indigenous influence on pragmatism. First, pragmatism's commitments to the values of interaction, pluralism, community, and growth can be found much earlier in Native American thought, particularly among the northeastern peoples whose lands bordered the original colonies that became the United States. Second, there were moments when the ideas of colonial thinkers clearly developed through a well-documented interaction with American Indian leaders and people; for example the Narragansett leader Miantonomi influenced Roger Williams's pluralistic vision of community, and Benjamin Franklin developed his understanding of democratic freedom through conversations with the Delaware leader Teedyuscung. Finally, Pratt explains how members of Native prophetic movements such as Neolin, Tenskwatawa, or Sagoyewatha developed a logic of place that emphasized pluralism and meliorism in resistance to the colonial attitude, which justified American progress—and thereby practices of "exclusion, intolerance, and attempts to eliminate difference"—by reducing "meaning to a single set of truths and a single hierarchy of value" (Pratt 2002: xiv).

Using this genealogy, Pratt developed throughout his work a borderland pragmatism, which reconstructed this tradition as a critical perspective that seeks to understand and ameliorate the problems that emerge when "radically different peoples meet and seek to coexist" (2002: xii). However, Pratt was not the first philosopher to carry out fruitful cross-border conversations, and his recent book with Erin McKenna (Pratt & McKenna 2015) offers an excellent survey of these conversations in a chapter titled "Red Power, Indigenous Philosophy."

The two authors begin with Felix Cohen's 1953 article "Americanizing the White Man," in which readers are reminded that the cultural exchange between settlers and natives has been mutual, although settlers conveniently forget or ignore the extent to which the ideas and practices of American Indians enabled their success, from colonization until the present. Best known as a legal scholar, Cohen devoted his career to lobbying for American Indian peoples and, with help from his father, Morris Cohen, litigated on behalf of many Indian nations with regard to land claims and federal land policies (McKenna & Pratt 2015: 286). He also drew popular support through the efforts of his friend Horace Kallen. Kallen did more than to support cultural pluralism for immigrants: in "On 'Americanizing' the American Indian," an article he wrote in 1958, he harshly rebuked US land grabs and assimilation projects and asserted that all nations should "recognize and respect the right of the tribal cultures—and the faiths and the works that express, embody, and fulfill them—to live on" (Kallen 1958: 472).

On the other side of the border, indigenous scholars also highlight the concepts and values they share with pragmatism. In a book titled *An American Urphilosophie: An American Philosophy before Pragmatism*, Robert Bunge (1984) thoroughly articulates several concepts from the Lakota, both to demonstrate the rich epistemologies and systems of metaphysics present in the western hemisphere before the arrival of Europeans and to bring them into dialogue. In his introduction he explains how the dominant political theories of Europe, as represented by John Locke and Thomas Hobbes, blinded the settlers and their nations to the values and sovereignty of the Lakota and other indigenous peoples. This effect was due to the settlers' inability to appreciate the land and other non-human beings as fellow persons rather than as material resources to be exploited (Bunge 1984: 13–23).

By contrast, the pragmatists could appreciate this deeper epistemological and moral connection to the land. Bunge states that the Lakota are "at once mystics and pragmatists" and "would agree with James' summation of the characteristics of a religious life with some modification," because his pluralism allows for the possibility that the purpose of human life is to bring the self and the community into harmony with our living spiritual universe, through practices that are mutually beneficial (1984: 63–65). He deepens this connection between the two traditions still further, while also highlighting what the pragmatists still need to learn from the Lakota: he does this in a short section on the work of the anthropologist Paul Radin, who was a student of Dewey and Boas at Columbia. Bunge argues that, in his 1927 book *Primitive Man as Philosopher*, Radin worked too hard to prove that indigenous people were practical and rational in order to defend their abilities and ways of life from the racist caricature of them as superstitious and backward animists, trapped in a less sophisticated phase of development (1984: 65–70).

Thus Bunge applauds Radin for recognizing the shared humanity of indigenous people and the sophistication of their beliefs and practices but accuses him of projecting the pernicious dualism of his culture onto the Lakota and others. Another reason why even a curious and sympathetic settler descendant fails to understand indigenous beliefs is the mistranslation of specific indigenous concepts or ideas. For example, Bunge soon explains the centrality of *wakán* to the life and epistemology of the Lakota. Although "sacred mysterious power" comes close to a proper rendering in English, much meaning is lost in translation, especially if one scrutinizes the translation using the reductive analytic tools of western philosophy. Bunge explains:

Unlike the Europeans, the Lakota never concerned themselves with fixing the boundaries of the knowable. They frankly acknowledged that there were limits but in an equally frank manner, acknowledged that they did not know these limits. The Lakota believed and still believe that there is much in the universe which is inaccessible to ordinary man or things that can only be known in a special way by special people. (Bunge 1984: 72)

Wakán is not an expression of superstition, obscurantism, or ignorance but a precise and sophisticated epistemological concept, rooted in fallibilism, that captures the feelings of humility, awe, and wonder we experience standing before the mysterious and limitless power of the universe. Anything can be *wakán*, for nothing in this universe is merely ordinary, but the religious ceremonies of the Lakota often coalesce around experiences of *wakán* in specific sites, where it manifests itself through the land. Consequently the best example of *wakán* would be the feeling one experiences upon seeing for the first time a majestic natural wonder, like the Grand Canyon. Consider, also, that such a site is as likely to inspire cosmic wonder in a scientist as it is to inspire divine gratitude in the pious (think of the kind of wonder that Carl Sagan described in 1985, in *The Varieties of Scientific Experience*). Thus *wakán* is neither a purely sacred nor a secular term, just as the Lakota are neither purely spiritual nor pragmatic, but all of these things, because the dualisms between the sacred and the profane, between the mind and the body, between the rational and the passionate are not essential features of experience or nature but the contingent conceptual tools invented by one culture to understand experience and nature. Given this fallibilist understanding of knowledge, the Lakota possess a pluralistic ontology rather than a realist epistemology:

Knowledge among the Lakota also includes what Europeans would consider "feeling" or "emotion"; yet this was all part of knowing. Any appearance or anything that could be perceived or apprehended by any or all of the faculties, critical or uncritical, was "knowledge." Some of this knowledge was immediately intelligible and was obtained in various ways, i.e., through direct daily observation, or through the various kinds of oral narratives. (Bunge 1984: 75–76)

Later on, in the chapter on axiology, Bunge explains that ultimately the Lakota determine whether or not something is true, not according to conceptual analysis, empirical verification, or technological achievement, but according to how well it allows people to live in accord with each other and the land (1984: 92). Bunge concludes his book by asserting that, while the Lakota may appear "backward regarding science and technology," through this pragmatic epistemology and pluralistic ontology they have developed "very advanced ideas about how to live in harmony with the universe and its people, both animal and human" (1984: 179).

Bunge also issues a warning that all readers should heed: soon the Lakota and the indigenous peoples of the world may become "teachers instead of the taught," and this may be "especially true in the areas of environmental control and human relationships" (ibid.). It must be said here that, according to anthropologists, the "10,000+ years of bison hunting on the Great Plains" practiced by the Lakota and other peoples "constituted the longest-sustained human lifeway in North American history" (Flores 2016: 44). For centuries, millions of bison ranged from the Arctic Ocean in the north to the Gulf of Mexico in the south and from the Catskills in the east to the Cascades in the west, as a result of the sustainable ecological practices that extended their range and their significance as the ceremonial animals around which countless generations of people organized their lives. True, we should not perpetuate the trope of the ecological Indian (as Shepard Krech calls it), as it springs mostly from the romantic imagination of settlers and, much like Radin's anthropology, distorts the actual histories, practices, and humanity of indigenous peoples, past and present. However, the success and longevity of this way of life is founded on a pluralistic rather than exclusivist ontology, which favors fallibilism and meliorism over justice and certainty. This is probably the most widely practiced form of an American pragmatism as well.

The pragmatists and the philosophers of all nations have far more to learn than from the indigenous peoples of our planet than they have to teach them. Sadly, colonialism has created and still maintains numerous impediments to cross-border dialogue. Ironically, the biggest barriers are not the deliberate destruction of the Mesoamerican libraries and codices, or the contemporary institutional structures, assumptions, and prejudices of academia. The highest barrier lies within our own bodies. Much like the white folk who attempted to ask DuBois, "What is it like to be a problem?," sympathetic settler descendants often lack the words, knowledge, sensitivity, or, tragically, the opportunity to converse with an indigenous person or to receive accurate and authentic information about an indigenous culture. And, like DuBois, an indigenous person may understandably lack the patience to entertain yet another awkward conversation on a painful subject merely to satisfy the curiosity of someone descended from the people who murdered his ancestors, stole his land, and destroyed his culture.

Fortunately, previous generations of indigenous philosophers devoted their careers to building the necessary ladders and bridges to transgress these spiritual and physical barriers. Not only does their work articulate various indigenous concepts but, more importantly, it contains the advice and etiquette necessary for fruitful dialogue. Brave and sincere scholars must begin their studies with the work of the Lakota theologian Vine Deloria, Jr. (1933–2005), who established the field of contemporary indigenous philosophy through his prolific essays, through activism, and through masterpieces such as *Custer Died for Your Sins* (1969), *We Talk, You Listen* (1976), *The Metaphysics of Modern Existence* (1979), *God Is Red* (1994), and *Red Earth, White Lies* (1995). However, his best advice for scholars of indigenous philosophy appears in "Philosophy and the Tribal Peoples." Written for the first collection of articles by American Indian philosophers, the essay is his answer to a question asked by the book's editor, Anne Waters: "Will the hegemony of professional philosophy allow assimilation without acculturation?" (Waters 2004: xvi). In other words, will mainstream philosophy, which Deloria describes as the "last bastion of white male supremacy" (Deloria in Waters 2004: 3), allow indigenous philosophers to participate in academic conversations and assimilate its preoccupations, without requiring them to give up their identity or interests?

Deloria answers first by presenting the risks to indigenous philosophers. If the answer is yes to assimilation but no to accommodation, then the price of recognition would be too high for them. If accommodation occurs, then there are several challenges that must be overcome. On the indigenous side of the border, colonization has been so thorough that the possibility of an authentic representation probably "ended for most tribes around 1900, when the last generation of people born free were in an elderly meditative stage of their lives" (Waters 2004: 4). Likewise, the process of professionalization and credentialing required for entering academic conversations runs counter to the values and ways of life of most indigenous communities. Therefore indigenous philosophers would risk either alienating themselves from their people or investing talent, time, and resources that could benefit their communities in more obvious, immediate, and practical ways (2004: 5).

Deloria then turns to the challenges faced by settler descendants interested in cross-border dialogue. First, nearly all popular fiction, from James Fennimore Cooper's *The Last of the Mohicans* in 1826 to Carlos Castaneda's *The Teachings of Don Juan* in 1968, should be avoided, as such creations usually represent the fantasies of settlers rather than the belief of native people. Second, settlers must possess a basic understanding of the stark differences between indigenous and western philosophy, of their separate assumptions about knowledge, the land, time, non-human persons, and the relationship between individuals and their communities (2004: 11). Despite these thorny obstacles, Deloria remains hopeful and insists that the rewards will be worth the risk. He concludes by saying that the quality of these conversations depends on two conditions. First, it depends on "the degree to which Indians take their own traditions seriously and literally" (ibid.). They must remain confident about the legitimacy of their cultural worldview, even when its claims conflict with contemporary science or professional philosophical assumptions. Second, those indoctrinated in western philosophy must accept that "all knowledge must begin with experience, and further that all conclusions must be verified easily in the empirical physical world" (ibid.).

In the same volume, V. F. Cordova (1937–2002), the first American Indian (Jicarilla Apache) to earn a PhD in philosophy, provides further advice for constructive cross-border dialogue. First, two dogmas of western philosophy must be overcome: that concepts can be separated from their culture of origin; and that abstract general knowledge is preferable to context-specific knowledge. This implies that both interlocutors have to learn about each other's context in order to be effective; otherwise meaning will be lost in translation, as in the earlier example of *wakán*. Second, an attitude of mutual respect must be established between participants. Indigenous beliefs can be questioned or challenged; but if a philosopher of settler descent does not genuinely believe that she has something to learn and is not willing to revise her own beliefs, then no meaningful dialogue can occur. Also, agreeing to disagree is fine, as long as real differences are not ignored but acknowledged "with equal weight" rather than insisting upon a "vast universal, absolute, Truth (with capital T)." Finally, she concludes that the purpose of cross-border dialogue should be "change" rather than "progress" (Cordova in Waters 2004: 27–33).

As demonstrated by the contents of the present volume, pragmatists come to cross-border dialogue with deep and genuine commitments on all these fronts. Therefore we should not be surprised that Scott Pratt and Horace Kallen are not the only pragmatists whose works are informed by American Indian thought. Thomas M. Alexander, one of the foremost Dewey scholars, argues that American philosophy and pragmatism "must be understood as a narrative, not an account of an 'essence,'" and should therefore include not only the discursive work of indigenous intellectuals, like speeches and essays, but also indigenous cosmologies, stories, and practices (Alexander 1996: 378). Alexander revisits the subject in several chapters of his most recent book *The Human Eros: Eco-Ontology and the Aesthetics of Existence*, where he reminds us that "the traditions of the original nations of the place—Fourth World, Turtle Island—should gain our attention, our ears. After all, they have been speaking to us for quite a while now" (Alexander 2013: 283). Another excellent example is Bruce Wilshire's *The Primal Roots of American Philosophy* (2000), which places Black Elk side by side with Thoreau and Emerson, as the deep sources of American philosophy and pragmatism.

More importantly, the exchange has been mutual, as proven by the work of contemporary indigenous philosophers who have used concepts from pragmatism to explicate ideas present in their cultures. For example, the Shawnee philosopher Thomas Norton-Smith builds upon the work of Nelson Goodman (1906–1998), another twentieth-century pragmatist, specifically upon his concept of a worldview, to create a general framework of American Indian thought as a "dance of person and place" based on the four most common indigenous themes: the circularity of time, the relatedness of all beings, an expansive concepts of persons, and the semantic potency of performance. Furthermore, when indigenous philosophers mounted an effective resistance to attempts by analytic philosophers to reduce experience to language and semantics, they did so with the help of pragmatist notions. The best example of this resistance to the linguistic turn can be found in Shay Welch's recent book *The Phenomenology of a Performative Knowledge System* (2019), which uses Mark Johnson's pragmatist conceptualization of embodied cognition to explain how the dance of indigenous peoples is not only a medium of expression and community but also a means of encoding and expressing ancestral knowledge that resides in the body, unconsciously and consciously alike.

Together, these scholars represent the beginning of an indigenous pragmatism, which is poised to understand, resist, and ameliorate the legacies of US colonialism; and they are not alone. If this version of American pragmatism creates philosophical alliances from within and across time, others have worked across geographic borders to create a new, inter-American pragmatism, which recruits adherents throughout the entire western hemisphere. The foundational text for this movement is a multicontributor volume titled *Pragmatism in the Americas* and edited by Gregory Fernando Pappas (see Pappas 2011)—who, like Thomas Alexander, has written extensively about Dewey. Pappas laments that pragmatism was not well received in the Spanish-speaking countries of the Americas for a variety of reasons unrelated to any philosophical disagreements, such as lack of translations of the pragmatists' works, prejudices based on caricatures such as the one discussed earlier by Horkheimer (whom Latin American scholars were more likely to read), and the reasonable association of American philosophy with US imperialism. Pappas sees this as an ironic missed opportunity as logical positivism was often used to "justify dictatorships and threaten values and beliefs dear to Latin Americans" and could have benefited from the resources pragmatism developed to resist these influence in the United States (Pappas 2011: 4).

While each contribution is magnificent and warrants further study, the work of two Latin American authors emerges as required reading for all current and future pragmatists. These authors are Enrique Dussel and Gloria Anzaldúa. In an article titled "Religiously Binding the Imperial Self," Alexander Stenh explains how both James and Dussel attempted to reconstruct American cultural identity away from imperialism, through appeals to their philosophies of religion. He concludes that James failed because his religious pluralism was too expansive while his political aims were too vague; by contrast, Dussel succeeded because his use of liberation theology "theorizes the religious *contraction* of the self as a necessary part of ethical and political life," in conjunction with a "more concrete and radically democratic philosophy" (Stenh in Pappas 2011: 298). In a later article, Alexander Sager and Albert Spencer make a similar argument, suggesting that Dussel could benefit from Dewey's experimentalism and that he "provides a corrective to Dewey's Eurocentrism and to his tendency to underplay the challenges of incorporating marginalized populations" (Sager & Spencer 2016: 1). Together, these sympathetic criticisms of pragmatism's foundational figures derived through comparisons with Latin American authors reveal the limitations of even the most visionary colonizers. We should not dismiss their work, but we need not repeat their mistakes if we wish to reconstruct American identity in the twenty-first century.

I conclude this section by turning to the work of Gloria Anzaldúa. In an article of his own in the multicontributor volume he edited, Pappas imagines that, if "Dewey were alive today, he would be interested in and supportive" of Latina lesbian feminists because their autobiographical works "reveal the experience of growing up with the constant pressure to define and identify themselves by exclusive categories that do not fit their lived experience" (Pappas 2011: 262–263). He begins with the work of María Lugones, who exceptionally articulates the "logic of purity," which she defines as demanding that "what is multiple is internally separable" and "thereby reducible to the units that compose it" (2011: 265). Those who internalize this logic "deny legitimacy and exercise control over those who are impure" by stigmatizing anything hybrid or ambiguous as deviant or impure. Consequently Lugones argues that Latina lesbians should resist the logic of purity by embracing their hybrid identity as a unique and coherent composition of their multiplicity (ibid.).

Pappas fully accepts Lugones's analysis and does not personally object to her strategy, but worries that it is vulnerable to criticism from the lovers of purity, because it does not reject their ontology—the proposition that the identity of a person or any other being can be reduced to parts and wholes. By contrast, Anzaldúa dodges this reductionism and proposes that there are no parts to one's identity, since there are no borders within experience. Pappas explains the difference with a masterful summary of Dewey:

> the view of cultures as pure, isolated, discrete, self-contained, atomistic wholes prior to their interaction is a false abstraction. This atomistic way of thinking about cultures is a consequence of a metaphysical tradition that Dewey criticized as not being based on experience. It is a philosophical tradition that regards ambiguity, vagueness, and continuities as not part of reality.

But in Dewey's ontological landscape, what is primary is the ongoing interactions of cultures with all of their raggedness and impurities. Cultures, just as with many other things in the world, have a center and fluctuating, indeterminate boundaries. These boundaries are fringes and are places of continuity and interaction between cultures ... we cannot draw a discrete line between or come up with criteria for when night ends and day begins, but who can say that there is no difference between night and day? (2011: 268–269)

Pappas reminds us of the central insight of James's and Dewey's method of experience: that we develop concepts to understand experience, therefore we must not expect experience to conform to them. Thus the fallacy into which all essentialists fall—be it metaphysical, epistemological, racial, cultural, political—is the fallacy of misplaced concreteness.

Just as we cannot deny the difference between night and day, we cannot deny that these conceptual tools enabled humans to perform fantastic technological feats and to reveal wonders hidden from our experience; and we cannot deny that the worst atrocities have been committed, or rationalized, through this simple and persuasive logic, which persists even though our experience continually falsifies it. Fortunately, Anzaldúa gives us hope by reminding us that, if our imagination invented these oppressive logics, it also has the power to dispel them by creating new identities. She expresses this insight best in a piece written in 2002, in resistance to the US invasion of Afghanistan: "Let Us Be the Healing of the Wound." Anzaldúa begins by rehearsing the wounding she felt inside herself when she saw the September 11 terrorist attack on television. She became fragmented and dissociated from herself as she watched the Twin Towers crumble.

After spending months to explore this internal and external wound, she realized that "sadly we are all accomplices," as we are all part of the web of relations that caused the wound. She realizes that America's "real battle is with its shadow—its racism, propensity for violence, rapacity for consuming, neglect of its responsibility to global communities and the environment, and unjust treatment of dissenters and the disenfranchised, especially people of color" (Anzaldúa

2009: 304). Once this problem is resolved, she describes her "job as an artist to bear witness to what haunts us, to step back and attempt to see the pattern in these events (personal and societal), and how we can repair *el daño* (the damage) by using the imagination and its visions" (2009: 304). She realizes that we each must choose either the path of *desconocimiento* (ignorance), which "leads human consciousness into ignorance, fear, and hatred," or that of *conocimiento* (knowledge), "the more difficult path, [that] leads to awakening, insights, understandings, realizations, and courage, and the motivation to engage in concrete ways that have the potential to bring us into compassionate interactions." *Desconocimiento* "creates the abyss; *conocimiento* builds bridges across it" (2009: 311–312).

Her solution, her path of *conocimiento*, is the Coyolxauhqui imperative. In Aztec religion, Coyolxauhqui is a goddess dismembered for her rebellion (see Figure 5.1); but in her earlier book *Borderlands/La Frontera: The New Mestiza* Anzaldúa presents this goddess as one avatar through whom the land manifests. Most importantly, she describes Coyolxauhqui as a syncretistic entity that does not discriminate between those to whom she manifests, later appearing to Spanish women in 1531, in the form *la Virgen de Guadalupe*, the Virgin Mary, in the same place where she was worshiped by the Aztecs (Anzaldúa 1987: 49–52). Consequently Coyolxauhqui has become "the single most potent religious, political and cultural image of Chicano/*mexicano*" and, like Anzaldúa herself, she is a "synthesis of the old world and the new, of the religion and culture of the two races in our psyche, the conquerors and the conquered" (1987: 52). She personifies "hope and faith," "sustains and insures our survival," and "mediates between humans and the divine, between this reality and the reality of spirit entities" (ibid.). Above all, she symbolizes the ethnic identity of Chicanos *mexicanos*—people of mixed race, people who have Indian blood, people who cross cultures—and the tolerance for ambiguity that characterizes such people (ibid.).

In Anzaldúa's later essay, Coyolxauhqui symbolizes the "necessary process of dismemberment and fragmentation,

Figure 5.1 Coyolxauhqui (Museo Nacional de Antropología, Mexico)

Source: https://commons.wikimedia.org/wiki/File:Coyolxauhqui_en_el_Museo_Nacional_de_Antropolog%C3%ADa.JPG

of seeing that self or the situations you're embroiled in differently" and the need to "heal and achieve integration" (Anzaldúa 2009: 312). It is her "symbol for reconstruction and reframing, one that allows for putting the pieces together in a new way"; and, since this is an "ongoing process of making and unmaking," she concludes that there is "never any resolution, just the process of healing" (ibid.).

In conclusion, if we truly wish to make America great again, then we must listen to her, we must listen to America, we must listen to Coyolxauhqui. She has been speaking to all the peoples of this hemisphere since the beginning, and she will never cease. She always knows what we need to do to heal ourselves. Many have heard her voice, answered, and heeded her guidance, but far too few know how to listen today. American pragmatism is but one story of newcomers who learned how to listen, but it is part of a conversation that remains open and through which more can learn the goddess's language.

Bibliography

Addams, J. (1894). A modern Lear. Speech delivered at the Chicago Women's Club and the Twentieth Century Club of Boston. Iowa State University Archives of Women's Political Communication. https://awpc.cattcenter.iastate.edu/2018/03/05/the-modern-lear-1896.

Addams, J. (1905). *Democracy and social ethics*. New York: Macmillian.

Addams, J. (1912). A modern Lear. *Survey*, November 2, pp. 131–137. Jane Addams Digital Edition. Transcript. https://digital.janeaddams.ramapo.edu/items/show/8932.

Alexander, T. (1987). *John Dewey's theory of art, experience, and nature: The horizons of feeling*. Albany, NY: SUNY Press.

Alexander, T. (1996). The fourth world of American philosophy: The philosophical significance of Native American culture. *Transactions of the Charles S. Peirce Society, 32*(3), 375–402.

Alexander, T. (2013). *The human eros: Eco-ontology and the aesthetics of existence*. New York: Fordham University Press.

Anderson, D. (2008). Peirce and pragmatism: American connections. In *Oxford handbook of American pragmatism*, C. Misak (Ed.). Oxford, UK: Oxford University Press, 40–59.

Anzaldúa, G. (1987). *Borderlands/ La frontera: The new mestiza*. San Francisco, CA: Spinsters/Aunt Lute.

Anzaldúa, G. (2009). Let us be the healing of the wound: The Coyolxauhqui imperative: La sombra y el sueño. In *The Gloria Anzaldúa Reader*, A. Keating (Ed). Durham, NC: Duke University Press, 303–317.

Aristophanes (2017). *Clouds*, I. Johnston (Trans.). http://johnstoniatexts.x10host.com/aristophanes/cloudshtml.html.

Bernstein, R. (2005). *The abuse of evil: The corruption of politics and religion since 9/11*. Malden, MA: Polity.

Bernstein, R. (2015). *Pragmatic encounters*. New York: Routledge.

Brander Rasmussen, B. (2001). *The making and unmaking of whiteness*. Durham, NC: Duke University Press.

Brandom, R. (Ed.). (2000). *Rorty and his critics*. Malden, MA: Blackwell.

Brandom, R. (2011). *Perspectives on pragmatism: Classical, recent, and contemporary*. Cambridge, MA: Harvard University Press.

Bunge, R. (1984). *An American urphilosophie: An American philosophy BP (before pragmatism)*. Lanham, MD: University Press of America, Inc.

Burch, R. (2014). Peirce's view of the relationship between his own work and German idealism. In *Stanford Encyclopedia of Philosophy*, E. N. Zalta (Ed.). https://plato.stanford.edu/entries/peirce/self-con textualization.html.

Campbell, J. (1979). *Pragmatism and reform: Social reconstruction in the thought of John Dewey and George Herbert Mead*. Stony Brook, NY: SUNY.

Carter, J. A. (2017). Race-ing the canon: American icons, from Thomas Jefferson to Alain Locke. In *Routledge companion to the philosophy of race*, P. C. Taylor, L. M. Alcoff, & L. Anderson (Eds.). New York: Routledge, 75–87.

Caute, D. (1970). *Frantz Fanon*. New York: Viking.

Coates, T. (2015). *Between the world and me*. New York: Spiegel & Grau.

Coates, T. (2017). *We were eight years in power: An American tragedy*. New York: One World.

Cordova, V. (2007). *How it is: The Native American philosophy of V. F. Cordova*, K. D. Moore, K. Peters, T. Jojola, & A. Lacy (Eds.). Tucson: University of Arizona Press.

Cotkin, G. (2003). *Existential America*. Baltimore, MD: Johns Hopkins University Press.

Cousin, V. (1866). *Course of the history of modern philosophy*. New York: D. Appleton.

Cresswell, T. (2004). *Place: A short introduction*. Malden, MA: Blackwell.

Cronin, C. (2006). Editor's preface. In J. Habermas, *The divided West*, C. Cronin (Ed. & Trans.). Cambridge: Polity, vii–xxi.

Curry, T. (2018). *Another white man's burden: Josiah Royce's quest for a philosophy of white racial empire*. Albany, NY: SUNY Press.

Davidson, D. (1973). On the very idea of a conceptual scheme. *Proceedings and Addresses of the American Philosophical Association, 47*, 5–20.

Deen, P. (2010). Dialectical vs. experimental method: Marcuse's review of Dewey's *Logic: The theory of inquiry. Transactions of the Charles S. Peirce Society, 46*(2), 242–257. doi: 10.1353/csp.2010.0009.

Deloria, V. (1999). *Spirit and reason: The Vine Deloria, Jr., reader*, K. Foehner & S. Scinta (Eds.). Golden, CO: Fulcrum.

Deloria, V. (2003). *God is red: A native view of religion*, 30th anniversary edn. Golden, CO: Fulcrum Publishing.

Dewey, J. (1981). *The philosophy of John Dewey: Two Volumes in One*, J. J. McDermott (Ed.). Chicago, IL: University of Chicago Press.

Dewey, J. (1984). From absolutism to experimentalism. In *The later works of John Dewey, 1925–1953*, vol. 5: 1929–1930. Carbondale: Southern Illinois University Press.

Dillon, M. (2014). *Introduction to sociological theory, theorists, concepts, and their applicability to the twenty-first century*. Oxford, UK: Wiley Blackwell.

DuBois, W. (1926). *Criteria of Negro art*. New York: Crisis.

DuBois, W. (1968). *Dusk of dawn: An essay toward an autobiography of a race concept*. New York: Schocken Books.

DuBois, W. (1996). *The Oxford W. E. B. DuBois reader*, E. J. Sundquist (Ed.). Oxford, UK: Oxford University Press.

DuBois, W., & Eaton, I. (1967). *The Philadelphia Negro: A social study, together with a special report on domestic service*. New York: Schocken Books.

Dunbar-Ortiz, R. (2014). *An indigenous peoples' history of the United States*. Boston, MA: Beacon.

Emerson, R. (2000). *The essential writings of Ralph Waldo Emerson*, B. Atkinson & M. Oliver (Eds.). New York: Modern Library.

Fanon, F. (2004). *The wretched of the earth*, R. Philcox (Trans.). New York: Grove.

Fesmire, S. (2003). *John Dewey and moral imagination: Pragmatism in ethics*. Bloomington: Indiana University Press.

Festinger, L., Riecken, H. W., & Schachter, S. (1956). *When prophecy fails*. Minneapolis: University of Minnesota Press.

Field, P. (2001). The strange career of Emerson and race. *American Nineteenth Century History*, 2(1), 1–31.

Flores, D. (2016). Reviewing an iconic story: Environmental history and the demise of the bison. In *Bison and people on the North American Great Plains*, G. Cunfer & B. Waiser (Eds.). College Station: Texas A&M University Press, 30–47.

Fried, A. (1997). *Communism in America: A history of documents*. New York: Columbia University Press.

Garrison, J. (1997). *Dewey and eros: Wisdom and desire in the art of teaching*. New York: Teachers College Press.

Garrison, J. (2008). *Reconstructing democracy, recontextualizing Dewey: Pragmatism and interactive constructivism in the twenty-first century*. Albany, NY: SUNY Press.

Goodman, R. (2015). *American philosophy before pragmatism*. Oxford, UK: Oxford University Press.

Green, J. (1999). *Deep democracy: Community, diversity, and transformation*. Lanham, MD: Rowman & Littlefield.

Gross, N. (2008). *Richard Rorty: The making of an American philosopher*. Chicago, IL: University of Chicago Press.

Habermas, J. (1989). *Jürgen Habermas on society and politics: A reader*, S. Seidman (Ed.). Boston, MA: Beacon.

Hamington, M. (2005). Public pragmatism: Jane Addams and Ida B. Wells on lynching. *Journal of Speculative Philosophy, 19*(2), 167–174.

Hamington, M., & Bardwell-Jones, C. (Eds.). (2012). *Contemporary feminist pragmatism*. New York: Routledge.

Hamner, M. (2003). *American pragmatism: A religious genealogy*. Oxford, UK: Oxford University Press.

Harris, L., Pratt, S. L., & Waters, A. (Eds.). (2002). *American philosophies: An anthology*. Malden, MA: Blackwell.

Hickman, L. (1990). *John Dewey's pragmatic technology*. Bloomington: Indiana University Press.

Hickman, L. (2007). *Pragmatism as post-postmodernism: Lessons from John Dewey*. New York: Fordham University Press.

Hook, S. (1959). Pragmatism and existentialism. *Antioch Review, 19*(2), 151–168.

Horkheimer, M. (1974). *Eclipse of reason*, rev. edn. New York: Seabury Press.

Hume, D. (2017). *A treatise on human nature*, Bennett, J. (Ed.). Early Modern Texts. http://www.earlymoderntexts.com/assets/pdfs/hume1739book1.pdf.

James, V. D. (2013). Reading Anna J. Cooper with William James: Black feminist visionary pragmatism, philosophy's culture of justification, and belief. *Pluralist, 8*(3), 32–46.

James, W. (1907). *Pragmatism: A new name for some old ways of thinking*. Auckland, New Zealand: Floating Press.

James, W. (1958). *The varieties of religious experience: A study in human nature*. New York: New American Library.

James, W. (1968). *The writings of William James*, J. J. McDermott (Ed.). New York: Modern Library.

Janssen-Lauret, F. (2018). Willard Van Orman Quine's philosophical development in the 1930s and 1940s. In W. V. O. Quine, *The significance of the new logic: A translation of Quine's O sentido da nova lógica*, W. Carnielli, F. Janssen-Lauret, & W. Pickering (Eds. and Trans.). Cambridge: Cambridge University Press, xiv–xlvii.

Jensen, K. (2016). The growing edges of beloved community: From Royce to Thurman to King. *Transactions of the Charles S. Peirce Society, 52*(2): 239–258.

Johnson, M. (2007). *The meaning of the body: Aesthetics of human understanding*. Chicago, IL: University of Chicago Press.

Kahneman, D., & Tversky, A. (1972). Subjective probability: A judgment of representativeness. *Cognitive Psychology, 3*(3), 430–454.

Kallen, H. (1910). James, Bergson and Mr. Pitkin. *Journal of Philosophy, Psychology and Scientific Methods, 7*(13), 353–357.

Kallen, H. (1915a). Democracy versus the melting pot I. *Nation, 100(2590)*, 190–194.

Kallen, H. (1915b). Democracy versus the melting pot II. *Nation, 100(2591)*, 217–220.

Kallen, H. (1957). Alain Locke and cultural pluralism. *Journal of Philosophy, 54*(5), 119–127.

Kallen, H. (1958). On 'Americanizing' the American Indian. *Social Research, 25*(4), 469–473.

Kautzer, C., & Mendieta, E. (Eds.). (2009). *Pragmatism, nation, and race: Community in the age of empire.* Bloomington: Indiana University Press.

Katzav, J., & Vaesen, K. (2017). On the emergence of American analytic philosophy. *British Journal for the History of Philosophy, 25*(4), 772–798.

Koopman, C. (2009). *Pragmatism as transition: Historicity and hope in James, Dewey, and Rorty.* New York: Columbia University Press.

Korzybski, A. (1933). *Science and sanity: An introduction to non-Aristotelian systems and general semantics.* Oakland, CA: University of California.

Kuklick, B. (1977). *The rise of American philosophy: Cambridge, Massachusetts, 1860–1930.* New Haven, CT: Yale University Press.

Lachs, J. (2014) [1976]. The transcendence of materialism and idealism in American thought. In *Freedom and Limits*, J. Lachs & P. Shade (Eds.). New York: Fordham Press, 97–112.

Lakoff, G., & Johnson, M. (1980). *Metaphors we live by.* Chicago, IL: University of Chicago Press.

Lakoff, G., & Johnson, M. (1999). *Philosophy in the flesh: The embodied mind and its challenge to western thought.* New York: Basic Books.

Lawson, B., & Koch, D. F. (2004). *Pragmatism and the problem of race.* Bloomington: Indiana University Press.

Lindberg, C. (1939). Aviation, geography, and race. *Reader's Digest, 34*, 64–67.

Livingston, A. (2016). *Damn great empires! William James and the politics of pragmatism.* New York: Oxford University Press.

Locke, A. (1968). *The new Negro: An interpretation.* New York: Arno Press.

Locke, A. (2012). *The works of Alain Locke*, C. Molesworth (Ed.). Oxford, UK: Oxford University Press.

Lysaker, J. (2012). Essaying America: A Declaration of Independence. *Journal of Speculative Philosophy, 26*(3), 531–553.

Madsen, D. L. (1998). *American exceptionalism.* Jackson: University Press of Mississippi.

Marcuse, H. (1955). *Eros and civilization: A philosophical inquiry into Freud.* Boston, MA: Beacon.

Marcuse, H. (1964). *One-dimensional man: Studies in the ideology of advanced industrial society.* Boston, MA: Beacon.

Martin, J. (2002). *The education of John Dewey: A biography.* New York: Columbia University Press.

McCumber, J. (1996). Time in the ditch: American philosophy and the McCarthy era. *Diacritics, 26*(1), 33–49.

McCumber, J. (2016). *The philosophy scare: The politics of reason in the early Cold War.* Chicago, IL: University of Chicago Press.

McDermott, J. J. (1991). Why bother: Is life worth living? *Journal of Philosophy, 88*(11) (special issue), 677–683.

McDermott, J. J. (1994). Ill-at-ease: The natural travail of ontological disconnectedness. *Proceedings and Addresses of the American Philosophical Association, 67*(6), 7–28.

McDermott, J. J. (2007). *The drama of possibility: Experience as philosophy of culture,* D. R. Anderson (Ed.). New York: Fordham University Press.

McDermott, J. J. (2010). A lost horizon: Perils and possibilities of the obvious. *Pluralist, 5,* 1–17.

McHenry, L., & Shields, G. (2017). Analytic critiques of Whitehead's metaphysics. *Journal of the American Philosophical Association, 3*(2), 483–503.

McIntosh, P. (forthcoming). *On privilege, fraudulence, and teaching as learning: Selected essays, 1981–2019.* New York: Routledge.

McKenna, E. (2017). The need for reciprocity and respect in philosophy. *Pluralist, 12,* 1–14.

McKenna, E., & Light, A. (Eds.). (2004). *Animal pragmatism: Rethinking human–nonhuman relationships.* Bloomington: Indiana University Press.

McKenna, E., & Pratt, S. L. (2015). *American philosophy: From Wounded Knee to the present.* London, UK: Bloomsbury.

Menand, L. (2001). *The metaphysical club.* New York: Farrar, Straus, Giroux.

Mills, C. W. (1951). *White collar: The American middle classes.* New York: Oxford University Press.

Mills, C. W. (1956). *The power elite.* New York: Oxford University Press.

Mills, C. W. (1959). *The sociological imagination.* New York: Oxford University Press.

Mills, C. W. (1997). *The racial contract.* Ithaca, NY: Cornell University Press.

Mills, C. W., with Schneider, H. (1948). *The new men of power: America's labor leaders.* New York: Harcourt, Brace.

Misak, C. (2013). *The American pragmatists*. Oxford, UK: Oxford University Press.

Moore, T. (2005). A Fanonian perspective on double consciousness. *Journal of Black Studies, 35*(6), 751–762.

Northrop, F. S. (1946). *The meeting of East and West*. New York: Macmillian.

Ortiz, S. J. (2011). Indigenous continuance: Collaboration and syncretism. *American Indian Quarterly, 35*(3), 285–293.

Pappas, G. (2008). *John Dewey's ethics: Democracy as experience*. Bloomington: Indiana University Press.

Pappas, G. (Ed.). (2011). *Pragmatism in the Americas*. New York: Fordham University Press.

Pateman, C. (2008). *The sexual contract*. Stanford, CA: Stanford University Press.

Pease, D. E. (2009). *The new American exceptionalism*. Minneapolis: University of Minnesota Press.

Peirce, C. S. (1992). *The essential Peirce*, N. Houser & C. Kloesel (Eds.). Indianapolis: Indiana University Press.

Philström, S. (2012). Toward pragmatically naturalized transcendental philosophy of scientific inquiry and pragmatic scientific realism. *Studia Philosophica Estonica, 5*(2), 79–94.

Pollan, M. (2018). *How to change your mind*. New York: Penguin Press.

Posthumus, D. (2016). A Lakota view of Pté Oyáte (Buffalo Nation). In *Bison and people on the North American Great Plains*, G. Cunfer & B. Waiser (Eds.). College Station: Texas A&M University Press, 278–309.

Pratt, S. (2002). *Native pragmatism: Rethinking the roots of American philosophy*. Bloomington: Indiana University Press.

Quine, W. V. O. (1960). *Word and object*. Boston, MA: MIT Press.

Raban, J. (1999). *Passage to Juneau: A sea and its meanings*. New York: Pantheon Books.

Rescher, N. (1998). Fallibilism. In *Routledge encyclopedia of philosophy*. Taylor & Francis. https://www.rep.routledge.com/articles/thematic/fallibilism/v-1.

Rivera, J. M. (2005). Introduction. In L. Zavala, *Journey to the United States of North America*, J.-M. Rivera (Ed.), W. Woolsey (Trans.). Houston, TX: Arte Público Press, vii–xxxiii.

Richardson, R. D. (1995). *Emerson: The mind on fire: A biography*. Berkeley, CA: University of California Press.

Rogers, M. (2009). *The undiscovered Dewey: Religion, morality, and the ethos of democracy*. New York: Columbia University Press.

Romano, C. (2012). *America the philosophical*. New York: Knopf.

Rorty, R. (1961). Recent metaphilosophy. *Review of Metaphysics, 15*(2), 299–318.

Rorty, R. (1967). *The linguistic turn: Recent essays in philosophical method*. Chicago, IL: University of Chicago Press.

Rorty, R. (1979). *Philosophy and the mirror of nature*. Princeton, NJ: Princeton University Press.

Rorty, R. (1989). *Contingency, irony, and solidarity*. Cambridge, UK: Cambridge University Press.

Rorty, R. (2006). *Take care of freedom and truth will take care of itself: Interviews with Richard Rorty*, E. Mendieta (Ed.). Stanford, CA: Stanford University Press.

Ross, E. (1914). *The Old World in the New; The significance of past and present immigration to the American people*. New York: Century.

Rowe, A. C., & Tuck, E. (2017). Settler colonialism and cultural studies: Ongoing settlement, cultural production, and resistance. *Cultural Studies ↔ Critical Methodologies, 17*(1), 3–13.

Royce, J. (1900). *The world and the individual*. New York: Macmillan.

Royce, J. (1908a). *The philosophy of loyalty*. New York: Macmillan.

Royce, J. (1908b). *Race questions, provincialism, and other American problems*. New York: Macmillan.

Royce, J. (1914). *War and insurance: An address delivered before the philosophical union of the University of California at its twenty-fifth anniversary at Berkeley, California, August 27, 1914*. New York: Macmillan.

Royce, J. (1916). *The hope of the great community*. New York: Macmillan.

Royce, J. (1969). *The basic writings of Josiah Royce*, J. J. McDermott (Ed.). Chicago, IL: University of Chicago Press.

Russell, B. (1958). *Portraits from memory*. London, UK: Allen & Unwin.

Russell, B. (1959). *My philosophical development*. London, UK: Allen & Unwin.

St. John de Crèvecoeur, J. (1912). *Letters from an American farmer*, W. B. Blake (Ed.). London, UK: J. M. Dent & Sons / New York: E. P. Dutton.

Sager, A., & Spencer, A. (2016). Liberation pragmatism: Dussel and Dewey in dialogue. *Contemporary Pragmatism, 13*(4), 1–22.

Santayana, G. (1936). *The sense of beauty: Being the outlines of aesthetic theory*. New York: Scribner's.

Santayana, G. (1942). *The realms of being*. New York: Scribner's.

Santayana, G. (1946). *The idea of Christ in the Gospels or God in man*. New York: Scribner's.

Santayana, G. (1949). *The last Puritan*. New York: Scribner's.

Santayana, G. (1986). *The works of George Santayana*, W. G. Holzberger, H. J. Saatkamp, & M. S. Wokeck (Eds.). Cambridge, MA: MIT Press.

Santayana, G. (2009). *The essential Santayana: Selected writings*, M. A. Coleman (Ed.). Bloomington: Indiana University Press.

Schneider, B. (2008). Boudinot, Emerson, and Ross on Cherokee Removal. *English Literary History, 75*(1), 151–177.

Seigfried, C. (1996). *Pragmatism and feminism: Reweaving the social fabric.* Chicago, IL: University of Chicago Press.

Shusterman, R. (2008). *Body consciousness: A philosophy of mindfulness and somaesthetics.* Cambridge, UK: Cambridge University Press.

Silko, L. (1996). *Yellow woman and a beauty of the spirit: Essays on Native American life today.* New York: Simon & Schuster.

Silva, G. (2018). "The Americas seek not enlightenment but liberation": On the philosophical significance of liberation for philosophy in the Americas. *Pluralist, 13*, 1–21.

Skowroñski, K. P. (2007). *Santayana and American values, liberties, responsibility.* Newcastle, UK: Cambridge Scholars.

Soames, S. (Ed.). (2014). The place of Willard Van Orman Quine in analytic philosophy. *Analytic philosophy in America and other historical and contemporary essays.* Princeton, NJ: Princeton University Press, 104–138.

Stack, G. (1992). *Nietzsche and Emerson: An elective affinity.* Athens: Ohio University Press.

Stikkers, K. (2008). An outline of methodological Afrocentrism, with particular application to the thought of W. E. B. DuBois. *Journal of Speculative Philosophy, 22*(1), 40–49.

Stuhr, J. (1997). *Genealogical pragmatism: Philosophy, experience, and community.* Albany, NY: SUNY Press.

Stuhr, J. (Ed.). (2000). *Pragmatism and classical American philosophy: Essential readings and interpretive essays*, 2nd edn. New York: Oxford University Press.

Sullivan, S. (2001). *Living across and through skins: Transactional bodies, pragmatism, and feminism.* Bloomington: Indiana University Press.

Sullivan, S. (2006). *Revealing whiteness: The unconscious habits of racial privilege.* Bloomington: Indiana University Press.

Sundquist, E. (Ed.). (1996). *The Oxford W. E. B. DuBois reader.* Oxford, UK: Oxford University Press.

Talisse, R. (2005). *Democracy after liberalism: Pragmatism and deliberative politics.* New York: Routledge.

Talisse, R., & Aikin, S. F. (Eds.). (2011). *The pragmatism reader: From Peirce through the present.* Princeton, NJ: Princeton University Press.

Taylor, P. (2004). What's the use of calling DuBois a pragmatist? *Metaphilosophy, 35*(1–2), 99–114.

Trout, L. (2010). *The politics of survival: Peirce, affectivity, and social criticism.* New York: Fordham University Press.

Vannatta, S. (2014). *Conservatism and pragmatism in law, politics, and ethics.* New York: Palgrave Macmillan.

Vaughan, K. (2018). Progressive education and racial justice: Examining the work of John Dewey. *Education & Culture, 34*(2), 39–68.

Voparil, C. (2010). General introduction. In *The Rorty Reader*, C. Voparil & R. Bernstein (Eds.). Oxford, UK: Wiley Blackwell, 1–51.

Waters, A. (Ed.). (2004). *American Indian thought: Philosophical essays*. Malden, MA: Blackwell.

West, C. (1989). *The American evasion of philosophy: A genealogy of pragmatism*. Madison: University of Wisconsin Press.

Westbrook, R. (2005). *Democratic hope: Pragmatism and the politics of truth*. Ithaca, NY: Cornell University Press.

Whitehead, A. (1933). *Adventures of ideas*. New York: Macmillan.

Whitehead, A. (1964). *The concept of nature: Tarner lectures delivered in Trinity College, November, 1919*. Cambridge, UK: Cambridge University Press.

Whitehead, A. (1967). *Science and the modern world*. New York: Free Press.

Whitehead, A. (1968). *Nature and life*. New York: Greenwood Press.

Whitehead, A. (1978). *Process and reality: An essay in cosmology*, D. R. Griffin & D. W. Sherburne (Eds.). New York: Free Press.

Wilshire, B. (2000). *The primal roots of American philosophy: Pragmatism, phenomenology, and native American thought*. University Park: Pennsylvania State University Press.

Wise, T. (2011). *White like me: Reflections on race from a privileged son*, 3rd edn. Berkeley, CA: Soft Skull Press.

Wittgenstein, L. (1922). *Tractatus logico-philosophicus*. Ogden, C. K. (Trans). London, UK: Kegan Paul, Trench, Trubner & Co., Ltd.

Wittgenstein, L. (1958). *Preliminary studies for the "Philosophical investigations" generally known as the blue and brown books*. New York: Harper.

Zavala, L. (2005) [1980]. *Journey to the United States of North America*, J.-M. Rivera (Ed.), W. Woolsey (Trans.). Houston, TX: Arte Público Press.

Zitkala-Sa (1921). Impressions of an Indian childhood. In Zitkala-Sa, *American Indian Stories*. Washington, DC: Hayworth Publishing House, 7–46.

Index

cognitive biases, 57
cognitive dissonance, 56–7
Cohen, Felix, 220
Cohen, Morris, 220
Confederacy, 126
continental philosophy, 69–70, 156
Colón, Gabriel Alejandro Torres, 116
Columbia University, 99, 105, 115, 116, 156, 190, 202–3
comparative philosophy, 8
Conant, James, 212
conceptual pragmatism, 157
conocimiento, 231
conservative, 4, 84, 110, 123, 125, 153
Cooper, Anna J., 83
Cooper, James Fennimore, 225
Cornell University, 162
cosmopolitanism, 119, 121–2, 202, 121–2, 125, 202
cosmopolitan society, 201
correspondence theory, 198
Cousin, Victor, 36
Cordova, V. F., 226
Coyolaxuhqui imperative, 219, 231–2
Crevecoeur, J. Hector St. John de, 142
critical race theory, 8, 131
Cresswell, Tim, 18, 21
The Crisis, 137
cross-border dialogue, 8, 224–6
Crummel, Alexander, 127
cultural appropriation, 136
cultural naturalism, 106, 114
cultural pluralism, 140–7
Curry, Tommy, 83–4

Darwin, Charles, 46, 48, 99, 107, 109, 110, 111, 112, 113, 114
Darwinian naturalism, 204
Darwinian understanding of nature, 123
Darwinism, 1, 107, 108, 159
Debs, Eugene V., 87

decolonization, 84
Delaware, 219
Deloria Jr., Vine, 22, 224–5
    Custer Died for Your Sins, 224
    God Is Red, 22, 224
    The Metaphysics of Modern Existence, 224
    "Philosophy and the Tribal Peoples," 224
    Red Earth, White Lies, 224
    We Talk, You Listen, 224
democratic pluralism, 141, 146–55
Dennett, Dan, 159
Derrida, Jacques, 199, 212
Descartes, René, 45, 47–8, 51–2, 55–56, 58–9, 61–2, 64, 77, 111, 166–7, 177, 198
desconocimiento, 231
Davidson, Donald, 188–9, 198
    "On the Very Idea of a Conceptual Scheme," 188
Deen, Phillip, 203–4
Dewey, John, vii–viii, ix, 2, 9, 12–14, 25–6, 41–3, 46, 49, 63, 73, 84–5, 86–9, 97, 99–116, 120, 130, 154, 158–61, 181, 198, 190, 192, 194, 202, 204, 207–8, 211–12, 221, 226, 228–30
    A Common Faith, 205
    cultural naturalism, 106, 114
    Democracy and Education, 113
    eclipse of the public, 205
    "Existence as Precarious and Stable," 113–14
    Experience and Nature, 113–14
    experimentalism, 207, 228
    Freedom and Culture, 205
    "From Absolutism to Experimentalism," 9
    Individualism Old and New, 205
    "The Influence of Darwin on Philosophy," 107–8

Wilshire, Bruce, 37–8, 200, 227
  A Fashionable Nihilism, 200
  *The Primal Roots of American
    Philosophy*, 227
Winthrop, John, 30
The Wire, 97–8
Wise, Tim, 131, 145
Wittgenstein, Ludwig, 170, 189,
  191–3, 195, 198
  Philosophical Investigations,
    192
  *Tractatus Logico-
    Philosophicus*, 191, 197
The Wizard of Oz, 122
Woodbridge, Frederick, J. E., 190

Woolf, Virginia, 78
Wordsworth, William, 36
World War I, 120
World War II, 119–20, 122, 150,
  155, 162, 202, 204
Wounded Knee Massacre, 143
Wundt, Wilhelm, 15

Yale University, 190
yellow journalism, 144

Zangwill, Israel, 141–2, 145
Zavala, Lorenzo de, 30–2
Zitkala-Sa, 144
Zea, Leopoldo, 10